THE BIBLE AND THE PEOPLE

For my faculty colleagues at the Claremont School of Theology, 1991–2005

THE BIBLE
AND THE PEOPLE

LORI ANNE FERRELL

YALE UNIVERSITY PRESS
NEW HAVEN AND LONDON

For information about this and other Yale University Press publications, please contact:

U.S. Office: sales.press@yale.edu   www.yalebooks.com
Europe Office: sales@yaleup.co.uk   www.yaleup.co.uk

Set in Adobe Caslon by IDSUK (DataConnection) Ltd.
Printed in the United States of America by Sheridan Books.

Library of Congress Cataloging-in-Publication Data

Ferrell, Lori Anne, 1957–
    The Bible and the people / Lori Anne Ferrell.
       p. cm.
    Includes bibliographical references and index.
    ISBN 978–0–300–11424–9 (ci : alk. paper)
    1. Bible—History. I. Title.
    BS445.F47 2008
    220.5—dc22
                                    2008026769

A catalogue record for this book is available from the British Library.

10 9 8 7 6 5 4 3 2 1

CONTENTS

ILLUSTRATIONS

ACKNOWLEDGEMENTS

I've long wanted to write something that opened on the road to Joshua Tree National Park and ended with a story about my maternal grandmother. But I would never have guessed that *that* something would be *this* book. What follows, then, is not only a long list of thanks but, in between every line, astonished pleasure.

The Bible and the People began with an invitation to guest-curate an exhibition on the Christian Bible at The Huntington Library in 2004: a foolhardy move on the part of Roy Ritchie, and one that launched me up one of the most precipitous learning-curves of my adult existence. It was also one of the most rewarding. And so I want first to express my deep gratitude to Roy, who, out of the blue, dropped this opportunity onto my desk and trusted me to take care of it (and for good measure, titled the exhibition, and thus by extension this book, for me). Along for the wild ride, packing their varied expertise, came the Huntington's Cathy Cherbosque, Alan Jutzi, Susan Lafferty, Mary Robertson, Randy Shulman, Lauren Tawa, Susan Turner-Lowe, and David Zeidberg: thank you, brave ones all.

Many thanks to the busy and jovial crew behind the scenes in the Huntington stacks, who never yelled at me when I got in their way (which was pretty much every time I was in the stacks). And to the WSs (they know who they are, and so the acronym will suffice) working around Dr. Cherbosque's warren of an office, me perched amongst them for hours at the only table long enough to hold several large, unwieldy books at a time, trying desperately to compose succinct, accurate, and interesting exhibit labels. Jessica Dupray, Jean-Robert Durbin, and Bob Herman, especial thanks for letting me read them out loud to you, for making those rude remarks about the Infant Samuel at Prayer, and for courageously looking over my shoulder at the more lurid specimens of Victorian biblical illustration without flinching.

In the end I learned that everybody at the Huntington Library – staff, curators, directors – eventually has a job to do in an undertaking of this complexity and size, and so I am grateful to them all: they put up with my general cluelessness about how exhibitions work and my interruptions at inopportune moments; they expressed interest in my endeavors on a regular basis; and they tactfully undid most of my errors of judgment. For these praises, I single out Stephen Tabor, the Huntington's curator of early printed books and the all-knowing, all-seeing, ever-vigilant, and remarkably generous co-curator of the Bible exhibit. Early on in our collaborative effort I overheard a piece of exhibit arcanum, which goes something like this: *That Curator whom the gods wish to test will find himself saddled at some point in his career with a Guest Curator.* Steve faced his tragic fate with epic stoicism, surpassing intelligence, and bone-dry humor; there are not enough words to express my gratitude – plus, as he had to keep reminding me, "only ten lines per label" – so I'll trust him to know the innumerable lines I could use in describing my debt to him.

Every one of my good friends, all my professional colleagues, and most of my students have heard me talk endlessly about the writing of the book that followed upon the heels of the exhibition. I have kinder friends than I merit, better colleagues than I could ever have imagined, and cleverer students than I can take credit for: I cannot possibly name you all. (It's a tricky business, this one of acknowledgement; someone is sure to be missed, only to be remembered too late in the proof-stage.) But thank you for listening, for your help and suggestions, and for remaining on speaking terms with me now that this vexing labor of love is finally finished.

My family went beyond the call of duty and provided loving hospitality of the sort that allowed me to visit libraries, consult archives, and, most essential, remain sane at those times when I was under-funded, under-fed, under-rested, and unnerved. Thanks, then, to Elizabeth Ferrell Wilson and Jennifer Ferrell Lo for their sororal sympathy; the guest rooms, sofa-beds, and couches in New York, London, and Boston (they have been nothing if not obliging when it comes to the places I need them to live); and the loan of affectionate nieces and affable brothers-in-law; and to Bonnie Ferrell, for listening to me whine on the telephone in that way one only can to one's Mother. Last and most important, in addition to all the other ways he enhances my life (mostly by remaining fairly indifferent to me as a scholar and very attentive to me as a human being), this year my son married into one of the kindest and most congenial families-in-law I can imagine. Thanks, Kev! You've always come through for us both.

One last thing about hospitality. Every important stage of this book was completed on long weekends at the 29 Palms Inn, truly the best place on earth to hike, write, think, tear out hair, rewrite, despair, finally finish a draft, and get fed and watered at the end of the day. The rooms on this oasis (in every sense of the term) in the high Mojave have no phones, no working televisions, no wireless; they are, however, equipped with plugs for the laptop and old but perfectly serviceable Gideon Bibles, which made for no distractions and one less book to pack.

On to other substantial forms of help: those of my colleagues and friends who offered advice, citations, or draft-reading. If this book informs, pleases, or makes sense, it is probably due to them. (And, of course, what has been left unsaid, said improperly, or said un-fluently remains my responsibility.) Andrew Cambers, Peter Carlson, David Cressy, Tom Freeman, Peter Lake, Scott Mandlebrote, Sammie McGlasson, Sara Moslener, Adam Rosenkranz, Tammi Schneider,

Marvin Sweeney, Dirk von der Horst, and David Wilson gave me cautionary advice, apt citations, and (in one case) a priceless YouTube link. Kathryn Wolford performed the duties of research assistant with meticulous skill. Henry and Vi Jones, bless them, provided me with digital pictures of their antique Methodist circuit riders' Bible. Maria Dowling and Edmund Green offered their London home on many occasions, as well as enduring friendship, hot suppers, and incisive questions about the progress of the manuscript. David Cressy, Jeff Groves, Mary Robertson, Stephen Tabor, Ann Taves, and Michael Winship read and commented on early drafts; Ben Christensen and Bill Sherman (who also took the picture of the modern-day church that opens the book) read the entire manuscript for the press, and offered both encouragement and many useful suggestions and criticisms. And Lou Ruprecht read a number of successive drafts with his typical keen insight and intelligence. His books, which I so admire, provided me with the working models for *The Bible and the People*. I am grateful he took such time with it, only wishing I could do adequate justice to his style of writing, and of friendship.

There are still more generosities to be acknowledged. My travel, research, and writing were made possible by several grant-giving institutions along with, most spectacularly, the support of the Huntington Library: the National Endowment for the Humanities, the British Academy, the Folger Library, the British Library, and the Honnold Library of the Claremont Colleges. (The Huntington, Folger, British and Claremont Libraries – and their staffs, curators, research librarians, and directors – exist, I believe, to make those of us who chose to remain in school forever happy we did so.) Changing jobs and job titles in 2005 required me to request sabbatical time in mid-stream from two cooperative administrations: thanks, then, are due to Jack Fitzmier and Patricia Easton, both of whom represent the gold standard of academic deanery; and to the presidents and trustees of Claremont School of Theology (then) and Claremont Graduate University School of Arts and Humanities (now) who ratified their decisions.

I was also remarkably fortunate in my press, Yale London, whose copyeditor, Beth Humphries, must surely be a red-pencil saint given I have never completely mastered the differences between English and American formatting (not to mention spelling). Rachael Lonsdale helped me with the intricacies of obtaining permissions and images. My editor, Heather McCallum, read this entire manuscript more than once with care and concern, helping me write a new kind of book, at least for me – generalist, broadly-cast, and, I hope, appropriately reader-friendly. For this reason, perhaps, it may also from time to time sound opinionated (actually, it would be more accurate to admit that it may sound opinionated because I *am* opinionated), and so I should also say my opinions do not always reflect those of my several Managements.

Which brings me to this last. That I could write this book at all is, in the end, because of the rigorous, if unplanned, remedial education I received after graduation: when the faculty of the Claremont School of Theology inexplicably decided to entrust the teaching of HC301 (REQ year 1), "Introduction to the History of Christianity," to a brand-new and dismayingly callow PhD who had never studied Church History, gone to Divinity School, taken a graduate course in Religious Studies, nor possessed even a modicum of teaching experience. Thus it was that my CST colleagues, from sheer necessity, put me through an intellectually demanding and philosophically liberal course of theological education between 1991 and 2005. They did so with unfailing grace and unstinting collegiality. I will not meet their kind again. I am grateful beyond words that I did. And I know of no other way to thank them, all of them, except to offer them the dedication to this book.

London, 1 June 2008

INTRODUCTION

The Bible and the People

It is a cool and sunny February morning in the high Mojave, on the road to Joshua Tree National Park. California Route 62, the Twentynine Palms Highway, is better paved than it was a decade or so ago, its roadside attractions much less dusty and perhaps even slightly less dubious. Twenty-four-hour bail bond services, tattoo parlors, and all-night liquor stores have given way in places to super-sized pharmacies, a Wal-Mart, even a Starbucks (drive-thru). The relative prosperity of the 1990s made its brief impact on even this hardscrabble region, now clotted with Bank of America kiosks and Nissan dealerships.

Nowhere is the once-rising tide more apparent than in the appearance of the churches that have always featured in this stark and impoverished landscape. Quonset huts and peeling storefronts with hand-lettered crosses have been turned into freshly painted buildings with electronic bulletin boards. A new church with a pitched roof and low stone wall catches my eye, and I pull over to take a longer look. Bolstering the steeple is a dramatic display: a huge block of wood ingeniously jigsawed and painted to resemble an open book. The left page displays the numbers "1611"; the right, the letters "KJV." Standing in the spine is the figure of a man in modern dress. He is forging a sword on an anvil.

1 Twentynine Palms Baptist Church, Twentynine Palms, California

This is the Twentynine Palms New Testament Baptist Church (independent), *circa* 2008, where a Bible named after the first Stuart King of England currently serves as the chief corner-stone.

My book takes its inspiration from that evidence of a long, strange journey, tracking the Christian Bible's translation not simply from one language into another but – more important for this retelling – from one hand into another. *Translation*, after all, goes well beyond the transfer of words; it invokes *movement*: from one word, one place, one form, one date in time, to another. A painted sign on the front of a twenty-first century church, proclaiming its fidelity to a very old, but neither ancient nor original, version of the Christian scriptures pays tribute to the restless, peripatetic text that is the Christian Bible: forever caught up in time out of mind, forever renewed, forever capturing the current with uncanny specificity.

This is something we cannot say for all holy books. And so surely this must tell us something about the Bible's readers, especially their willingness to swap one sense of origin – *its* beginnings – for another: *theirs, now*.

This book, *The Bible and the People*, began its life as a collection of books, not as a collection of historians' notes on people's lives. But if books, like people, have biographies – and *this* cultural historian surely thinks they do – their narratives can also be recounted in the language of origins and endings, actions recorded, generations marked, and relationships to their times. Books provide the intersecting, material link uniting writers with readers, which can communicate through successive generations. These moments constitute the creative lifespan of any book, and they are documented in many ways. *This* book may have begun, in other words, with *books* – one particular Book, in fact – rather than recorded histories, but it cannot end there, for every book, especially this one, not only tells a story but shares many more.

The Bibles considered here, and their makers and readers, have been reassembled to form a cast of characters who feature in interlocking historical narratives from the eleventh century to the twenty-first. The first story begins in very familiar territory: a standard, in fact, in the annals of Protestant history. This is the tale of the Bible as a book once held captive in a strange tongue, a book laypersons had the duty and thus should have had the right to read. Consequently, it was wrested from the Roman Catholic Church and finally returned to ordinary believers by translators and reformers eventually called Protestants.

This tale, which we could title "The Battle for the Bible," is no fiction, and I feel no need to challenge its basic plotline. I do, however, intend to read that plot from new perspectives. Yes, the western medieval Bible was in Latin. A powerful Church claiming an indisputable jurisdiction over a generally illiterate Europe and Britain worked to prevent it from being owned or read by anyone other than powerful clerics – and, in time, by a very few, very wealthy, very educated laymen. And, yes, from the fourteenth century, men and women fought for the right to translate it into their everyday tongues – and were sometimes persecuted and occasionally killed – until in certain countries their cause, no longer called "The Bible in Translation" but "The Protestant Reformation," prevailed.

My particular take on this brave time begins, however, with an observation based on long study of the progress of reformation in England: even rendered in familiar language, the Bible could remain stubbornly closed, its message surpassingly strange, to new readers. To have it in the language of everyday life was not the same as to have it make sense *to* everyday life. In fact, as we shall see, this could make the Bible's messages more frustrating and confusing, caught between the familiar world of the everyday and the jarringly alien expressions and exotic worldviews of both Testaments.

What makes this paradoxical story so thrilling, however, is the undeniable fact that people still wanted to read this impossible book, creating new theological and political problems for the very reformers and monarchs who had once claimed common cause – or at least *this* cause – with the laity. The Bible's strangeness spoke to readers otherwise mired in the day-to-day. The voice could sound inspiring, radical, or terrifying. The creative energy marshaled into the pursuit of "The Word" stood and still stands as remarkable testimony to the very human desire to understand the Bible. Translated scripture remains worthless and out of reach, after all, unless people learn to read it; intend to make meaning out of its theological claims, indecipherable commands, or exotic tales; are willing to produce, sell, purchase, or transport it; or make themselves acquainted with persons who can explain it with sensitivity, relevance, and persuasiveness.

This brings us to a second strand of the story. Step back a bit and we see that, in all those biblical endeavors – literacy, interpretation both scholarly and informal, production and distribution, pedagogy – the history of the Christian Bible has been inextricably entwined with the history of Christianity, with beliefs that inspired and drove people to seek out and make the words of what they called the Old and the New Testaments their own. It is virtually impossible, then, to tell this story without knowing the doctrines and practices that both depended upon and often transformed scripture; without these, we have only a thing of paper, ink, and leather covers, connected to its readers by forces and claims we would fail fully to comprehend or calibrate.

From a historical-cultural point of view, the Christian Bible became a sacred text because its readers were, and are, Christians. Any influence Christian scripture has had on secular culture – and admittedly, its effects have been Legion – still stem from the expectations Christians have brought, not only to its pages but also to their cultures and societies. Each chapter of this book, therefore, unpacks one or more of the general tenets of Christian belief or practice as it played out in the history of the Bible's interactions with Britain and America from the Middle Ages to the present day: the meaning of "tradition" and church authority; the meanings of orthodoxy, heresy, reformation, and schism; the mandate to mission; the significance of "canon"; and, inevitably, the impact of secularism, denominational diversity, and consumer culture as the modern age gave way to the post-modern. These, as we will see, had and still have very real consequences for how the Christian Bible was (and is) regarded, and its ideas broadcast, in every era.

Finally, in the pages that follow, we will also assay the Bible as, quite simply, a *book*: material object and as such an ever-transforming physical delivery system for spiritual and secular ideas alike. *The Bible and the People* is, in fact, primarily based upon a specific set of books: those held by the Huntington Library in San Marino, California, whose founder, Henry E. Huntington, decided in the early twentieth century to found a world-class library, drawn mainly from British (and, in time, American) presses, private libraries, and manuscript collections. To that end, he and his agents famously bought a pricey Gutenberg Bible on vellum, as well as first editions of nearly every important Christian Bible translated into English.

For that reason this book will not examine many Bibles from the European continent, any Bibles representing eastern orthodoxy, or the sacred texts of other religious traditions, like Judaism or Islam: Mr Huntington simply did not collect them in significant numbers. Not the most comprehensive or, perhaps in this day and age, the most politic heuristic strategy to limit the scope of a subject so vast, but, given that vastness, a pragmatic one. Now, however, the Huntington Library's original Bible collection has expanded with significant, if not always world-famous, additions. Entire libraries purchased by Mr Huntington and his agents, or donated to subsequent curators, accidentally and fortuitously brought to the Library such items as salesmen's Bibles, children's Bibles, Bible concordances, Bibles bound with hymn and prayer books, Bibles illustrated with reproductions of famous paintings, to name only a few.

The physicality of the Bible thus has a powerful and well documented analog in the materiality of historic Christian belief and western consumer culture alike. *The Bible and the People* takes, then, what was once in the hands of people – and then preserved on shelves and exhibited in glass cases – and, finally, draws it into the realm of cultural history. It will trace some of scripture's many forms and, shaped by these, its diversity of messages, along the two narratives I have already described: of access and of desire.

Before 1066

It's most accurate to say that the Bible is not a book but a library of books. The oldest extant versions of this collection's oldest books, those that comprise the Hebrew Bible (the Old Testament, to Christians), are captured in crumbly fragments of scrolls dating from around the first century of what we now call the Common Era (AD, or *anno domini*, "the year of our Lord," is falling out of use). Some of the texts of these books were in use in Jerusalem, however, six hundred years before that – in 621 BCE ("Before the Common Era": BC, "Before Christ," is also falling out of use). The smaller collection of books Christians call the New Testament was written over a hundred years between the middle of the first century CE and the middle of the second. The earliest versions we have of these Christian texts, also in fragmentary state, date from the later second century. No originals of the Hebrew Bible or the Christian scriptures exist.

"That the Bible was not written in English," the editor of the *New Oxford Annotated Bible* notes with a certain hint of understatement, "is a fact not always appreciated": wry testimony to the fact that, for the majority of its readers, whether educated or not, the Bible's expressive origins are as indecipherable as its material ones are irretrievable. The Bible was originally written in three languages: the Hebrew Bible in Aramaic and Hebrew; the Christian New Testament in Greek. The Hebrew Bible had also been rendered into Greek by the third century BCE for the use of non-Palestinian Jews who spoke and read Greek rather than Hebrew; this version became known as the Septuagint, named for the seventy scholars who, according to tradition, had made the translation. Greek was the language of philosophy and theology in the Roman Empire, the birthplace of Christianity, but as the Empire foundered, so did its grounding in the Greek language. Latin, the homelier tongue of legal and business transactions, became the language of everyday life in the Empire.

By the third century of the Common Era, the far-flung, disorganized (and mostly clandestine) Christians of an enormous (and mostly hostile) Empire were consulting a number of different versions of what they considered scripture. Some assemblies used nothing but the Greek version of the Hebrew Bible; some believed in nothing but the Gospels and rejected the Jewish scriptures of a common past; still others revered writings that told stories of Jesus that challenged doctrines espoused by church leaders, who issued directives from places safely far away: Rome, Milan, Jerusalem.

But by the middle of the fourth century, the Christian Church, now with the backing of the Emperor Constantine, found a source of singular power and a uniform voice, using both to build tightly organized hierarchical structures and win an extraordinary degree of state recognition, support, and, finally, control. Armed, sometimes literally, with these distinct advantages, its leaders decided it was time to regularize its sacred text by deciding which of its books could be regarded as authentic. Their standard of judgment took into consideration the protection of the newly official Christian doctrines of Jesus' humanity and divinity, the prophetic nature of the Hebrew scriptures, and the need to trace the texts of a new testament to apostolic origins.

In the year 382, the leader of the Christian Church based in Rome, Damasus, proclaimed the Christian Bible's canon: a word that means both "measuring rod" and "catalogue," excellent terms to describe an approved list of books containing rules of the faith. From Genesis to Revelation, if not always listed in the same order, Pope Damasus's list contained the same books that together we know as the Christian Bible today. (This event might have occurred earlier, but it took a lot of time and discussion before church leaders recognized the controversial Book of Revelation as authentically Holy Writ.) Papal declarations notwithstanding, it was centuries before this "official" Bible was recognized and taken up throughout the western Christian world. Other versions continued to circulate, and not everybody was satisfied with the list as it had been promulgated in the fourth century. Theologians argued, for example, throughout the Middle Ages about the official place of several books of Jewish scripture found in the Septuagint Greek but not the Hebrew scriptures. These books, the Apocrypha, had achieved a middling status in the Christian Bible: adjudged non-canonical, they nonetheless remained in the book, texts for liturgy but not for believing in. It would take a reformation to dislodge them – or, in the case of the English Church, to send them to the back of the book.

Still, these disparities were less influential than this supposition: that the Bible described by Pope Damasus was the only authentic text of the scriptures in the Latin-speaking world. The western empire fell to Germanic invaders in the fifth century but that particular Bible, like the Roman Church, remained. What was once the Roman Empire became in part the Holy Roman Empire by the ninth century, and, after that, a collection of kingdoms, but the same Bible, like the same Holy Catholic Church, remained. In the process Latin became the language of European ecclesiastical learning and liturgy, and the language of everyday life had become a hodgepodge of regional languages and local dialects.

This history of the English-language Bible begins, then, in a time and place when most people were illiterate and probably thought the Bible was written in the language of the Roman Church. The version they recognized, mostly by ear, was the one originally commissioned by the same man who had proclaimed its canon in 382: Damasus, who, in tandem with his concern about different versions, had also decided there were too many different translations of scripture circulating in the western Christian world. Along with declaring the canon, then, he also commissioned an official translation.

This new Latin translation of the Bible, designed to replace a myriad older and differing Latin versions – by the later fourth century few ecclesiastical scholars in Rome read Greek well, if at all – was undertaken by Jerome, one of the finest scholars of the early Christian Church and, in contrast to his peers, a superb linguist. He wrote on parchment or papyrus pages bound together into books called codices and his version was consequently transmitted in hand-copied texts (Christians apparently were the first to use the codex format; scrolls remained in general use for everybody else until much later) until the invention of the printing press eleven hundred years later.

For his base texts Jerome used existing Latin translations of the Hebrew Bible and a Greek manuscript of the New Testament. In other words, this consummate scholar translated the most lasting and influential Bible in Christian history out of already corrupted versions of its books. Jerome's scriptures were finally collected into one single book, whose existence is testified to in the writings of a Roman senator who founded a monastery – and, by extension, a monastic library – in the sixth century. Senator Cassiodorus's Bible is lost to us, but the oldest full manuscript copy of Jerome's Bible, the "Codex Amiatinus," may well have been copied from it in the late seventh century, in a Benedictine monastery between the Tyne and Wear rivers in Britain.

Thus by a roundabout if well-worn path we find ourselves in early medieval Britain, regarding a book transmitted with remarkable devotion, persistence, and skill but no particular claim to originality, accuracy, or general accessibility. What Jerome's fourth-century Bible translation did have was authority, if only the authority granted by custom and usage until 1546, when it was articulated at the Fourth Session of the Council of Trent. An official edition of the Vulgate Bible was printed in 1590, in the papacy of Sixtus V. Nevertheless, two years later Sixtus's Bible had to be recalled by Pope Clement VIII: it required more than three thousand corrections.

The Council of Trent ratified the Vulgate Bible officially for the first time in 1546 because, for the first time, it had to: Protestantism was gaining ground in Europe and Britain, people were demanding the Bible in their own language, and so the Roman Catholic Church's response was to undertake some reformations of its own. To that end, it abandoned many of its obsolete or less doctrinally justifiable practices, but it also formally declared its uniform and unshakeable truths, one of which was that the Vulgate Bible, in use since the fourth century, was the only authentic version of the scriptures. And it would remain in Latin, now declared the only authentic language of the scriptures.

Authentic is not the same as *original*, as Protestant translators would find out in their quest for earlier – and thus presumably less corrupt – biblical texts. The Bibles translated by Protestants from older versions of Hebrew and Greek scriptures into vernacular languages like English required as many if not more corrections and updates throughout the sixteenth century and after. Jerome's fourth-century plight was the same for all who followed his vocation: more than a millennium later, in the second great age of biblical translation, fifteenth- and sixteenth-century translators – humanist and Protestant alike – did work with older manuscripts than Jerome had at his disposal. But these were not original and so also corrupt, for the contents of handwritten books invariably shift during transmission.

The printing press made the Bible easier and cheaper to produce, but it could ensure neither the accuracy nor the stability of the text itself. The Protestant Bible would continue to be corrected, and it would eventually go on to appear in a multiplicity of formats and a diversity of translations and paraphrases. By the middle of the twentieth century, the Catholic Church would also undertake the task of translating the Bible out of Latin and into new formats for lay study. Change is, after all, the fate of any text, however divinely inspired and reverently believed in, that has been translated and transmitted over centuries by human means.

This paradoxical condition of simultaneous transience and permanence sets the tone for *The Bible and the People*. In the pages that follow, I will argue that the medieval Bible was neither as elite, nor as inaccessible, as has often been claimed; that the reformation Bible was neither as popular, nor as accessible, as has often been taught; that England's Bible made its greatest impact when it became an American Bible; that designing Bibles to fit the modes of secular culture does not, necessarily, make them secular; and that it was not widespread biblical understanding, but biblical *unknowing*, that had a galvanizing effect on the emerging early modern culture of vernacular knowledge. Throughout its history, the Bible has been tailored to fit its readers' needs and expectations without losing its special status as a sacred text. What I will not do is attempt the impossible task of explaining divine inspiration, nor will I presume to justify Christian practice and belief. For the past several years, though, I have been as captivated by the Bible and its believers, makers, and readers, as I was by the task of tracing their intersecting paths.

CHAPTER ONE

THE EYE OF THE BEHOLDER

The English Bible, c. 1066–1200

In the monasteries of the medieval age, The Word became Book. Here, in purpose-built rooms called scriptoria, men and women pledged to conduct their lives by counsels of perfection – poverty, chastity, and obedience, to work daily and pray without ceasing – copied the lines of the Christian scripture. The creators of medieval Bibles occasionally embellished this holy script, populating their text with fantastic beasts that clawed at the margins and gilded capital letters that framed lively little narratives in one act. Completed over years of labor, produced for immensely powerful patrons or ecclesiastical foundations, designed to honor apostles, saints, or the Mother of God, the worth of such illustrated manuscripts was just as immense then as it is today. Illuminated Bibles are now considered works of art. They are owned by museums, research libraries, and private families (many of whom eventually sell them for tax reasons to museums and research libraries). The most lavish of these assured and arrestingly lovely books represent only a small fraction of the Bibles once produced by hand in western Christendom. They constitute nearly all of the ones we view today on public display.

Which may lead us to miscalculate the value and misunderstand the work of the Bible in the Middle Ages.

Pretty is, after all, as pretty does. The Latin Bible was a hard-working text in an age wherein the Christian Church claimed universal jurisdiction over all aspects of society and culture. The language of scripture permeated the world of the medieval West. Its lines formed a basis for theology and literature and created a template for daily liturgies and weekly sermons. Its phrases underpinned basic catechisms, epic poetry, and the investiture of emperors. Gleaming from a rich cathedral dais or humbly unadorned in a shadowy clerical study, a Bible's worth was primarily calculated by how well it did its job of representing the divine, rendered incarnate in vellum and ink.

A modern curator of medieval manuscripts will run a practiced eye, then, not only over a medieval Bible's illustrations but also over its most precious asset: its lines. Are they evenly spaced and neatly penned? Are the letters consistently legible and reliably accurate? Do they reflect the work of one scribe or many? One style of handwriting or many? A well-made Bible is, first and foremost, a collection of well-wrought words on a page.

All manuscripts are handmade: not merely rare but unique. Any consideration of their worth begins, then, with an appraisal of the labor, skill, and artistry that went into their making. These humane values transcend the worth of even the finest materials used in the construction of books – animal hide, colorful inks, gold leaf, precious gems. Vellum, tougher than paper, lasts for ages but the illuminators of medieval manuscripts do not, and usually remain mysterious figures. The work of their hands too often constitutes the sum of their biographies and so we name them after their labors: "Master of the Stammheim Missal," "Master of the Louvain Psalter."

In any case, an infinitesimal number of medieval manuscripts were illuminated by a single genius; most were neither intricately nor ornately illuminated, if at all. The Bible was too long, too complex, too important, and too necessary a text to be produced inefficiently. A monastic team of scribes could work far more quickly. The very best of these collaborators were trained in several formal styles of handwriting and would trade turns on the same book without sacrificing its clarity or uniform appearance.

This is not to say, however, that even a well-made manuscript Bible was a marvel of perfection. (No book, whether hand-copied or printed, ever can be.) Despite their remarkable material durability, every manuscript remains a human artefact: exasperating, poignant testament to the many frailties to which the human is heir. Manuscript Bibles were often inaccurately transcribed. The monks and nuns of the scriptoria were trained in the exacting skills of reproducing text, but not always in the elite art of reading the Latin language. Working from faulty texts, possibly unable to recognize or comprehend the words they copied by rote, scribes routinely transmitted the errors of previous generations and then added flaws of their own fashioning. Vellum being too valuable to toss out or scrape overmuch, the mistakes that were detected had to be corrected, directly and obviously, on the page.[1] Sometimes a subsequent reader undertook the responsibility. Few if any of these otherwise punctilious students felt obliged to match the color of the ink or the style of the original hand.

When we open medieval Bibles, then, we are confronted with a veritable riot of words, images, and additional markings, which can make these books seem as kinetically charged and noisy as a room filled with several generations of loudly busy human beings. This is their glory – and *our* consequence. The hand-inked pages link centuries of successive readers in an ongoing conversation, of which we are the most recent and least interactive participants. For we no longer correct medieval manuscripts directly on the page (at least not if we wish to exit the research library under our own steam and not in the custody of security guards – and, quite possibly, psychiatrists). Instead we write a polite note to the curator and, if we are wise, think gratefully upon the mistakes and the misreadings that make up the messily believable beauty of the Past. These "flaws" rip the opaque veil that separates us from places and times now out of mind, and an age once lost to us is suddenly and powerfully revealed.

One such time and place is the earlier Middle Ages (*c.* 800–1100 CE), an era characterized by the extent of the political and religious influence of the papacy. Before the advent of Protestantism shattered the unity of western Christendom, the Christian Bible was in the care of this Church based in Rome, whose primary concern was to protect the faith by expounding it responsibly and preventing its beliefs from degenerating into heresy. This means that only one characteristic of the pre-Reformation "official" Bible was, in a sense, standard: it was supposed to be rendered in Latin, transmitted from scribe to scribe, from generation to generation, out of a fourth-century translation from the Greek made by the North African scholar and churchman Jerome.

Beyond the certainty of finding a text more or less derived from Jerome's translation, not much else in a Bible made before the thirteenth century was standardized. Its books were not always set in a particular order: they could be placed in differing sequences depending on regional norms, local liturgical practice, or peculiar working conditions. Scriptures were unevenly and confusingly formatted; text divisions often went unmarked; individual verses were unnumbered until the later sixteenth century. At least medieval sentences were lightly punctuated, a nicety not observed in the codices of an earlier age. This explains, incidentally, why silent reading was so rare at the time: it is virtually impossible to make sense of an unpunctuated passage without reading it aloud. The fifth-century churchman Ambrose's ability to read a book without moving his lips was seen by some of his contemporaries as nothing short of miraculous (and by others of his acquaintance, no doubt, as a slightly annoying episcopal parlor trick).[2]

These irregularities explain, at least in part, why we find the kinds of decoration we do in a medieval Bible. Far from being shiny add-ons, images and emphasized capitals had useful purpose. In a read-aloud culture, wherein books were generally scarce, literacy always low, and liturgies lengthy, a lector had to be able to find his or her place swiftly. The first letters of the first words of the books of the Bible required signposts; illumination and other decorations marked the reader's way.

They were sorely needed, as were those relatively few expositors and lectors. Like all medieval books, the medieval Bible was an inaccurate and irregular artefact. It was written in a language only a very few people could read, in an age when the language spoken by the people was itself a language only a few could read. It was confusing, unwieldy, expensive, and unlikely to contain many helpful illustrations. Yet it formed the basic script for sacred and secular life in the western Middle Ages, an era best described from our currently secular vantage point as scripturally saturated and biblically aware.

How do we comprehend the impact of this confounding, para-doxical work – both so esoteric, odd, and user-unfriendly and also so essential, well known, and revered – on its own age?

Explanations for the Bible's powerful hold on medieval society and culture in western Christendom most often center on the power of its message or the power of the ecclesiastical institution charged with its protection and dissemination. These are good but incom-plete answers. The first can assume too much about the clarity and universal theological appeal of the Christian scriptures and the second can, and usually does, assume the worst about the universal authority claimed by the Catholic Church in the Middle Ages. There are other ways to account for the Bible's success, and so I will begin with a consideration, not of brightly illuminated pages, but of the gentler light generated by the pages of a deceptively plain scriptural manuscript.

The Biography of a Bible

The manuscript to which we now turn is material proof of the paradoxical fact that, in the age before printing presses, Protestant reformation, and widespread vernacular literacy, the Bible was both a rare luxury item and a widely known, hard-working text in daily use. The oldest book in the holdings of the Huntington Library in San Marino, California, is the manuscript known as the "Gundulf Bible." It dates from the second half of the eleventh century. Notes on the first pages of each of its two volumes identify an early owner as Gundulf, who was Bishop of Rochester, in southern England, from 1077 to 1108. This particular book appears in the catalogue of the Rochester Cathedral library for the years 1130 and 1202, information that fixes the book in a place with a documented history and allows us to trace the genealogy of a medieval Bible.

While the English Church described by Bede in 731 was not exactly the moribund institution that the apologists for William the Conqueror would claim after 1066, Rochester Cathedral was no place to go seeking evidence of pre-Norman ecclesiastical vibrancy. Rochester was the oldest and smallest of the bishoprics that effectively functioned as dependencies of the great southeastern archiepiscopal see of Canterbury. Founded in 604, the second-oldest religious foundation in England, Rochester endured the depredations of Mercian and Danish incursions in the seventh and eighth centuries – the unhappy fate of so many Anglo-Saxon foundations erected near Britain's southern coastlines. By the eleventh century, battered by invasion and neglect, the cathedral was worn down and outmoded – as, undoubtedly, were its four remaining priests.

In the late eleventh century, Gundulf, a Norman monk and trained architect who built the Tower of London for William the Conqueror, was named Bishop of Rochester by Lanfranc, the new Archbishop of Canterbury. Gundulf took up his post and almost immediately made his name as a man of surpassing energy and ambition. He remade the cathedral into a soaring model of Norman architecture and replaced its residential priests, or "seculars" (so called to distinguish them from priests bound by monastic rule), with a resident order of Benedictine monks like himself. His decision, not only to rebuild the structure but also to redirect the work of the community that it housed, made Rochester Cathedral into an abbey and Bishop Gundulf into an abbot. Gundulf now had charge not only of the secular churches and clergy in his region but also of all monastic communities including, most authoritatively, his own. His decision to install a religious order in the environs of Rochester Cathedral thus placed him in a position of great power and influence.[3]

It was power and influence secondary only to that of his contemporary, England's formidable Archbishop of Canterbury (c. 1005–89).

The two had been novice monks together in France, which may explain their collaborative success in reforming religion in the south of England. In medieval terms the word "reformation" always means a unification program: conforming the disparate Christians – whether alienated monks, ignorant priests, or willful laypeople – of the many regions of western Christendom to a set of common beliefs and practices deriving from Rome. Medieval reformations thus were, and still are, judged on how well they accomplished that work of uniformity and that claim of Roman universality, which may surprise those of us more used to thinking of reform as sectarian critique and the word "reformation" as necessarily attached to the modifier "Protestant." Lanfranc's reforms in England included regularizing ecclesiastical law and defending the doctrine of the Eucharist as approved by Rome, but these projects emerged from a deeper ambition: to correct England's many different circulating biblical texts – all Latin, but few Jerome's – to orthodox standards, thus "bringing them," as one scholar points out, "into line with that of eleventh-century Europe."[4]

Four hundred years before the advent of print, the Bibles of the British Isles were a traditionalist's nightmare: not only had they accumulated a mass of textual errors, they could be found in any number of unsanctioned versions reflecting regional practices, preferences, and geographical isolation. A fierce defender of orthodoxy and a stalwart ally of the western papacy, Archbishop Lanfranc reformed English Christianity by building upon foundations laid by his corrections of scriptures and his sponsorship of the production of an official, church-sanctioned version of the Latin Bible in England.

For his part, Gundulf concentrated on translating Lanfranc's large ambitions into the small world of Rochester. The library, like the cathedral fabric itself, was in parlous shape upon his assumption of the episcopate. So, in addition to replacing its priests in 1080 and rebuilding the cathedral in 1082, Gundulf also oversaw the construction of a world-class library: a task that would necessarily include not only commissioning and copying texts from other scriptoria but also training Rochester's monks to become scribes.

Here, as seemingly everywhere else, Gundulf's efforts swiftly bore fruit. The pre-Norman book lists of the cathedral note the presence of only six books; by the 1202 assessment, Rochester housed more than ninety. Most came from Canterbury's scriptorium, either directly or as texts copied by Rochester monks. The Bishop had successfully transformed a moribund institution into a vibrantly bookish one. The worship of God would thereafter proceed in acts of copying and preservation.

The Gundulf Bible

The most noteworthy thing about the Gundulf Bible is not that it is a one-thousand-year-old book (although that simple fact in itself is surely deserving of admiration), but that it has been considered an ancient book for nearly all of that lifespan. On the front flyleaf we find the following note, penciled in a modern hand: "The famous Gundulf Bible/Described as *old* in the catalogue of the library of Rochester Cathedral in 1202!" Other less exclamatory but still enthusiastic inscriptions can be found on the first folio page of its first volume, unfolding testimony to this Bible's successive owners and the fierce possessiveness that disputed claims can inspire. Here at the upper right hand we find the following warning to would-be thieves, penned thickly in a script that probably dates from the thirteenth century:[5]

> *First part of the bible, courtesy of Gundulf, bishop of Rochester, of good memory. This book belongs to the cloister of Rochester, and he who may steal it from there, or who may hide it once it has been stolen, or who may erase this ownership note fraudulently, is hereby excommunicated, with the sentence carried out by the afore-mentioned holy bishop, the prior and the individual priests of the chapter of Rochester.*[6]

This pre-emptive strike was aimed less at strange burglars than at rapacious cathedral administrators, and reflects the complex situation at Rochester that followed Gundulf's transformation of the cathedral into a Benedictine abbey. By the later twelfth century, secular bishops rather than monks took charge of Rochester, with the inevitable clash of interests, pulling of rank, and jurisdictional spats. Studious of their honor and jealously possessive of the abbey's property – as Benedictines, they were not allowed to possess individual wealth, which seems to have rendered them indefatigable in defense of their corporate holdings – the monks of Rochester began to label their books and write their history: already time-honored ways of establishing precedence and ownership. In order to make themselves and their tenure at Rochester unimpeachably ancient, the monks made their precious, newly acquired books ancient as well.

No matter how successful they were at protecting their authority and property from greedy bishops, the monks were finally no match for a determined Renaissance king. Rochester Abbey was dissolved, like all English religious houses, in the reign of Henry VIII, falling victim to Henry's determinedly administrative and fiscal approach to religious reform. Some five hundred years after the establishment of monks within its walls and a few short months after their disestablishment, the cathedral was resupplied with a secular Dean and priests in 1542. The books of the abbey, the Gundulf Bible among them, were catalogued by the king's agents as valuable property and dispersed, some to the king's library (now housed under the same name at the British Library in London) and some into private hands.

So by the sixteenth century what the monks feared had become reality, and their precious book left the cathedral library with no sign that the dire mishaps called down by their curse would take effect. Later in the century, the Gundulf was acquired by a John, Lord Lumley, who may have penned the directive we find underneath the monks' now toothless Latin imprecation.[7] In an impeccably neat Renaissance hand is a set of precise instructions in English:

Memorandum this Bible is perfecte which I would wishe to be safelye kepte togither with ye booke in written hande called Reductorium Bibliae in quo moralizantur omnes figurae Bibliae. *The booke is covered in wood and white leather.*[8]

This notation of its condition along with the precise details of its physical appearance, the instructions on its storage, and the mention of its inclusion within a system of classification surely set the Gundulf on a new stage. All of the above suggest that, by the time it made its way into his collection of "books in written hand" (thereby distinguishing it from printed books), the Gundulf Bible had ceased being a valued working text, a *book*, and had instead become a valuable collector's *item*. It was now a rare object, a remembrancer to the world of print and Protestantism, testifying to a bygone age of universal Catholic faith and of books produced manually.

At this point, centuries of stable existence gave way to a busy life of scholarly and commercial exchange. The Gundulf crossed the water to the European continent some time in the seventeenth century, moving between the libraries of theologians and the shelves of Dutch bookstalls for more than a century, not returning to England until the nineteenth century. There it acquired a new binding of blue leather, stamped with the motto of its Victorian owner, Theodore Williams (*Deus Alit Me*, "God will strengthen me"). Williams subsequently sold the manuscript to Thomas Phillipps in 1827, after which it migrated to America. It was acquired by Henry Huntington from the book-seller A.S.W. Rosenbach in 1924, during the heyday of Huntington's collecting career, as this turn-of-the-century railroad magnate avidly pursued books that would stock a world-class library dedicated to the western literary tradition.

What did Mr Huntington (or his agents) find to covet in this particular manuscript of two volumes (besides, perhaps, the inspiring glimpse of another, earlier quest to create a great library)? At first encounter, we might well wonder. The Gundulf is a "plain style" Bible, reflecting the distinctly unflashy book culture of the French priory of Bec where both the future Bishop and his Archbishop were bent to the taut bow of the monastic life. It boasts no illuminations and no original pictures. Later marks sketch out a few figures in pencil – animals, a seated man, a lonely knight – but these were never finally executed. One catalogue calls the decorations "small and competent," surely a cautious compliment. The

2 Monastic admonition, the Gundulf Bible.

rubrication is correct and contained. In a very few places the initials have been outlined in silver or show touches of red or purple. The effect, though, is still anything but lavish. It has, instead, an elegant, un-showy simplicity, which allows the reader better to appreciate the restrained beauty of fine workmanship.

This Bible's classy appeal actually begins with its heft in the hand. The Gundulf provides tactile pleasures often lacking in modern versions. To render the profusion of words that make up "the Bible" with careful clarity in this age meant placing larger, well-spaced letters on the page: fewer words, more pages per volume, making this work substantial in terms of its size – and its worth. The vellum pages are thick and silkily-smooth; treated animal hide feels like velvet to the touch but it also feels considerably sturdier than the cloth or wood-pulp paper in books made after the 1500s. The leaves of medieval manuscripts, unlike the printed pages of the Victorians, will undoubtedly outlast all others and rise up to greet Judgment Day.

What stands out most, perhaps, is the appearance of the words on almost every page of the Gundulf. They are penned in minuscule display scripts in two sizes and styles, prologues and introductory materials thus distinguished one from the other, each letter set accurately within ruled lines a reader can still discern faintly traced on the page. The lines are presented in two columns, with the largest colored initials indicating the start of every book. The effect is balanced and orderly, and almost perfectly proportionate. In the margins, roman numerals and smaller capitals in brown and red mark the start of scriptural passages, assisting readers who needed to navigate a lengthy, complex manuscript without frequent or numbered verse divisions. The simply decorated letters serve the same purpose as luxurious gilded ones – to mark beginnings and endings in a long, complex book not yet divided into numbered chapters and verses.

This Bible was designed, then, not only for aesthetic pleasure but also for ease in reading. Here it is important to remember that reading was not a private act in the medieval period. The many unique abbreviations in the Gundulf may betoken an "insider" clerical readership, but the rubrication that highlights the lines of the Psalms, carefully marking the start of every liturgical phrase, reminds us that these were sung daily in a ritual that at Rochester would have had an audience made up of locals as well as of monks and priests.

This should also remind us that biblical knowledge could never be the sole property of a learned clergy, in this or any other age. If by "reading" we mean individual apprehension and comprehension of words on a page, it is true that in the Middle Ages the Bible could be read only by those very few individuals who possessed a working knowledge of Latin. Their acts of reading, however, were not aimed at the solitary acquisition of private scriptural knowledge. Instead the men and women, nearly all of them clerics or monastics, who read the Bible in this era did so in order to enlarge its audience: those people, lay and religious, who heard it recited in the Mass or at monastic mealtimes or who listened to its precepts and stories in parish sermons or retold in midsummer biblical plays.

Which brings us to the slightly less orderly nature, perhaps, of this particular Bible. The first chapter of Genesis in the Vulgate opens with the Latin *In principio* (In the beginning). In the Gundulf Bible this iconic opening line is marked prominently with an intersecting, rubricated I and N. The effect is orderly, stately, and geometric. What may be most impressive about the opening page of the Gundulf Genesis, however, is just how messy it looks around the edges and between these opening lines. This particular page is thickly annotated – more heavily, in fact, than any other page of the Gundulf (although there are annotations on many other pages as well). Notes in several hands (especially heavy at the top left) provide evidence of scholarly interaction with its pages over generations. And if annotation is evidence of use – and heavy annotation the evidence of heavy use – we might be tempted to posit that this page was the hardest-working page of the Gundulf Bible.

And it may well be, if we judge only by how heavily it is marked up in a number of hands. But this would be evidence of a different kind of work, as the Book of Genesis was not, like the Psalms,

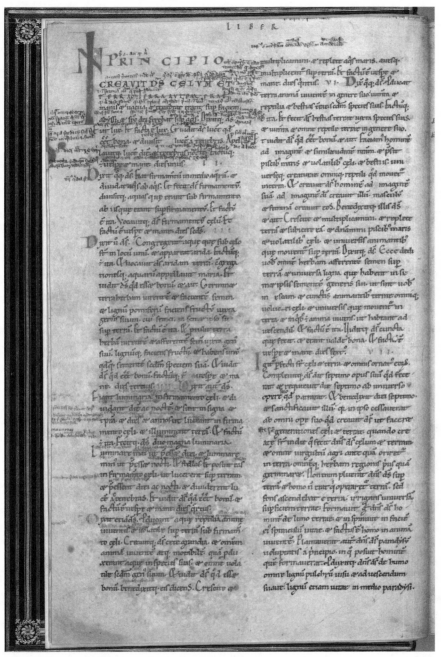

3 The Gundulf Bible, Genesis 1:1.

in daily liturgical rotation. The annotations, in fact, appear to be amplifications on the meaning of the text rather than corrections (it requiring none as the text is accurately faithful to the orthodox version), or enlargements on its many clever abbreviations (which, as most are unique, betoken an "insider" audience who arguably would not need them). It is tempting to hypothesize: that this first page of the first book of the Bible, with its iconic opening line and its almost hypnotic repetition of *dixit Deus fiat . . . et vidit Deus quot esset bonum*, "God said Let there be . . . and God saw it was good," formed an initiation of sorts, with the well-known story of Creation used for lessons in scriptural reading and exegesis.

Conclusion

The elegant if restrained Gundulf Bible is a fitting start to a study of the second millennium of the Bible's history. It reminds us that the scriptures are inextricably bound to the people who own and copy and translate and interpret and read them – and that this, in effect, means that books, like people, have biographies: lives that intersect with other lives, shape them and are in turn profoundly shaped *by* them, generation after generation. In the pages that follow, we will trace those intersections and generations, between the Bible and the people, and between the Bible and other books.

CHAPTER TWO

ON THE ROAD AND IN THE STREET

THE ENGLISH BIBLE, *c.* 1200–1500

By the year 1300, the very middle of the Middle Ages, the Bible should have been the exclusive property of a few high-level clerics and a small cohort of Latin-educated elites – nearly all of them male.[1] Each Bible could only be produced by hand, individually and occasionally. And those that had been so produced were shelved in cathedrals, churches, and monasteries: hardly the private haunts of even the most pious laypersons. The Church's official disapproval of any version of the Christian Bible save the Latin of Jerome's Vulgate pitted the power of absolutist authorities against those who would have their Bible not in the Church's but in their own language. Not that this would have mattered: few people in the medieval West, rich or poor, could read their own language either.

Despite these facts – and they are undeniable – the Bible was never the exclusive property of any institution or any one social class, even at this time. Lively participants in a scripture-saturated culture, the vast majority of medieval folk were both illiterate *and* deeply familiar with Holy Writ. This will not seem such a startling paradox if we enlarge our notion of what might constitute biblical understanding and how it might have been acquired in the age before print and Protestantism. It is true that relatively few people had access to the Bible, if by "The Bible" we mean "a text to read" or "a book to own." We can redefine "access," however, in ways that do not require people to have owned or to have read the Bible in order to have taken it to heart – and mind.

Medieval laypeople heard the Vulgate Bible spoken aloud, week in and week out, over the entire course of their lives. When they encountered the scriptures as part of worship, whether in liturgical readings or in set prayers, they would first have experienced the strange-sounding words as auditory impressions. In the evocative setting of the cathedral or parish service, where Latin words were buttressed by sacred images and accompanied by grand priestly gestures, the cadence of certain repeated sounds – *Pater noster . . .*; *In nomine domino . . .*; *Beatus vir . . .*; *pro ora nobis . . .* – would have coalesced into a composite language, comprehensible to audiences destined never to read nor to write Latin, transforming what should have been mere gibberish into the practice of piety. As a vernacular religious treatise from 1375 stated, even "when not understood, the power of God's word still avails."[2] This aural and somatic experience of the sound of the Vulgate Bible would have formed an essential aspect of popular biblical understanding.

This chapter examines three formats for the scriptures that lent a more material form to biblical understanding in the later Middle Ages, an era as significant to the history of scriptural access and outreach as the age of translation yet to come. Between 1200 and 1500, the scriptures escaped the confines of churches and monasteries to move into hands and onto the road. In the 1200s, Bibles shrunk to fit the hands and pockets of mendicant monks. In the 1300s, the scribes who had made clerical Bibles portable then turned to the domestic market, producing small, exquisitely decorated private Psalm books for laypersons with the money to buy them. And by the 1400s, Bible stories were being staged in the city streets, often riotously, by merchants and tradespeople. All these transformations predate the age of print and Protestantism; as we shall see, they forged a necessary path to the reformations of the sixteenth century.

The Rise of the Mass-Produced Bible

Every manuscript is unique, but some manuscripts were less unique than others. Even a casual glance at these French Bibles from the thirteenth century reveals the degree to which, by the later Middle Ages, the work of scribes had become regularized and scriptorial styles of illuminating and decorating distinctively uniform. These Vulgate Bibles are very subtly different, of course, but overall they share so many characteristics that they appear almost mass-produced. Indeed they are so much alike that they force us to reassess the qualities of singularity that we often say distinguish a manuscript Bible. After all, the elegantly idiosyncratic Gundulf Bible was a Vulgate Bible – and, as such, material evidence of the Church's successful drive for orthodox conformity in eleventh-century Britain. So we might want to ask: *Was the Bible ever designed to be exclusive?*

And the answer would have to be: *No, of course it wasn't.* But at this time the form of its words *were.* The Bible had claims to special protection, and for understandable reasons, given the situation of western Christendom in the Middle Ages. There was only one legitimate and recognized form of Christianity in the medieval West and it was regimented and rigorously institutionalized. What we would now call the Roman Catholic Church, therefore, can just as easily and surely more simply be referred to, in that period and in that place, as "the Church," for it neither recognized, would have tolerated, nor was actually troubled overmuch by, any serious and sustained Christian competition.

This does not mean the Church never felt called upon to defend itself: identifying and eradicating what it considered "heresy" was the method it had always used to define what it considered "orthodoxy," and this era proved no exception to that rule. Its particular kind of thought-policing is hard to come by in the western world nowadays, which makes it hard for us to understand the mind-set of an earlier, fully Christian culture. In today's America and Europe, where the practice of religion is currently voluntary, habits of thought generally post-Enlightenment, and approaches to matters of the soul typically

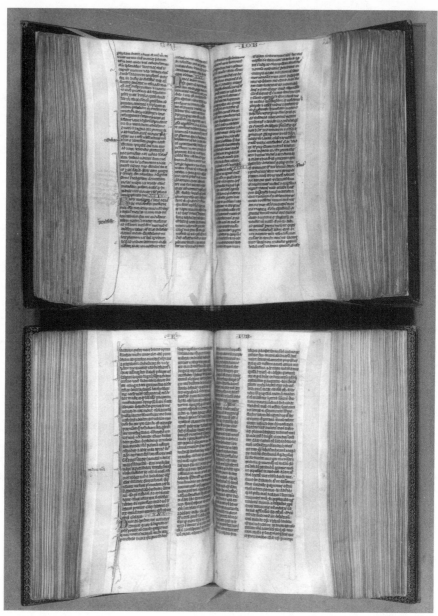

4 Two nearly identical manuscripts, Vulgate Bibles, French, thirteenth century.

post–Freudian, "heresy" and "orthodoxy" are not even considered relative terms: they are instead treated as improbable, culturally constructed, archaic categories that in and of themselves make little sense and have no reality. This is true even for conservative, evangelical, and even fundamentalist Christians, who are more comfortable wielding the language of sin than the language of heresy.

We cannot make this statement in the past tense with integrity, however. In the Middle Ages, true belief and true practice existed – for the simple reason that medieval people believed in both. To understand them best, then, we need to honor their certainties even if we cannot share them. They knew without a shadow of a doubt that a true Church charged with the protection and dissemination of true belief and practice oversaw western Christendom. Outside that true Church, they knew, there was no salvation. These were living, working, realities. Medieval Christians, ecclesiastic and lay, understood that "heresy" and "orthodoxy" were authentic categories. They set their religious expectations accordingly.

Best, then, to suspend the practice of enclosing those two powerful words in the condescending inverted commas of historical analysis, at least for now. For this cultural knowledge, of true and false – which are, after all, much more interesting categories than right and wrong – applied to the medieval Bible, both in terms of its endorsement or definition of true and false religion, and also and more simply, in terms of its actual content, which was limited to the Latin Vulgate. According to the western Church, no other version of the Bible could convey the truth of Christianity.

Throughout the history of Christianity, however, stating what *wasn't* to be believed has always proved a more straightforwardly successful task for the Church than explaining what *was*. Before the reformations of the sixteenth century, which transformed and redesigned the complementary notions of heresy and orthodoxy altogether, heresy (defined as "the formal denial or doubt of any defined doctrine") tended to be local in its effects and sporadic in its occurrence.[3] Heretical ideas were, for the most part, faulty ideas about God and humankind – sincerely meant miscalculations in doctrinal reasoning easy enough to make in any age, given the ongoing difficulty of explaining and justifying any of the ways of an omniscient God to an ignorant humankind.

The nature of the Deity and the operation of divine action in the world had been defined in an overwhelming array of doctrinal statements ratified – and sometimes subsequently undone – by church councils since the early centuries of Christian history, testimony not only to the exhilaration of theological reasoning, but also to the realities of corporate decision-making. In the Middle Ages, these approved doctrines of the Church required belief in (amongst other similarly paradoxical but slightly less important ideas): a threefold Divinity which nonetheless was to be accounted as an indivisible Singularity; the fact that ordinary bread and wine in the communion service became the actual, ingestible body and blood of the son of God; that this son of God was both entirely human and entirely divine at one and the same time without damage done to either of those essential and indivisible natures; that a world created by an omnipotent and beneficent God was always unsafe and often wildly wicked; and that humans could be saved from the finality of the death that so obviously and consistently came for all living things, from generation to generation. So complex and improbable were these tenets that educated, mainstream theologians in the lawful employ of the Church could still find themselves on the wrong side of ecclesiastical law just by trying to explain them better or understand them more thoroughly.

Pity, then, the uneducated folk who could get in trouble simply for trying to work them out for themselves, or for being poorly acquainted, due to their own ignorance or that of a particularly doltish local priest, with those doctrines in the first place.

Educated or uneducated, however, most medieval Christians didn't fall into gross heresy, and those who did were generally open to instruction or re-instruction on basic matters of doctrine and practice, were it to be had. And while a few well-known and well-documented heretics did become obdurate in defense of ideas they saw as superior formulations of the doctrines espoused by the institutional Church, even fewer originally intended either to challenge the legitimacy of the western Church or the idea that the rigorously focused theological worldview called "orthodox" existed. For most people, such a challenge would have been, simply, unthinkable.

For one thing, to have thought anything else would have been far too dangerous. In the world of the Middle Ages, heresy was an affront to God and thus by extension a spreading stain on any society pledged to live by God's laws. It was akin to contagion in the medieval mind and, like contagion, was considered as implacable, deadly, and liable to lead to an epidemic if not swiftly diagnosed, treated, and ruthlessly eradicated. The penalty for obstinate heresy could be (at best) a hefty fine, or (at worst) a grisly death meted out by the State, which worked in conjunction with the Church on such unavoidably violent matters. But the Church did not delight in ferreting out and prosecuting heretics, which, after all, was a path to social unrest almost as sure as that paved by heresy itself. One way to avoid unnecessary bloodshed and tumult was to make sure the Church's approved teachings were reaching everyone within the bounds of its purview.

No inconsiderable task, that. The Church based at Rome drew an enforceable spiritual jurisdiction along boundaries that at this time covered a vast number of kingdoms and an empire or two. This far-flung Church aimed at making its doctrines tenable. It was required to deliver its professions to the Christians of an impressive number of countries – each speaking different languages and engaged in different social practices. How to speak univocally to such a polyglot, multicultural congregation? For one thing, it helped if everyone heard the same teachings in standard form, issuing from every church, cathedral, and monastery in western Christendom.

It was the view of the Church that its singleness of voice and purpose could only be communicated if its entire corps of personnel worked from the same texts. And so, to promote unity of belief and uniformity of practice, the Church transmitted its official documents and pronouncements in a single language: Latin. Latin was the language of its doctrines; Latin was the language of its laws; and Latin was the language in which its sacred text, the Bible, was legitimately conveyed. Moreover, the Latin of this Bible couldn't be just any set of

Latin translations of the older Hebrew and Greek texts of the Old and New Testaments. It had to be Jerome's translation, known as the "Vulgate," as ratified in church councils over the centuries since its first appearance in the latter part of the fourth century: the era that also witnessed the establishment of Christianity as an imperial religion able to enforce its doctrines by the power of the State. Claiming singular, non-transferable, and unchanging power, the Church found it most logical to base those claims not only on eight centuries of corporate decision-making under papal authority but also on one single, immutable text.

As the populations of Western Europe expanded and migrated in ever-larger waves in the 1200s, the Church at Rome accordingly became concerned about how to protect its doctrines in changeable times. The highly mobile conditions of the century were conducive to outbreaks of less than orthodox thinking, and so the Church had to broadcast its teachings with clarity, efficiency, and a reasonable degree of uniformity. Given the fact of mass illiteracy, the primary delivery system would have to be person-to-person. Books were still few and far between, after all, but people were everywhere in this age.

Not only that; many were on their way somewhere else. By the thirteenth century, Europe's economic culture, based on feudal land-holding, was increasingly dependent upon itinerant labor. Its religious culture was characterized by the crusading impulse and the success of pilgrimage industries both international and domestic. Its secular culture was beginning to reflect the astoundingly rapid growth of urban centers such as London, Paris, and Cologne. This was no cozily settled age. It was, arguably, one of the wanderlustiest periods in the entire history of western civilization.

Rich woman, poor man, beggar child, thief, at any given moment these people might just be on the road in the Middle Ages. Their intents could be far-fetched: going overseas to lead – or follow – a crusade or to visit a pilgrimage site; running off to the nearest city to find work or to study theology or read law at the university. They could be local: out to the same old fields to sow; on to new fields that offered the possibility of better harvests. The majority were leaving the countryside to try their vocational luck in the city. Still others were trudging dustily back from the travels that had once promised to be so salvific, beneficial, or exciting. And, of course, certain other enterprising souls on the road were simply there to rob, con, beg from, sell to, or otherwise take advantage of all these busy seekers after salvation, education, crops, or fortune. Traveling players shared the byways with wayfaring knights and wandering cutthroats – and lucky the vagrant who could tell one from the other. Coming or going, wealthy or not so, successful or less so, the people of late medieval Europe were in seemingly perpetual motion.

On the well-tramped roads surrounding the cities were also monks freshly sprung from claustration: the new religious orders of Dominican and Franciscan friars. The followers of Francis of Assisi (1181–1226) and Dominic Guzman (1174–1221) made vows even harsher than those once devised by the father of western monasticism, St Benedict (480–550). In addition to personal wealth, conjugal sympathy, and the dubious liberty of self-determination, Franciscans and Dominicans also gave up their right to own even communal property or accept money by any means except begging, thus consigning themselves to a permanently unsettled existence. Pledged to a kind of sanctified state of restlessness, they set out in search of under-counseled souls in transit. The new religious orders thus created a monastic version of the culture at large that both reflected and exacerbated the itinerant and urbane tenor of later medieval life.

Occasionally the friars mirrored the times a bit too well. The popular literature of the day often suggested – less than politely and with a good deal of salacious speculation – that these newly footloose monks were little more than shifty and rapacious confidence men with tonsures. But for the most part they were the dedicated and nimble advance men of late medieval popular orthodoxy. The Franciscans and Dominicans brought a distinctively religious cast to the two representative locales of the late medieval western world. They could be found (especially the Franciscans) on city streets, creating popular interest in church teachings by preaching homely sermons and instituting the myriad new devotional practices – for example, meditating on the fourteen "stations of the cross" – approved by Rome in this period. And they could also be found (especially the Dominicans) lecturing to the students of the new urban universities, where monks taught subjects as varied as philosophy, geometry, logic, law, and rhetoric, in addition to theology.

Leaving the monasteries – which, in search of sanctified solitude, had been built far from urban centers – meant being without resources to hand. Lacking a monastic library, these new monastics needed books they could pack and carry – even if they could not actually own them. And they needed them in far larger numbers, too: one for every monk rather than one or two for every corporate house.[4] The social conditions of the second half of the thirteenth century thus can seem almost providentially designed to take advantage of an emerging new format for the scriptures, but it is more accurate to say that production shifted rapidly to serve a powerfully emergent market. By the end of the twelfth century the lavish decorations and regional eccentricities that distinguished the occasional products of the scriptoria had begun to give way to newly styled Bibles: increasingly standardized, portable, and available.[5]

These neat little Bibles, primarily created for monks, were no longer made by monks. They were the creation of secular scribes in Paris, where, by the middle of the thirteenth century, the art of efficient and innovative book-making flourished as it did nowhere else in western Christendom. The scribes turned out books of all sorts with a hitherto unknown degree of efficiency and dispatch. The scriptures crafted by these stationers were called "Paris Bibles," even when copied by workmen operating out of London or Bologna. The one-name-fits-all reflects these Bibles' remarkable similarity of content, look, layout, and organization.

This is a good time to pause and contemplate the challenge of producing a portable Bible in the age before typeset printing and modern paper. After all, twenty-first-century paperback versions printed in stupefyingly tiny type on the flimsiest of paper stock are still not sized for many people to read easily and hold unobtrusively at the same time. Paris Bibles represented an enormous advance. Their script was minute, yet exact and legible, featuring the very latest in standardized abbreviation. They were copied onto a type of vellum scraped or split so thin as to resemble soft, pliable tissue. The smaller, slender letters, crowded deftly onto those thin pages, made for fewer pages: the lightening of the scriptural load was apparent with every lift into a monk's hands or drop into his traveler's pouch.

In books, portability is the first and most characteristic sign of user-friendliness. But the ingratiating qualities of a Paris Bible went well beyond its reduction to personal scale, extending to content, layout, and internal structure. For the first time, the order of the books of the Bible, with the exception of the Psalms, became almost entirely uniform. For the first time, running heads in blue and red routinely identified the books of the Bible on the top of each page. For the first time, scriptural chapters came numbered and distinctly marked, with bright marginal letters keyed to glossaries and other helps included at the end of the book. For the first time, every Bible came supplied with a standard set of prologues and auxiliary texts (concordances, lists of Hebrew names) in an appendix. Every Paris Bible thus not only looked but also worked like every other Paris Bible. (With exceptions, of course – these were still manuscript books, after all, each one hand-made separately and thus uniquely imperfect.) As Christopher De Hamel reminds us, Paris Bibles represent the first great transformation of scriptural format since scrolls unfurled to become page-bound books, assuming the structure and layout we still expect from Bibles today.[6]

Paris Bibles also remind us that, while majesty of appearance characterizes books created for lectern readings and liturgical settings, ease of use is an attribute of *textbooks*. By the end of the thirteenth century, the bulky, multiple-volume Bible of the cathedral library had become a compact reference book of one volume. Eleventh-century Bibles like the Gundulf reflected the idiosyncratic genius of a particular monastic scriptorium or scribe; that archaic, eccentric note no longer sounds upon the opening of Paris Bibles. Instead, our eyes light upon – and upon, and upon, and upon once more – the many properties that later medieval Bibles have in common: the regular, exquisitely tiny, and scrupulously accurate rows of words; the meticulous, restrained decoration, the exact same "helps" found in exactly the same place in, seemingly, every single book.

The monks were primarily responsible for the scriptural saturation of a still overwhelmingly illiterate culture, but at least one aspect of their work was probably more than a little unwitting. Portable Bibles in hand, mendicants went out to instill or reinforce scriptural orthodoxy. When preaching or teaching they could now find their places quickly without fumbling, adeptly and impressively proof-texting their sermons with direct quotations from scripture. They could take this new scriptural dexterity on the road and into the schools. But before they had opened their mouths – even as they lifted their good book, pointed to it, and opened it – they had already made the Bible into a physical icon: a portable, material, ubiquitous emblem of the Church's singular and all-encompassing authority. At the same time, they demonstrated to a public audience just how easy the Bible could be to handle. The monks thus instilled orthodox piety with the one instrument virtually guaranteed to undo it: not the Bible itself, which was still a formidable engine of orthodoxy – but the demonstrable idea that anyone could, quite literally, *grasp* it. The new smaller-scale, practical Bibles were, therefore, not only the harbingers but also the primary symbols of a changing, increasingly intimate relationship between the Bible and ordinary people.

Lay Bibles for Private Devotions

This intimacy was reflected in a remarkable upswing in private book ownership. Literacy rates remained discouragingly low in this period, and even quite wealthy people without a career in the Church were, for the most part, illiterate – in both Latin and their vernacular language. For that matter, many who worked for the Church were poorly educated in their mother tongue and could only rattle off essential bits of the Latin Mass by rote. By the 1300s, nonetheless, we begin to find increasing numbers of books, secular and sacred, in the inventories of private households. Most of these were "Psalters": devotional books, in smaller, often luxurious, formats containing the Psalms used in the daily prayer services of the Church. Such decorated books of scripture were designed not for public but for private, even lay, reading. They signal a sea change in the relationship of books to people that predates by several centuries the invention of the printing press.

The sumptuously but whimsically decorated Vulgate Psalter pictured on these pages is a luxury book from the fourteenth century. We have no direct record of its creation, nor of its owners before John Egerton (1579–1649), first Earl of Bridgewater and an assiduous collector of old books in manuscript in the early seventeenth century. All clues to this Psalter's life prior to its residence in Bridgewater's Library must be surmised from a careful look at the decorations and notations on its pages. We know from the style of its script and decorations that it dates from the first half of the fourteenth century, but not before the year 1316, for the most recent pope listed on its calendar is John XXII, who reigned from that year until 1334. Other clues hint at an English provenance. The liturgical calendar marking holidays for the month of December, for example, features the English saint Thomas à Becket, Archbishop of Canterbury (1120–70). The day of his martyrdom is written in gold at 29 December, glistening clue to the Psalter's national origin.

In the absence of early records of its ownership, and with no helpful signatures on its flyleaves, we have to hypothesize about the origins of Egerton's Psalter. Because of its small size, it might be posited that this book was first owned by, perhaps even commissioned for, a layperson. A cursory assay of its contents, however, would probably not lead us outright to that educated guess. This book is filled with texts that would seem to be more suited to church than the home: hymns, a calendar of ecclesiastical holidays, litanies (including the Office of the Dead). The Psalms in these settings seem at first glance to be unsuitable for the private use of the laity.

But let us look again, a bit more closely. Psalters are conveyances for the Book of Psalms. And as such, they played (and still play)

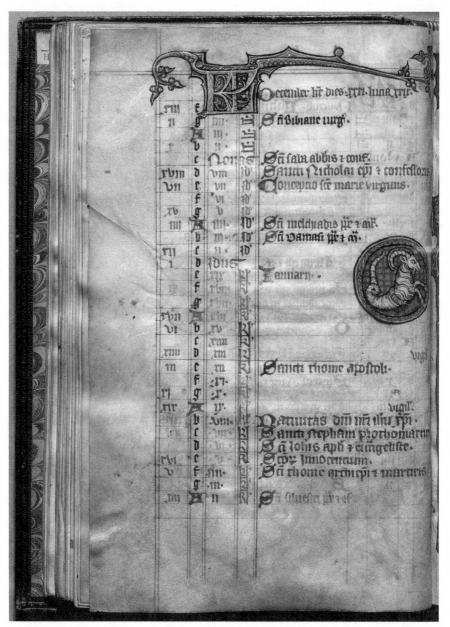

5 Egerton's Psalter (known as the "Ellesmere Psalter"), December calendar of saints and martyrs.

a central role in both Jewish and Christian worship. The public recitation or singing of Psalms was a distinct feature of early Christian worship; secular[7] churches and cathedrals built morning and evening public prayer around them. In monastic houses, the Psalms were sung even more rigorously, parceled out into seven separate services in every twenty-four-hour period. By the 1200s, all churches followed this more demanding arrangement, which meant that the entire Book of Psalms was publicly sung through on a weekly, year-round, basis in western Christendom. This organized round of daily prayers was set out in standard form for medieval clerics and monks in breviaries, large manuscript manuals containing Psalms, hymns, and lessons.

Of all the books of the Bible, then, the Psalms would have been most familiar to medieval people: both the clergy who recited them and the laity who heard them – repeated, in Latin, with clockwork regularity. So essential to worship were the Psalms that the Church was forced to come up with a strategy for all those wayfaring Christians of the later Middle Ages to continue to access them in transit. By the 1300s, Rome allowed Franciscans, Dominicans, and university students to pack a smaller version of the breviary for personal use, thus explicitly authorizing travelers far away from their parishes to observe forms of private worship. In so doing, the Church implicitly authorized others with more sedentary itineraries and less theological education to follow suit and begin practicing their religion privately rather than in community.[8]

With their intensely personal tone and unsurpassed ability to express human praise, thanksgiving, and lament, the Psalms were equally well suited for the voicing of private, individual prayers. And so, by the end of the fourteenth century, they were finally produced in a smaller format with fewer auxiliary texts for lay purchasers. Along with the portable Bibles we have already encountered, these simpler Psalters, also called "Books of Hours," soon were being turned out by the same secular book-makers who had so deftly taken over the business of making and selling the new, small-format Bible. The market for these little scripture and picture books swiftly extended beyond the educated elite of Church, monastery, and royal courts to include laypeople of the elite and merchant classes. Psalters became the most widely owned books in the Middle Ages.[9]

It would be a fairly safe guess that the Ellesmere Psalter had a lay owner, and with that, we can extend a set of conjectures as we examine a few of its pages. From evidence of a very lovely and elaborate historiated, or inhabited, initial that marks the beginning of one well-known Psalm included in the book, we can speculate that the first owner of the Huntington's Psalter may well have been a laywoman.[10] In the center of a large C (*Confitebor*, the word that opens Psalm 111, "I will give thanks to the Lord with my whole heart; in the company of the upright, in the congregation . . .") we find a kneeling woman, clad not in the garb of a nun but in a red gown. Her head is covered; in her hands is an open book with the words *Ave Maria, plena gratia* plainly scripted across its pages.

The woman's face is rendered in fine detail, portraying her gaze as on the book rather than on the figures on the altar or pedestal before her. These figures are the Virgin and Child – who blesses the woman with outstretched right hand. The Mother and Baby figured here appear sculpted, but there is just enough delicate ease, just enough interpretive room, in the painted image to suggest that the pedestal is an altar that hosts Mary and Jesus in person rather than stone. In any case, the figures together form a model of piety, wherein the viewer is shown how private acts of devotional reading can lead to the bestowal of divine grace – and, quite possibly, the granting of revelatory visions.

If this is indeed a portrait of the first owner of this Psalter, the book the woman holds in her hands is the book we now survey.[11] The woman portrayed in the initial is not the subject of the biblical verse she decorates; she is its object. Seemingly out of place in the Psalms, she is in fact unquestionably in place as the central figure of a portrait: the person, most likely, for whom the book was made.

To speculate further about the life of a woman who might be able to see herself mirrored in such a luxuriously designed and decorated book, we need to turn back a few pages, to the opening page of the

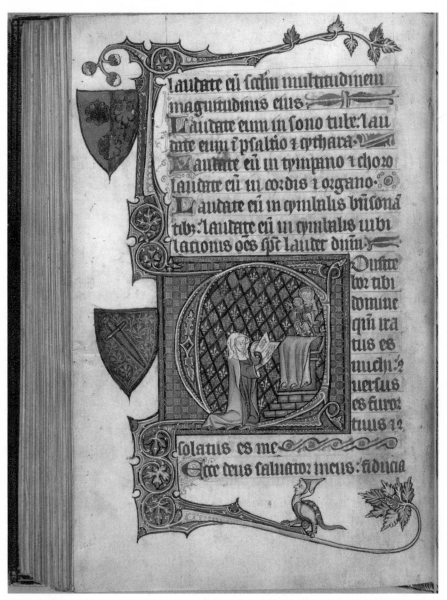

6 The original owner of the Ellesmere Psalter?

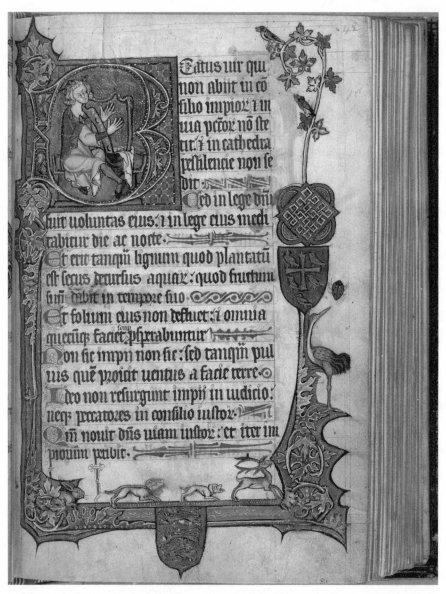

7 Harp-playing and a day's hunting illustrate the Ellesmere Psalter's Psalm 1.

Psalms, where we find a more conventionally historiated capital B (*Beatus vir*, or "Happy the man," the words that open Psalm 1). Inside it, against a stippled gold ground, David, who inhabits all the rest of the initials in this book, plays a harp carefully balanced against his knees, his shapely legs fetchingly on display. We should not be surprised to find David playing the holy songs traditionally and conventionally attributed to him, but the rest of the page might give us a bit of a start. It presents a very different kind of scene, one that would seem more suited to a secular book. At bottom left, the multicolored leaves in a herbaceous border partially conceal a clever rabbit from the notice of two determined hounds. They are chasing a panting stag, who pulls back, tongue out, in what appears to be confusion and ultimate capitulation.

Happy the man – or woman – who would have found that scene gratifyingly familiar, for hunting was an elite pastime in medieval England, allowed by law only to people with game-laden grounds and the horses to course them. If this book was designed for a lay patron, the illustrations in its margins relate to that reader, showing her or him how the scriptures could reflect the realities of a life – not only in providing familiar Psalms for solace and praise, but also by being the vehicle for images drawn from personal experience and social status.

Not all the decorations, however, conform to experience, at least not rational experience. Look once more at the right margin of this same page, where a stork stands on one leg, peering quizzically at an improbably large ladybug.[12] The page-edges of this Psalter and others like it displayed dozens of similarly witty visual diversions, amusing, off-scale *mise-en-scènes* – to say nothing of many marvelous hybrid creations called "grotesques" which show an unholy affinity with the manifold nooks and crannies of minuscule script. At the very heart of devotion, we find giddy slapstick performed by "lascivious apes, autophagic dragons, pot-bellied heads, harp-playing asses, arse-kissing priests, and somersaulting jongleurs," in the words of the great historian of medieval art, Michael Camille.[13] As we laugh out loud, we also realize that this book was designed to inspire surprised delight as well as recognition, and wicked grins as well as piety and reverence.

The Bible Embodied

The Bible may have been increasingly sized to the private hand in this era, but small Bibles and individual Psalters provide examples of how book technology appeared in advance of social change: *privacy* itself was a concept impossible to conceive of in the Middle Ages, and so even individual reading remained a public act, wherein wealthy book owners read their books in busy chambers crowded with servants, family, and other hangers-on.[14]

Likewise, the less wealthy and the unwealthy learned their scriptures amidst a cacophony of street voices and swirls of activity. The Bible's dramatic and comedic turns could be delivered on a variety of stages. The scriptures were expounded weekly, in the vernacular, in sermons preached as part of the regular church service. By the 1300s, as we have seen, these homilies not only issued from pulpits but from rural roadsides and city streets as Franciscan and Dominican priests took their messages more directly and informally to the people. Popular preaching pandered to popular taste, and most medieval sermons, whether delivered from the pulpit or the paving stone, would not have featured explications of the trickier passages of, say, the Pauline epistles or Hebrew prophets. Successful preachers instead specialized in fabulous, hortative, and often hair-raising stories of saints and miracles nowhere to be found in regular scripture. But some portion of a friar's sermons would have been based on biblical texts, generally the stories of the Creation of the world and its first inhabitants as recounted in the Old Testament's Book of Genesis and the life of Christ as found in the New Testament's gospel accounts. This was, at least in part, because these scriptural stories were themselves uplifting, hortative, hair-raising – and side-splittingly funny.

The residents of many cities and towns would also have witnessed these vivid stories from the Bible acted in the streets, performed in the language and conveying the attitudes of everyday life. These plays, sometimes referred to as "miracles" or "mysteries," flourished as a characteristic form of English religious expression from the early fourteenth century until their decline and suppression in the late sixteenth century. They were performed on movable stages in processions of stories or "cycles" that traced the biblical narrative. The audience staked out places along the streets; the plays came to them, one after another, unfolding in unrelenting narrative sequence. A full biblical cycle could comprise as many as twenty-four plays, from the Fall of Lucifer to the Last Judgment, and could last as many hours – or up to three days.[15]

In England, this day most often was the Feast of Corpus Christi, a festival in the season known as Whitsun.[16] Whitsun marked the end of the season of Eastertide and Corpus Christi celebrated the gift of the communion, making this day doubly appropriate for spiritual celebration. But by this date the people of England could also be absolutely sure of longer daylight hours and reasonably sure of pleasant weather, facts of time and geography that promised that the celebrations would be lingering ones. With its gaudy processions, festive decking of altars and churches, and – hardly inconsequential – the promise of a day off from work while the alehouses remained open, Corpus Christi offered the laity a chance to celebrate the sacred in ways both reverent and rowdy. The Church's attitude towards this festival, and the plays that graced it, was benignly supportive for the most part, evidence of its acquiescence to many of the creative and fanciful expressions of popular piety that were such a feature of the Christianity of the later Middle Ages.

When, exactly, the plays began to be known as "mysteries" is a fact which itself is clouded in mystery. The term may merely be affectedly antiquarian, postdated from the revived interest in this form of drama in the 1800s. Contemporary records most often call the plays, simply, "pageantes." In fact, the earliest known use of the term "mystery" only dates to 1555, by which time the plays were well on their way out of favor.[17] If, however, real usage predates first recorded usage, the term offers a neat example of the way certain words seem designed to carry a freight of interlocking meanings. To begin with, the term "mystery" has always been used to express a number of theological ideas, most powerfully among these the definitions "a revelation of the faith" and "a Christian sacrament." Both phenomena are truths that cannot be comprehended in full by human reason; the faith that confirms them as true is what sets Christians apart from non-Christians.

In the Middle Ages, however, "mystery" also referred to the practices of merchants and craftspeople: mastery of the skills and arts for which they had once been apprenticed and that set them apart from the rest of the laboring world.[18] The notion of religious arcana and specialized secular knowledge must have eventually merged to name the plays themselves – clever, given that for much of their short history in England the pageants were almost exclusively performed by city trade guilds, organized associations of medieval craftsmen and merchants. Seeking civic honor as well as the rewards of religious piety, guilds vied to stage those stories best suited to their vocational skills. Lay audiences thus learned the Bible from the plays, but, perhaps more important, lay performers sometimes wrote the plays – and they constructed the sets, sewed the costumes, and performed the roles: the hands-on approach to biblical education.

The texts of four great English cycles have been preserved, each named for the city in which it was performed: York, Coventry, Wakefield (also called the Towneley Cycle, after the first owner of the play manuscript), and Chester. The earliest copies of the English plays have long since disappeared; our scripts come from antiquaries who, starting in the later sixteenth century, ceremoniously and elaborately wrote out manuscript copies to preserve the memory of a tradition already suppressed by the combined forces of official religious disapproval and changes in popular taste.

But this is the rare case when the originals, no matter how endearingly and authentically bedraggled they may have been, would not have served us so well as these postdated works of sentimental reminiscence. What we see preserved in the affectionate if valedictory memories of the antiquaries reflects not only bare words spoken by the players. The memory-scripts also incorporate, both in and between the lines, the scribes' recollections of the conditions of playing itself: particularly vivid acting; innovative set design; the feel of a bright summer day darkened by observing the Fall of Man recreated on the streets of Coventry, or Chester, or York. A talented actor's take on the character of "Raging Herod" or the response, on and off-stage, to a lifelike depiction of the Crucifixion will find a way into the documentation. And thus the play of memory can catch the best, most accurate glimpse of the way people understood their Bibles in the medieval era: both in and between the lines, and, as we shall see, past them.[19]

The cycles are our best written record of how well and in what way the mostly unlettered people of medieval England knew their scriptures. The plays were based upon biblical stories, but for the sake of dramatic logic and comic effect even the ones that were written by priests inevitably strayed from strict retellings of the scriptural text.

A close look at one will show exactly how acts of textual infidelity betray a popular knowledge of the scripture that, while possibly unlettered, can be deeply relevant and powerfully insightful. It comes from Chester, a walled city in the northwest of England situated near the Welsh border. And while it may originally have been written by a thirteenth-century monk of Chester Abbey named Randall Hegnett, by the early fifteenth century it was played yearly by some of the "citizens of Chester," a trade guild known as the "The Waterleaders and Drawers of the River Dee," who by this time had doubtless placed their stamp on the story.[20]

The earliest manuscript copy of this biblical cycle was produced well after its theatrical productions, which may have begun as early as 1422 in the city of Chester.[21] This copy is the earliest known complete manuscript of the Chester Cycle, but even so it is of a much later date, which suggests that it was transcribed to preserve an older tradition. The scribal hand is singular, clear, and not only neat but decorative: another clue that what we have here is no player's copy (which would have been subject to such hard usage that it is no real surprise that we lack working copies of the medieval mysteries). The character's names – "God," "Noah," "Noah's wife" – are enclosed in neatly drawn boxes, the stage directions are enclosed in larger boxes, and each speech is set off by carefully drawn lines,

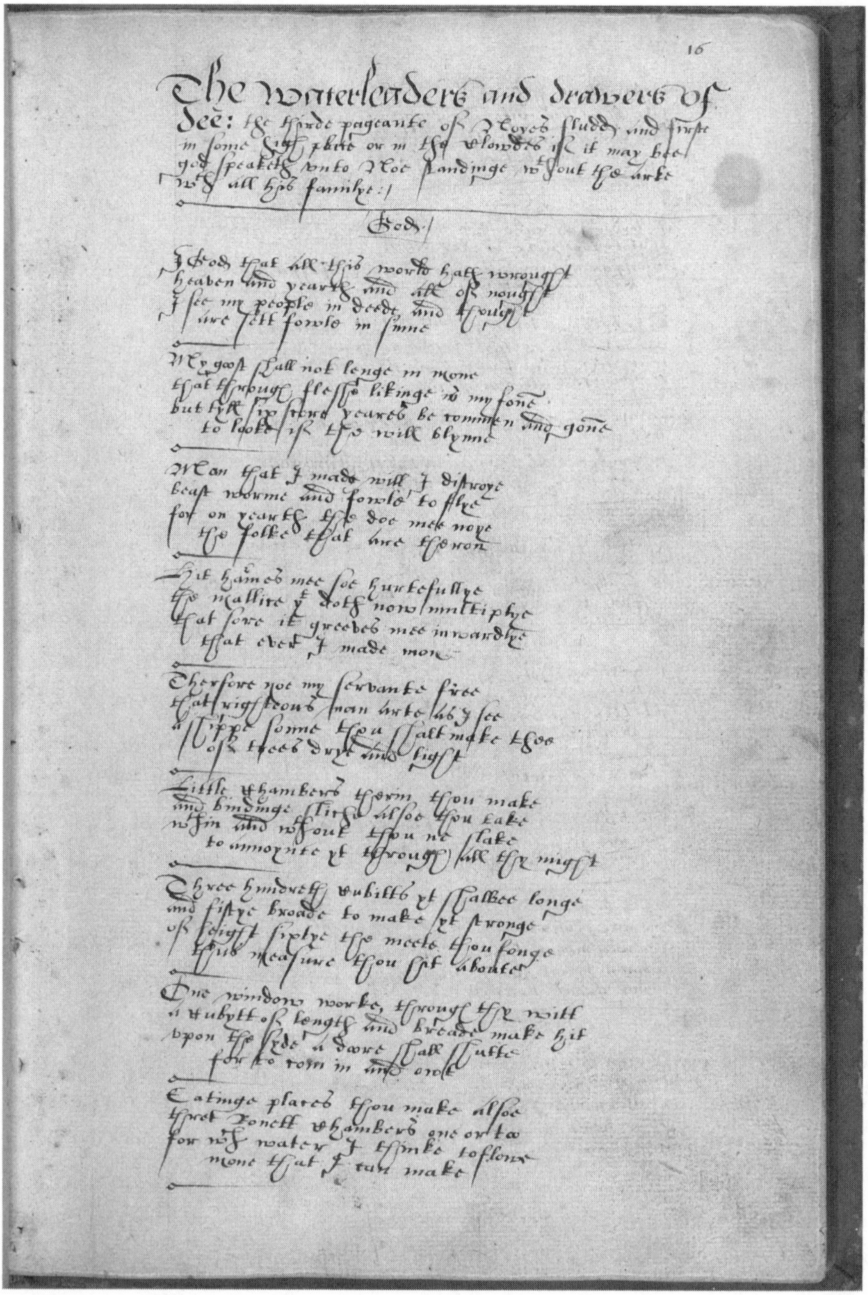

8 Act One, The Chester Play of Noah's Flood.

another hint that this was a "fair copy" rather than an actor's prompt book.

The title of the play, "The Waterleaders and Drawers of Dee: the third pageant of Noah's Flood," gives the guild top billing over the story. It was a clever collaboration. "Leaders" and "drawers" haul water for drinking; the Dee was the river alongside which the town was situated. By choosing to put on the pageant of Noah, the Waterleaders' Guild not only added the luster of a successful and impressive civic entertainment to their accomplishments, but also demonstrated their own skills in tricky water management and small craft construction through their identification with the ship-building and navigational skills shown by Noah in the story. The irresistibly apt conjunction of guild and tale, then, would have been very amusing – and very good advertising.

In the end, however, the Chester play of Noah is about the theological meaning of the Flood, not the work of waterleading. It affords us the chance to compare a popular retelling of a Bible story to the story as recounted in the scriptures. The Waterleaders' play is dramatically astute, theatrically lively, and wonderfully humane. It departs from scripture in a few very telling ways – and when medieval mysteries depart from their scriptural base text, we have just happened upon a historical moment of lay theologizing.

The play opens with an impressive flourish – ". . . and first in some high place or in the stands if it may be; God speaking unto Noah" – and a theatrical paradox. In beautifully disciplined rhyming couplets, God speaks of the disorder and disobedience of the world he created. "It harms me so hurtfully/The malice that doth now multiply," he states sorrowfully, "That sore it grieves me inwardly/that ever I made man." Noah, as every member of the audience would have known since childhood, is the righteous man who is the exception to this rule. And, as in the Book of Genesis, he is straightway ordered to build a ship and fill it with every kind of beast, bird, and fish.

The divine order allows the Waterleaders to build a boat on their movable stage in preparation for the promised deluge. But the play's *tour de force* is neither the building of an ark nor the rendering of a flood on stage but a hard-driving, torrential exchange between Noah and his wife – the leading lady in this drama despite the fact that she is only mentioned six times in all of Genesis (chapters 6–9) and then only with the brief appending words "and his wife".

Here, though, Noah's Wife is brought to irresistibly snappish life, given a substantial number of lines to speak, and an essential role to play. Consider the set-up: docile animals, an enormous number of them (all denizens of the English countryside), described by the cast and depicted on large painted boards, have been successfully loaded onto the ark, two by two.[22] So have Noah's sons and *their* amiable wives: again, two by two. But Noah's Wife, a woman more apt to brandish a two-by-four than submit to any enterprise requiring two-by-two, refuses to come aboard. A pragmatic, cranky woman, it's clear she considers Noah a dreamy fool for building a boat on dry land, and she simply will not be ordered about like her tractable, obedient daughters-in-law. Besides, Mrs. Noah has good women friends on shore, and they have a large bottle of sweet wine to pass around as the rain begins to fall.

As the rain falls ever more steadily Noah's Wife continues to berate her husband, standing alone and forlorn, the only unpartnered creature on the ark. Despite his pleas and cajolings, she declares that she will not leave her increasingly terrified – and increasingly inebriated – neighbors behind, one of whom has begun wailing, inconsolably, "for fear of drowning I am aghast . . ." Finally Mrs Noah is carried onto the boat by her strapping sons, a brave feat that requires all three of them, against her will. When greeted by her husband with the gracious line, "welcome, wife, into this boat," she promptly boxes his ear, replying in scanning rhyme, ". . . and have thou *that* for thy note." (The stage direction reads: "she gives him a blow.") Noah's rueful if less poetic response – "Aye, marry, this *is* hot" – seems guaranteed to compel the actor to rub the side of his head – and the crowd to burst into gales of laughter.

Forcibly reconciled to her family, Mrs Noah does not long remain obdurate at sea. The Punch and Judy by-play has ended with the clout, and from this point the stormy tone of play turns markedly calm and increasingly formal and solemn. Noah's next line, "It is good to be still," refers both to his silenced wife and the rising waters that have finally set the ark afloat. At this point the scribe indicates that Noah and his family move behind the walls of their ark, blocked from the view of the audience: "Then shall Noah shut the window of the ark and for a little space within the boards they . . . sing . . ." And what is it this dysfunctional but reunited family sings? It is Psalm 69: "Save me, O God," familiar from the Latin Mass but now rendered into English.[23]

Noah and his family may have been spared, but their play, like all the plays at Chester and other English towns, was not. Still flourishing at the beginning of the sixteenth century, the mysteries died out by that century's end.[24] They were suppressed in some localities by a newly Protestant ecclesiastical order and in others by newly and enthusiastically Protestantized city councils, both of whom would have considered the plays blasphemously unbiblical and their audiences drunk and disorderly. Compared to what came before them – scriptural orthodoxy as backed up by the Vulgate Bible; *and* what came after – scriptural orthodoxy as defined by Protestant reformers – plays like Chester's could easily appear to us, too, as quaint artefacts of vernacular ignorance: inappropriate, naïve, perhaps even immoral.

But the play tells us, surely, something more complex about lay understanding of the Bible in the Middle Ages. The Chester play of Noah – indeed the entire mystery play tradition – stands as eloquent testimony to the depth of lay interest in the Bible and to ordinary people's extraordinary capacity to make scripture relevant to lived experience. (This is a characteristic they share with the Ellesmere Psalter, which furnished the happy man of the first Psalm with all the genteel accoutrements of a day's hunting.) The Noah play underscores biblical precepts with an empathetic – if dizzily slapstick – portrayal of the human condition, in order to engage an audience who knew exactly what was so wonderful and what was not-so-wonderful about going through life two by two: the pains as well as the pleasures of married life.

So the players made Noah's wife more than the "and his wife" phrase appended to the word "Noah" in the Book of Genesis. She represents one understandably puzzled, all-too-human respondent to the mystery of the conjugal bond and to the unfathomable expression of God's enduring justice. She questions the limits of human obedience and of divine grace; she tests the boundaries of loyalty to community and family. In other words, Noah's Wife stands in for the medieval biblical audience – who, like Mrs Noah, do not get to speak *in* the Bible but now get to speak *to* the Bible. She and the play in which she takes such an unprecedentedly starring role represent how very well medieval laypeople knew their Bible, how astutely they navigated its problems and demands – and all without being able, perhaps, to read a single word of it.

Conclusion

The Bibles and Bible-related activities of the later Middle Ages remind us that in an age of orthodoxy it was still possible for a wide range of people to lay claim to the Bible and make it their own. This could begin with a purely physical claim, as the pocket Bibles of mendicant preachers, the eccentric designs of an aristocrat's Psalter, or the stage properties of un-Latined players in England's towns attest. In each case, the scriptures took on the attributes and desires of their owners, reflecting their lives of vocation and belief and, in so doing, remaking the Bible's narratives into familiar, contemporary stories: of life on the road, prayer in a great house, belief on the streets.

That these many familiar forms could flourish is a fair tribute to the acceptance of Christian orthodoxy in the West rather than evidence that most people chafed at its requirements. This is an important point to make before considering the changes wrought by religious reformation in England. The medieval Bible was not exactly kept in the kind of Babylonian captivity Martin Luther would claim in 1520; here we see evidence of its dissemination and its application to everyday life, even by an illiterate populace.

What medievals did not possess, however, was a version of their Bible in the vernacular. This was not true of an earlier age. In

Jerome's time, it should be noted, Latin was the language of ordinary life – this is why his Bible was called *vulgar* in an age wherein Greek was the tongue used for fancy business and philosophical reasoning. But merely translating scripture into the language of everyday life did not guarantee that every man and woman could or would seek out and understand the unmediated Word of God. In the chapter that follows, we will trace how ordinary biblical understanding was transformed – but neither initially nor generally improved – by the biblical translation projects of humanists and Protestants in the sixteenth century.

CHAPTER THREE

THE POLITICS OF TRANSLATION

THE BIBLE IN ENGLISH, *C.* 1500–1700

Matthew Parker (1504–75) was Queen Elizabeth's first Archbishop of Canterbury, one of the major architects of her restored Protestant Church, the general editor of the "Bishops' Bible" of 1568, and an adept in both the living language of ecclesiastical Latin and the dead one of Anglo-Saxon. In 1571, Parker produced a translation of the four Gospels in this last, one of Britain's ancient and nearly forgotten tongues. Parker's native British Bible was, as even its preface admitted, "most strange."[1] Printed in quaintly decorative, largely unfamiliar characters and punctuated by an over-ingenious system of "prickings," *The Gospels of the Fower Evangelistes, translated in the olde Saxons tyme out of Latin into the vulgare toung of the Saxons* was Holy Scripture tricked out as ancient British history.

To assist its readers, who surely would have required the help, the book featured a prefatory page of comparative alphabets and an explanation of Saxon forms of punctuation, plus marginal English transcriptions in black letter and numbered verse-divisions throughout. The additions reveal Parker's true intent in producing such a selectively arcane document, a book more indebted to the pedagogical books of the late sixteenth century than to the scriptural manuscripts of the late ninth. For one thing, verses were not numbered in

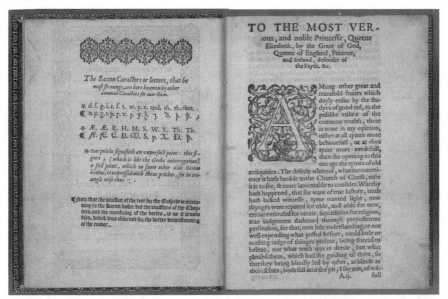

9 Archbishop Matthew Parker instructs Queen Elizabeth in Anglo-Saxon Religious History, 1571.

Anglo-Saxon Bibles; they weren't routinely numbered in any Bible produced before 1560. Such scholarly aids were instead typical of the educative focus and user-friendliness of the books, including the Bibles, which now issued in rapidly increasing numbers from later sixteenth-century English printing houses.

The historic nature of this particular Bible was, then, a bit contrived. So, in a sense, was its scriptural nature. Despite its textbookish look, this was no primer of Old English, nor was it an offering primarily aimed to increase scriptural knowledge; it was a shrewdly timed piece of Protestant propaganda. The queen had been excommunicated in 1570 by Pope Pius V, and in response her Archbishop deployed Anglo-Saxon scriptures as proof-texts against the legitimacy of that papal act.

Parker's might now seem to us a rather esoteric solution, considering the gravity of the threat. Newly Protestant monarchs feared papal excommunication every bit as much as they had when, not so long ago, they were Catholic monarchs. According to Roman Catholic political theory, subjects not only could but should rebel against an excommunicated ruler, and, generally speaking, early modern rulers feared political uprisings, always a real possibility, more than the damnation of their eternal souls, seemingly a more distant prospect. But Parker needed to fend off the Pope's claim that the queen's governance of the English Church not only placed her kingdom outside the ecclesiastical jurisdiction of Rome but also separated English believers from the ranks of orthodox Christians. In response, the Archbishop deployed the literary weapon of revisionist history.

Parker's foray into the British history of the scriptures underscores a truism: momentous religious change leads some people to rethink doctrines and others to restructure practices, but it also sends many people back to their desks to consult and then rewrite church history. Otherworldly as its spiritual desire has always been, Christianity is at the same time a religion originating in a historical place and specific moment that centers on the revealed transcendence of a human life. From this homely beginning, the faith has generated historical narratives one after the other, polemical justifications of the singular truth expressed in increasingly disparate Christianities. The core of Christian orthodoxy may have formed around one powerful idea, the indivisibility of humanity and divinity in the person of Jesus, but the establishment and dissemination of this remarkable notion required an essential and paradoxical proviso: that the faith established in first-century Judea required no subsequent updating. In short, nothing new could actually be true, which explains why men like Matthew Parker felt it necessary to argue so strenuously that the English Reformation was no novelty, but a return to purer days.

And so the preface to the *Evangelistes* argued that the conversion of the Church of England to Protestantism represented "no new reformation of things lately begun," but a long-overdue return to the autonomy the British Church enjoyed in the centuries before the Norman Conquest. Viewed from such a perspective, the papacy's rule over English Christianity represented a form of recent usurpation. Plucked from the ancient accounts and preserved "monuments" of Anglo-Saxon Christianity, Parker's Bible proclaimed the origins of a self-governing *English* Church of England.[2] Moreover, its singularity did not stem from the easy fact that such a set of Gospels existed – after all they had been, as even the title had to admit, translated *out of Latin* – but from the more complex claim that, some time back in the ancient recesses of England's past, an Anglo-Saxon translator had found it important to challenge the overarching Latinity of the Bible.

In the second half of the sixteenth century, the mere presence of Anglo-Saxon characters on the page of a religious book became a typographical hallmark of a certain kind of defiantly native English Protestant prose. Many keen-edged Protestants appear to have thought that their queen required remedial lessons in Early British Ecclesiastical History, and were more than happy to deliver them – without, it should be added, any particular encouragement from Her Majesty. "There [was] nothing ... more needful," John Foxe wrote in the hectoring address to Elizabeth that opens *Fower Evangelistes*, than to teach England's new Protestants "the times of old antiquity."[3] Anxious to prove himself a most stalwart Protestant champion, Robert Dudley, Earl of Leicester, had a copy of *Fower Evangelistes* bound with his coat of arms – materially aligning his own religious opinions with those of the sovereign who loved him so well.[4] By 1580, anonymous tracts with titles like *The Ruinate Fall of the Pope Usury, derived from the Pope Idolatry, [as] revealed by a Saxon of Antiquity*, pointedly dedicated to Elizabeth or her advisors, could be found on the shelves of many London bookstalls.[5]

Between the brave lines of these newly devised Christian histories ran a persistent undercurrent of anxiety that betrayed the fragility of Protestantism's infant grasp on English society in the early decades of Elizabeth's reign. Calling upon ancient precedent, Matthew Parker and John Foxe could affirm the independence of England's Church and deny the Pope's supremacy all they wanted; what they could not do was *ignore* the papal threats they so belligerently defied. Malingering Catholicism at home and militant Catholicism abroad continued to pose serious political threats to a kingdom as recently – and, in some ways, as reluctantly – converted as Elizabeth's.

Odd and idiosyncratic as it seems, Parker's quirky little artefact of Protestant politics provides us with a narrow but precisely illumined insight into the role that English-translation Bibles played in the English Reformation. Whether radical, mainstream, or sidelined, every act of scriptural translation in this era was an act of biblical interpretation, essentially religious at its core and thus unfailingly political in its effects. And so this chapter surveys the acts of interpretation, both licit and illicit, that punctuated an age of dramatic religious change, and the conflicts with authority that necessarily attended on such transformations.

Protestantism and the Bible

In the sixteenth century, Protestantism, with its perhaps overly optimistic doctrine of the "priesthood of *all* believers," was a powerful inducement to social change, shattering the unity of western Christendom and sparking fierce, often violent controversy between – and within – every one of its kingdoms. The Bible, and the role it played in the life of Christians, occupied the very heart of this contested territory. Reformers called for the scriptures to be translated from Latin – the language of a small, pan-European (including the British Isles), university-educated and well-connected ecclesiastical class – into vernacular languages like German or English. The Roman Catholic Church responded swiftly and definitively by reaffirming the solely orthodox status of the Latin Vulgate Bible at the Council of Trent on 8 April 1546.

On the face of it, the request for the scriptures to be expressed in the language of everyday life might seem innocent enough, and reformers were certainly quick to claim that their pleas were benign and reasonable. They were being entirely disingenuous. As both sides knew perfectly well, implicated deeply in both Protestant demand and Roman refusal were powerfully opposed views: not primarily on the importance of the Bible to Christian life (a doctrine also strongly reaffirmed at Trent), but on exactly the extent, and exactly the sort, of access Christians should have to that Bible. Translating the Bible thus became not only a religious but also a political act, as kings, emperors, and clerics struggled to control the influence of the new religion and, with it, the Bible itself.

No member of the Catholic ecclesiastical establishment had ever formally taught that the Bible was anything less than a source of truth central to the doctrines and practice of Christianity. What the Roman Church forbade, citing the difficulty such a sophisticated, complex, and often quite puzzling text would pose to ordinary readers, was unsupervised access to the Bible. Theirs was not an unreasonable fear, as Protestant clergy were to learn. Protestant doctrine asserted that the scriptures should be readily available to all, but this claim worked better as propaganda than as parish reality. Nowhere is this paradox more apparent than in the records of England's reformation. For all their social optimism and educational activism, the first generations of English Protestant clerics soon discovered that much of their reforming energy was inevitably spent negotiating waywardly unpredictable lay interpretations of scripture. The "Bible alone" may have been the much-vaunted "religion of Protestants," but, like all potentially dangerous objects, it was best handled with caution – and locked up at night. Soon Protestant authorities were just as alarmed as their Catholic counterparts had been, as subjects' radical or overly exuberant biblical interpretations threatened the political and social order.

In fact they may well have been more alarmed, considering they had brought the problem upon themselves. In all of Europe, only England went so far as to try to restrict its vernacular Bible's distribution to "authorized" versions – though this is hardly surprising, given that the pre-reformation English Church and State had also spent a singularly extraordinary amount of time and energy tracking down and punishing people who produced, distributed, or owned vernacular translations of the Bible. Laws against Bible translation distinguished late medieval England from all other European countries. They also make the story of England's religious transformation, and the Bibles that shaped that lengthy process, unique in the annals of the Protestant Reformation.

Archbishop Parker *was* on to something in 1572. In one sense, English singularity does begin with Anglo-Saxon, which was employed as a literary and religious language long before the common languages of other European countries rose to the same level of expression. Perhaps for this reason, vernacular literacy rates were higher for England than for the continent in the late medieval period. But even with scriptures to feed them, Readers do not necessarily make a Reformation. We might think a kind of elective, natural affinity would link a precociously literate country to a Protestantism that claimed an authority based solely on a text it often called, simply, "The Word," but in fact England embraced its English reformations with less initial enthusiasm than it embraced its English Bibles.

This may be because England's first concerted Bible translation project predated the Reformation by more than a century, and whilst it was certainly radical, it was not particularly forward-looking.[6] Like many orthodox medieval churchmen (especially those whose lives were more devoted to the pursuit of philosophy than the cure of souls), John Wycliffe (1330–84) made a career denouncing the corruptions of the Church and questioning the legitimacy of the papacy's claim to universal Christian jurisdiction. Unlike most medieval clerics, however, Wycliffe consistently asserted that his critique was based on a close reading of the Bible and a belief that ultimate ecclesiastical authority rested in the eternal verities of scripture rather than the transient pronouncements of a succession of human and very fallible popes. This was outspokenness made doubly dangerous by its correlative proposal of the Bible as an alternative to papal authority in an age when the authority of the papacy was already under unusually vigorous attack.[7] Wycliffe's energetic criticisms won him many adherents within Oxford university, where he was doctor of divinity. Their admiration was costly. Wycliffe's doctrinal opinions were eventually condemned by the English branch of the Catholic Church meeting in regional synod in 1382. The condemnation not only got Wycliffe fired from the university; it also made his acolytes heretics.

Wycliffe's promotion of the Bible as a source of doctrinal authority surpassing Rome's inspired his followers at Oxford to produce a translation of the Bible in English, and generations of Protestant historians have attributed not merely the inspiration for that translation but the actual work of commissioning or even translating to Wycliffe himself. This has proved a claim impossible to substantiate – and, in the end, one that seems not merely less accurate but also less revealing about what exactly was so radical about Wycliffe's influence.

Taking forced retirement in the small Leicestershire town of Lutterworth, Wycliffe continued to issue irascible denunciations of his ecclesiastical adversaries. Despite this proof of his intransigence, the church authorities must have assumed that – as with most teapot-tempests created by university professors – the mood Wycliffe had inspired would not long survive his rustication. This time the authorities were wrong. Two years later Wycliffe died, more perishable than his ideas – although, as we shall see, the authorities were a little less convinced of this corporeal reality. By the early fifteenth century Wycliffe's radical opinions about the Church, and the vernacular Bible now associated with those opinions, had become impossible for the authorities of the English Church and State to ignore.

As governments with absolutist ambitions invariably come to learn, ideas in themselves are impossible to control but ideas in material form make steadier targets. Aided by the English government, which had passed a law in 1401 stating its intention to enact secular punishments on those adjudged to be heretics, the Church decided to extirpate Wycliffe's influence by condemning the specific practices – and books – associated with his teachings. In 1409, the Archbishop of Canterbury, Thomas Arundel, banned the making or reading of Wycliffite Bibles without prior approval by the Church. While that proviso seemed to keep open the possibility that English translations might be allowable in the future, this seems never to have been the case – and the ban remained in force until 1529, when it was superseded by an even more subtly qualified form of royal censorship. What the 1409 ban *did* do, however, was form a useful pretext for search and seizure of heretical books and persons by the English authorities.

In one case at least, the search – and the seizure – were more than usually unsavory. In 1415, the Church, gathered in international council at the Swiss city of Constance, formally declared Wycliffe's doctrines heretical. Wycliffe could not answer the charges personally; he had been dead for nearly forty years. Undeterred by practical considerations, England duly followed up on the condemnation, exhuming Wycliffe's moldering corpse and publicly burning it in 1428: final, ugly confirmation that the Wycliffite cause had long left the ivory tower for the mean streets of England.

Which brings us to the people who took up that cause in the early fifteenth century, most of whom Wycliffe would not have recognized, even while alive, as fellow travelers. For the most part (but with some revealing exceptions that proved the rule), these renegades were no longer university-trained scholars but artisans and less wealthy members of the urban class. Called Lollards, their criticisms of the Church, its practices, its rules, and its wealth generally skipped the niceties of formal philosophical debate to express a more generalized religious and social unrest. Soon the term served to label any person who had the temerity to criticize the extent of the Church's secular and monastic property, the exercise of its political authority, or its capacity to effect the cure of souls.

Bible-reading in English, though, was what made a Lollard a *Lollard*. With its foolish, blubbery sound, the word is an onomatopoetic insult (one that reminds us why English is such a satisfying mouthful of a language to translate ideas into in the first place). Imitating a roomful of laypeople clumsily mumbling the scriptures in English, the epithet ridiculed both the people reading the Bible and the sound of those scriptures rendered into English. A word like *lollard* reminds us that, in the years leading up to the Reformation, most people still thought the Bible should sound like Latin.

The nickname also underscores the powerful association of vernacular scripture with Lollard – if not particularly Wycliffe's – beliefs.[8] Typical university philosopher and theologian that he was, Wycliffe was primarily concerned with the authority of the Bible, not the English Bible. But when they defied the traditional authority of the Church, appointing their own religious leaders and allowing laypersons to preach and deliver the sacraments, Lollards claimed to be acting directly upon the dictates of a Bible recast in – and on – their own terms. Consequently their Bibles not only sounded illegitimate; they were illegitimate: defining motifs of a particular heresy, these books were dangerous objects to own or to make, with late medieval ecclesiastical courts (in the words of one historian) "displaying more interest in the heretics' books than in their doctrines."[9]

Ban notwithstanding, however, they must have been produced in droves: more than 250 manuscripts, most of these truncated copies of all or part of the New Testament rather than whole Bibles, have survived to this day, making Wycliffite biblical texts the largest cache of medieval English literature extant. The library-owned manuscripts are, generally speaking, in decent shape, which suggests that they represent only a small percentage of those produced in the late fourteenth and fifteenth centuries. These were Bibles designed for use, after all, and most must have been handled to bits. And yet there are currently more than twice as many handwritten Lollard scripture texts available in research libraries than the Gutenberg Bibles that issued from a printing press.

This preponderance of material evidence has in all likelihood skewed our sense of Lollardy and its general influence on subsequent religious events in England. Lollardy was neither a nascent nor a premature reformation. It was local, even individual, in its expression; it did not advocate a stable set of doctrinal, social, or ecclesiastical opinions. Lollards did not seek to change the institution of the Church; their individual acts of piety and scattershot anti-clerical criticisms are typical malcontent behavior for this era. We are not even sure exactly how many Lollards actually made, owned, or read the scriptures in English; the true number is probably dismayingly small. In short, when viewed on their own terms, Lollards were interesting if eccentric medieval heretics, not proto-Protestants.

Except, perhaps, in this one particular. No matter how many or how few Lollards owned or read the scriptures, the heresy called Lollardy was forever after associated with the idea of a vernacular

Bible. This single characteristic provided a substantial material link between the biblical aspirations of the medieval era and the biblical ambitions of the Reformation.

Like all manuscripts, every Wycliffite Bible is a singular creation. And at first glance a well-wrought Wycliffite Bible can look exactly like that other contemporary Bible meant for good, hard use, a "Paris" Vulgate. Both feature neat, small script, abbreviations, running heads, the standard prologues and adjuncts, and chapters and books distinguished with blue and red inks and decorated capitals. Look closely at the words, though, and you'll see that Paris style now clothes English scriptures.

Wycliffite Bible-makers were translators, not transcribers. They started with no sanctioned production space and only the spiritually exhilarating and politically risky determination to turn the Vulgate Bible into an English-language book. At first they kept closely to the Latin: too close, perhaps, for comfort in the reading. First-generation Wycliffite translations from the late 1380s have a nearly literal dependence on the Vulgate. Not only rendered word for word

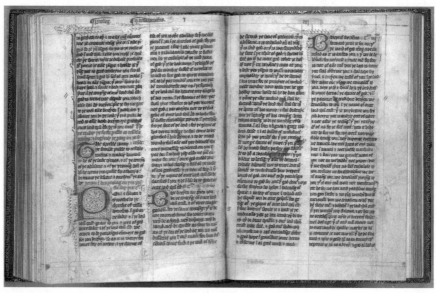

10 A Wycliffite manuscript Bible, *c.* fifteenth century.

but also word order for word order, the English in these early Bibles can sound simply nonsensical in many passages, as if the scriptures had served as no more than so many Latin primers.[10]

And, in fact, that's what it appears they may have been. Wycliffite Bibles produced after 1388 are less stilted, more assured, and even more idiomatic, which suggests that the translators, working from a first-generation vernacular version of the Vulgate, now felt the freedom – or the communicative necessity – to make readers a Bible they could relate to.[11] The second-generation translators labored, as all good translators must, to render not only accurate terminology but also, and more important, their true sense of scriptural passages, both recast in different words and reset to a different cultural tone. Given the words available to them in late medieval English, a language that manages to pack a good deal of winsome charm into some memorably homely locutions, these later versions (to this native English-speaking American at least) sound utterly strange but at the same time weirdly familiar: truly original and very, very down-to-earth.

Take, for example, the Wycliffite story of the nativity of Jesus as told in the second chapter of the Book of Luke:

> . . . & shepherds were in the same country waking and keeping the watches of the night on the flock & lo the angel of the lord stood besides them & the clearness of God shined amongst them and they dreaded with great dread/and the angel said to them why ye dread for lo I preach to you a great joy that shall be to all the people/for a savior is born today to you: that is christ the lord in the city of david & this is a token to you/ ye shallen find a young child wrapped in cloths: & laid in a cratch & suddenly there was made with the angel a multitude of heavenly knighthood hearing god and saying / glory be in the highest things to god & in earth peace be to men of good will . . .[12]

Anyone raised on the Gospel of Luke's Christmas story as recounted in a modern version of the scriptures will readily recognize its turns of plot in this Lollard Gospel: rough men working outdoors are interrupted on the night shift by a terrifying, blinding vision. They are given a miraculous message and the means to confirm its truth for themselves: precise descriptions of the geographical coordinates and the social condition of a Messiah appearing on earth in human form. The skies above them erupt with the ecstatic voices of angels whose glorious show confirms the divinely authoritative origin of the message.

What stand out in this particular rendering, though, are the sturdily descriptive expressions that affix the details of the story. The reiterated "dreaded with great dread" perfectly conveys the shepherds' awestruck double-takes; its alliteration recalls not only the conventions of medieval vernacular English poetry but also the darkly comic lines of medieval Christmas pageants like *The Second Shepherd's Play*. How better to explain an encounter with divinity not only so bright and shining but also so purely informative than to say it radiates a kind of "clearness"? How better to convey the job description of the angelic host to a feudal society than to call them a "heavenly knighthood"? How better to laud the coming to earth of a god in form so poignantly and vulnerably human than to claim he lies in a rough "cratch"? The Wycliffite Christmas story reminds us that to translate is to employ metaphors once removed, exchanging not only terms but cultures in what Daniel Rodosh has aptly called "thought-for-thought" rather than word-for-word translation.[13]

The Wycliffite Bible is, then, a marvelous medieval – not proto-Reformation – creation. It had long been the Church's contention that ordinary laypeople shouldn't read the Bible directly because they couldn't understand the Bible, at least not without priestly intercession. But of course ordinary laypeople already *did* understand it, thanks in large part to that same Church. After all, it was the Church that had sponsored lay access to the scriptures for centuries through a number of innovative modes. It was the Church that had ensured that people heard vernacular scripture in Sunday worship and in the homely and vivid popular sermons preached by wandering monks, and allowed biblical street theater on long, warm(ish) summer nights. The problem, of course, was how people would comprehend a direct infusion of English words in an English Bible instead of in vernacular preaching or plays originally inspired by the Vulgate Bible: whether a new, powerfully intimate, folk-inflected, vernacular familiarity would breed contempt – not for the Bible, but for the Church. The division between Latinate and vernacular religious culture so decried by the reformers may not have preceded the Reformation; in fact, there's a good deal of evidence to suggest it was one of the effects of having the Bible in translation rather than its cause.

Largely on the run by the middle of the fifteenth century, Lollardy missed the reformations of the sixteenth century. Its critiques of the Church and its clergy persisted faintly in popular memory, however, making the early reformers' jobs easier in certain English localities – and ensuring that a few religious renegades of a precociously Protestant stripe were labeled Lollards by authorities who were behind the times. But while Lollard ideas faded away, Lollard Bibles remained behind: tangible, graspable relics of the attractions of the vernacular word. Long after these late medieval heretics passed to their reward, their scriptures remained behind, holding place for the new versions of the sixteenth century.

That the attraction lingered can be seen in a royal proclamation printed for public distribution and display on 22 June 1530, wherein Henry VIII (1491–1547) demanded that his English subjects surrender all copies of "pestiferous English books" to their local curate or bishop within fifteen days. Royal proclamations carried the force of law and such public pronouncements, generally speaking, were voiced in the uncompromising and straightforwardly confident tone of absolute monarchy. But Henry's statement of 22 June is filled with cautious provisos and a number of carefully qualified promises that offset its harsh threats and imperious demands. The oddly conflicted tone of this statement offers, then, intriguing glimpses into the king's governing strategies when faced with what appears to have been – for him, for his clergy, and for his government ministers – a religious and social issue of unusual subtlety and complexity.

To confront it, Henry formed a task force of statesmen to advise him, and their concerns and deliberations form most of the text of the proclamation. The easiest issue for the royal commission, apparently, was what to do about books of disputed theological or political views written or translated into English. Such works, the committee assured their sovereign, were "books of heresy . . . worthy to be damned and put in perpetual oblivion." So much for religious propaganda; the problem posed by the English Bible, however, was not so summarily dispatched. "[R]eport is made," the proclamation goes on, "that it were . . . necessary to have in the English tongue both the New Testament and the Old, and that his highness, his noblemen, and prelates were [bound] to suffer them so to have it." This came dangerously close to sounding like an intemperate and imperious demand on the part of the king's subjects. Of particular interest to Henry, therefore, was the answer of his learned committee to this question: whether it would be "expedient," given an apparently importunate public, to allow "the administration or divulgation of the Old and New Testament translated into English."

The king decided that while his subjects' desire for the Bible in English was not in itself untoward, their impatient call for it was disrespectful and disruptive, prelude to an uprising. Luther's ideas, flowing into England from the continent, seemed to be unsettling the kind of people who were best served by having their Bibles "expounded to them by preachers." Only "superiors," therefore, could exercise the discretion to decide when, and how, the English people would get a Bible in English; they would not get it by clamoring for it. The proclamation then concluded with a qualified, but nonetheless startlingly conciliatory, promise:

Albeit if it doth appear hereafter to the king's highness that his said people do utterly abandon and forsake all perverse, erroneous, and seditious opinions, [along] with the New Testament and the Old corruptly translated into the English tongue now being *in print*, and that the same books . . . be clearly exterminate and exiled out of this realm of England forever: *his highness intendeth to provide* that the Holy Scripture shall be by great, learned, and Catholic persons translated into the English tongue, *if it shall then seem to his grace convenient so to be.*[14]

For Henry, his clerics, and his ministers, then, the primary issue was not *whether* an English Bible but *which* English Bible – and *when*. As the text of the proclamation makes clear, that *when* would come after the king's subjects turned in the contraband Bibles they already possessed. Then, and only then, would they get licit ones – that is, if and when the king approved the translation.

Some of the English Bibles now so dangerously familiar to Henry's subjects might have been leftover Lollard Bibles, but by 1530 it is more likely they were copies of a new translation of the New Testament by William Tyndale (1494–1536). Tyndale Bibles certainly looked like contraband: generally quite small (one-eighth or even one-sixteenth the size of the Bibles owned by churches), they were purpose-built to fit into hands and pockets, easily made clandestine. Tyndale's scriptures had to be printed abroad, often by printers operating under pseudonyms. Forced to flee England in 1524, Tyndale had kept up an ambitious schedule of religious tract writing while working on new translations of biblical Hebrew and Greek. His other illicit writings included proto-Protestant and anti-clerical tracts, all of which were vigorously attacked in England and all of which he just as vigorously defended. Like Wycliffe, Tyndale believed in a Bible that alone validated the doctrines and practices of Christianity. His public reputation as a man of dangerously radical ideas was secured in the 1530s when he entered into a bitterly scathing print debate with Lord Chancellor Thomas More, which set the legitimacy and authority of the Catholic Church against the legitimacy and authority of the Holy Bible.

What most distinguished a Tyndale Bible from a Wycliffe Bible – besides, of course, the consequential fact that the latter was a manuscript book and the former a printed one – was announced on its title page: *The new Testament diligently corrected and compared with the Greek by William Tyndale: and finished in the year of our Lord*

Of S. John.   Fo.Cxxii.

✠ John bare witnes of him and cryed sayin
ge: This was he of whome I spake/he that
cometh after me/was before me / Because he
was yet then I. And of his fulnes have all we
receaved/even (grace) for grace. for the lawe
was geven by Moses/but grace & truthe ca
me by Jesus Christ. No mā hath sene God at
eny tyme. The only begottē sonne/which is in
ẏ bosome of ẏ father/he hath declared him.
✠ And this is the recorde of John: When
the Jewes sent Prestes and Levites from Je
rusalem/to axe him/what arte thou? And he
confessed/and denyed not/and sayde playnly:
I am not Christ. And they axed him:what
then? arte thou Helyas? And he sayde:I am
not. Arte thou a Prophete? And he answered
no. Then sayd they vnto him:what arte thou
that we maye geve an answer to them that
sent vs: What sayest thou of thy selfe? He
sayde: I am the *voyce of a cryar in the wyl-
dernes/make strayght the waye of the Lorde/
as sayde the Prophete Esaias.
And they which were sent/were of the pha
risees. And they axed him/& sayde vnto him:
why baptisest thou then/yf thou be not Christ
nor Helyas/nether a Prophet? John answered them sayinge: I baptise with water: but
oneis come amonge you/whom ye knowe not
he it is that cometh after me/whiche was before me /whose sho latchet I am not worthy to vnlose. These thinges were done in
Bethabara beyonde Jordan/where John dyd
baptyse.

D.ii.   ✠The

Marginal notes:
John ba-
re witnes
(Grace)
all grace:
& all that
is pleasa
untin the
sight of
god/is ge
uē vs for
Christes
sake only:
euen oute
of the ful
nes & abo
undaunce
ofthe fa-
uoure th-
at he rece
aueth
with his
father.

*Voyce.
thatis: I
am that
I preache
I am sent
to proue
you synn-
ers & to
crye on y-
ou to amē
de that ye
maye rece
aue Chr-
ist & his
grace.

11 A page from William Tyndale's 1534 New Testament, showing his translation of the Gospel of John and his marginal commentary on the doctrine of grace.

God 1534 in the month of November. The key words here are, of course, *corrected and compared*, not to mention *diligently*; Tyndale found the Vulgate too riddled with errors of both translation and transmission that had built up over centuries. He went back to the Greek texts originally translated in the fourth century by Jerome and started over. The title also fixes Tyndale's labors to a particular time and place, proclaiming a new biblical age that was not so much post- as pre-Vulgate.[15] As the preface to Parker's Anglo-Saxon Gospels would declare some thirty years later, "no new reformation lately begun": Tyndale had replaced England's Roman Catholic history with an older, purer past in order to ensure its future.

Tyndale's preface to the 1534 New Testament was a testament in itself, describing not only the gravity and risk of his enterprise but also the painstaking process of producing accountable biblical translation. In it, he expresses an acute sense of responsibility, not only to the readers to whom he had promised the saving Word of God rendered more purely, but also to the very concept of what "purity of the scriptures" would mean for those readers. The best and most perfect translation, Tyndale conceded, could not always yield up its meaning to even the best and most motivated reader. There were passages in the Bible that were simply impenetrable, in Latin or in English. Juxtaposing metaphors of darkness and imprisonment with light and liberation, a stylistic device indebted to Martin Luther in the German reformer's infamous tract of 1520, *The Babylonian Captivity of the Church*, Tyndale tacitly acknowledged that, far from settling theological issues, a new translation could simply open up new problems of comprehension and interpretation.

To factor into the actual translations themselves the explanatory latitude to address these issues, however, would be to risk marring the pristine nature of the original. In hard cases he thought it "better," therefore, "to put a declaration in the margin than to run far from the text." He called this "set[ting] light in the margin to understand the text by,"[16] a technique that effectively made Tyndale's New Testament into a delivery system for his doctrinal opinions, which by now had been condemned by the Church.

For translating and publishing religious texts without authority, William Tyndale was found guilty of heresy. After fifteen months' imprisonment, he was finally executed in Belgium in 1536. The sentence was death by burning, but in view of his religious celebrity the authorities allowed him, mercifully (and never doubt that this was anything but the profoundest mercy), to be strangled at the stake before being fed to the flames. A woodcut illustration from John Foxe's *Acts and Monuments* shows the great translator with a rope around his neck at a public stake, one of the many illustrations that ensured that *Acts and Monuments* would soon commonly be better known as "Foxe's Book of Martyrs." It documents Tyndale's last words: "Lord, open the king of England's eyes." Light and liberation may have been the theme of his life's endeavors, but in the end the language of confinement and darkness was to define Tyndale's death for generations of Protestants.

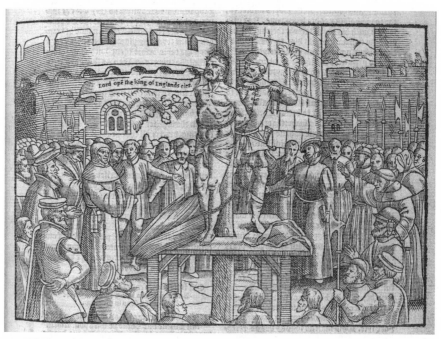

Lord opē the king of Englands eies.

12 William Tyndale prays for Henry VIII at his execution, as depicted in a sixteenth-century copy of "Foxe's Book of Martyrs".

Another, grimmer irony underscores this event – or, at the very least, it provides one more example of the absurd sense of timing that irregularly punctuates England's reformation history. By the mid-1530s, Henry VIII and his government ministers had already engineered the Church of England's break with the papacy, a bold act that made Henry the Supreme Head of his Church on earth (and had famously sent Lord Chancellor More to the scaffold for defying the king in this matter a full year before his erstwhile adversary Tyndale met his own untimely end). By 1536, then, William Tyndale's crime was, in effect if not judgment, treason. Tyndale's translation of the Bible was not the reason he went unconscious to the flames: his translation without official permission, complicated by the many written proofs of his heretical doctrinal opinions in the margins of that Bible and elsewhere, was what doomed him. Yet, given the dangerously unstable cast of the times, and the stubborn and self-righteous cast of his mind, it's not clear that Tyndale could have chosen – or would have chosen – to dodge his fate.

The example of one of Tyndale's contemporaries supports this conjecture. Miles Coverdale (1488–1568) was an assistant to Tyndale who managed both to avoid Tyndale's grisly end and to profit by the experience. (Coverdale's safety was also ensured by Henry VIII's second marriage in 1533 to the committed Protestant Anne Boleyn and the consequent fact that the bishops of the English Church petitioned the king for a translated Bible in 1534.) Translating from the Latin Vulgate and the vernacular Bibles of Martin Luther and Tyndale, Coverdale completed the first complete English Bible under the new queen's patronage. The first edition of his *Biblia* was printed abroad in 1535, while Tyndale languished in prison. Politic additions to the text aimed at ensuring its eventual safe passage into England: Coverdale's preface wisely did not dally with high-flown metaphors of light and liberation but instead opened with a flattering dedication to Henry suggesting that, by reading the Bible in their own language, his subjects would learn to be more obedient to both God and king.

From this point, the case for an official Bible in English moved swiftly. By 1537, Coverdale's Bible was being printed in London. By

1538, Henry VIII had issued a proclamation requiring every church in England to purchase a copy of the Bible in English. And by 1539, the king made provision for this by ordering into print *The Byble in Englyshe*. Henry's "Great Bible" (the name by which it became better known) was the first Bible to announce on its title page the fact of its publication by monarchical authority, a validating claim that has set English Bibles apart from European ones ever since.

Cum privilegio, however, was only one way – and not even the most direct way – that the Great Bible's title page announced its authorized status. The page in its entirety serves up a remarkable portrait of power. (The importance of words and pictures on title pages, like the value of modern real estate, begins and ends with location.) This image, then, like all elaborate title-page images from this period, should be read from the top down. To begin: Henry VIII sits enthroned at upper center, taking the place once occupied by the image of God in Miles Coverdale's Bible.[17] The Savior's outstretched arms create an arcing shape that repeats, and reinforces, the curving sweep of Henry's throne. While the Christ who blesses this endeavor is markedly smaller than the king, this is not the blasphemous depiction of relative status some recent commentators have suggested it is. Rather it is an attempt to convey, despite the limitations placed on the art of perspective by the flattening medium of woodcut printing, the idea that Jesus has blessed the king and his actions, which here take pride of place.

Thus beatified, Henry hands copies of the Bible to churchmen at the reader's left and statesmen at the right. They in turn pass these books on to the lesser clerics and pious laypeople who populate the middle and bottom of the page. At bottom left we find a cleric preaching to a cross-section of the people of England – young and old, male and female. At bottom right, even the bars on the windows of a brick prison fail to keep out the Word. The people receive the Bible with upturned hands and cries of *Vivat Rex*.

Vivat Rex. Stop. Look again. "God Save the King" – in *Latin*. Nearly everyone on the title page, and there are more than fifty figures, is depicted with words issuing from his or her mouth. All but

13 Henry VIII dominates the title page of the "Great Bible" of 1539.

two speak in Latin. This is due neither to editorial sloppiness nor ecclesiastical hypocrisy; the non-vernacular title page has a message to deliver. This large, expensively produced Bible may have been translated into English, but it was designed to be read by priests – for whom this imposing image was pointedly intended. Never mind his laypeople: Henry's churchmen, all of whom had begun their careers as Roman Catholic priests loyal to the papacy, were likely to have been Henry's most problematic subjects, at least when it came to accepting the king's defiance of the Pope's ecclesiastical authority over the Church of England. The first authorized Bible in English, then, in a neat twist on Wycliffe's and Tyndale's fundamental notion of biblical authority over the Church's, was designed as a vehicle to proclaim the king's authority over *his* Church.

But royal supremacy equals Protestantism no more – nor less – than papal supremacy equals Catholicism. Reformation requires transformation of doctrine, sacramental practices, and methods of worship. And those are only institutionally mediated actions: knowing when people's hearts can be called "reformed" is altogether a different, and generally inscrutable, matter. Historians will always debate whether Henry's Church could be called "Protestant" or "Catholic." Safest to say, perhaps, that the set of legislative initiatives passed by Henry's parliaments in the 1530s was bold enough to sever the Church's ties with Rome but not thorough enough to transform the religious temper of the kingdom – nor, in the end, of the king. In 1547, after a period of religious oscillation in which Henry seemed first to favor the cause of religious reform and then to repudiate it (he eventually restricted access to the scriptures in order to exclude most women and poor men), Henry VIII went to his eternal reward. He died a good Catholic, at least by this gold standard: his will left money for prayers to be said for his soul.

The English people then faced major confessional change with every Tudor succession of the sixteenth century, reflecting the fluctuating fortunes, both religious and parturient, of the relicts of the Henrician dynasty. For eleven years, Henry VIII's successors were childless and short-lived, their accession parliaments undoing and remaking religious legislation with dizzying rapidity. A brief period of radical Protestantism under Henry's only son Edward VI ended abruptly in 1553 with the unmarried king's death at the age of sixteen. During this short reign, Edward's government finally ordered the churches of England actually to purchase copies of the Great Bible.

More important, Edward's Archbishop of Canterbury, Thomas Cranmer, headed the effort to render the Church of England's services into English. The Book of Common Prayer produced in 1549 was a conservative affair, to some ears merely a translation of the traditional Catholic Mass into the vernacular. Nonetheless, linking everyday words in familiar cadence to embodied practices of long standing, the new Prayer Book – not the Great Bible – was what finally made the Church of England *English*. And it placed Coverdale's translation of the Psalms at the heart of the Church of England's ritual worship, where it remains to this day.

A more radically Protestant version of common prayer was produced in 1552: leaving time only for acrimonious debate before its rescission when Edward died, painfully young and without progeny to carry out his reforms. Edward VI's half-sister Mary – eldest daughter of Henry VIII and like her mother, Henry's first wife, Katherine of Aragon, a devout Catholic – inherited his throne. She returned England to Roman allegiance, earning for her conservative scruples an undeserved reputation – her father, an equal-opportunity religious persecutor who executed both Protestants and Catholics, had her beat on this score – as England's bloodthirstiest religious bigot. The reports exaggerate, but then again, Christian history attests time and again to the evangelistic power of the minority reports called "martyrdom narratives."

In fact most English men and women, preferring a legitimate ruler to a Protestant one any day, and having learned in volatile times to take things as they found them, readily conformed to the re-imposition of the old ways. Many were delighted by the return of their colorful and comfortable old religion. All Englishmen and women, in any case, were required to attend the services of the re-established Roman Catholic Church of England whether or not they cared to. Some of Mary's committed Protestant subjects did *not* care to, risking persecution and, in some cases, execution for their contumacious heresy. Those with a different kind of courage – or money, or advantageous connections – left England altogether to reside in reformed communities on the continent.

No English Bible was printed domestically during Mary I's reign. The campaign to translate and print an English Bible instead shifted to lands where "vernacular" meant "French" or "German": for a time, then, the English Bible was produced in exile. The most enduring of these exilic versions was first commissioned by William Whittingham, a Protestant firebrand who, having fled the religious persecution of Mary's government, led English congregations in Frankfurt and, later, the Swiss city of Geneva. Whittingham, who advocated a form of Calvinist religion so unpleasant and uncompromising as to blight his later career as an Elizabethan bishop, oversaw the production of an English New Testament at Geneva in 1557. But by the time his Bible had acquired an Old Testament to match the New, his nemesis Mary I was dead. The entire version, completed in 1560, was thus dedicated to the Protestant successor, her younger sister Elizabeth.

The Bible and Holy Scriptures conteyned in the Olde and Newe Testament, or the "Geneva Bible," resembled Tyndale's in its political and doctrinal opinions unsubtly expressed in the margins. It soon became clear that Elizabeth's Protestantism and the Geneva's were going to be at odds. As befits, perhaps, a book originally designed for unhappy and alienated people on the run from government surveillance back home, the Geneva's marginal notes tended to make the weak and sinful monarchs who crowd the pages of the Hebrew Bible over into types of anti-Christian usurpers, ripe for divine comeuppance. Take, for example, its description of Jehoram, the king of II Chronicles, chapter 21: "as some write, he was not regarded, but deposed for his wickedness and idolatry ..."[18] Or this gloss on Romans 13: 5 ("ye must be subject, not because of wrath only, but also for conscience sake," a verse usually much beloved of kings):

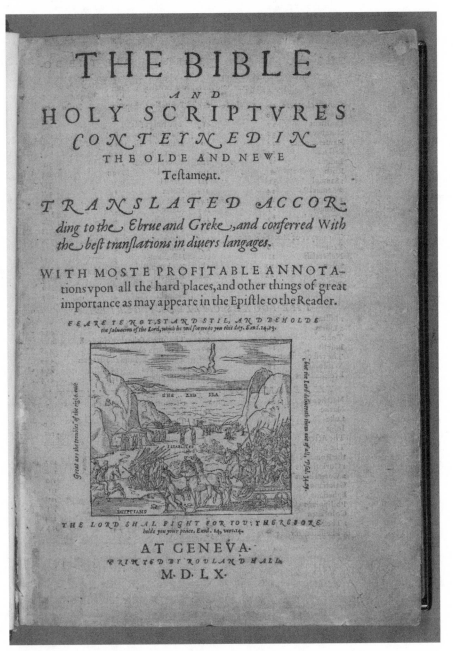

14 Title page, the Geneva Bible, 1560.

"here [Paul] speaketh of *civil* magistrates [i.e. not monarchs], so that Antichrist and his [minions] cannot wrest this place to establish their tyranny over the conscience." The margins of the Geneva Bible thus provide excellent lessons in the religious and political controversies of a shifting age.

But the controversies were not all interconfessional; many reflected matters intraconfessional: Protestant versus Protestant. The notes to Exodus chapter 14, for example, include the following remarks alluding to internal dissensions: ". . . the ministers of God following their vocation shall be evil spoken of, and murmured against, even of them that pretend the same cause and religion that they do."[19] In dangerous and unsettling times, the exiles were also liable to turn suddenly and savagely upon each other in crisis, as congregational fights led to ugly schisms like the one that took Whittingham to Geneva from Frankfurt. The Geneva Bible margins paint a portrait in words of a Geneva Bible reader, transferring its original sense of embattlement and internal dissension to the wider audience it gained once it was produced in London print shops.

But complexly theological, deeply political, and entirely insiderish as it was in its marginal words, the Geneva Bible was something else altogether in its overall format. It was produced in hand-portable quarto rather than lectern-sized folio. It was the first English Bible to be printed in easier-on-the-eye roman type. It was also the first English Bible (and one of the first Bibles altogether, in any language) to feature numbered verses in addition to chapter divisions, thus allowing people to find their places in the text with swiftness and ease.[20] Alongside the marginal lessons on Protestant theology were explanations of difficult words and citations of similar scriptures elsewhere in the Bible. The Geneva boasted informational illustrations that strove to duplicate the descriptions in the books of Exodus and Leviticus of archaic buildings and devices in ancient times: the dimensions of the Temple, or what the Ark of the Covenant might have looked like. It also featured fold-out maps, including one that tracked the wanderings of the children of Israel in the desert as described in Numbers chapter 33 and one that

This mappe properly apperteineth to the 33 Chap. of Nombres.

This mappe declareth the way, which the Israelites went for the space of fourtie yeres from Egypt through the wildernes of Arabia, vntil they entred into the land of Canaan, as it is mencioned in Exod. Nomb. & Deuter. It conteineth also the 42 places where they pitched their tentes, which are named Nomber, 33 with the obseruacion of the degrees, concerning the length and the breadth, and the places of their abode set out by nombers.

15 A fold-out map tracking the movements of the Israelites in the wilderness, part of the Geneva Bible.

disclosed the division of the land of Canaan as set out in Joshua chapter 15. It was replete with useful tables and well-marked indices.

The Geneva was, in short, a book that today undoubtedly would be titled *The Bible for Dummies*. This multitude of "helps," along with its compact size, made it the first Bible designed to assist the common English reader, which in turn made it popular on an unprecedented scale. Its very user-friendliness ensured, however, that religious radicalism would be indelibly associated with individual, private biblical accessibility in future.

The last of the Tudors, Mary's half-sister Elizabeth, took the throne in 1558, speaking cautiously about the value of both her father's and her brother's religion and forcing her auditors in Parliament and Privy Council to imagine what those vague and, practically speaking, paradoxical claims might actually signify. They soon found out that

Elizabeth had inherited Henry's conservative religious temper along with his preference for being sole head of the English Church, and that she intended to harness these characteristics to a style of worship scripted in a Book of Common Prayer that toned down the more radical elements of its 1553 predecessor. Hers was a placatory strategy, arguably for good reason: Elizabeth Tudor had inherited a religiously divided and politically confused kingdom, and her claim to rule her kingdom was contested by Spain even before Pius V denounced her as a heretic. She came to her throne more assured of the support of England's Protestants than of its Catholics. Many of these loyal Protestant subjects, however, wanted more reform of the Church's administrative structures, liturgical practice, and official doctrine than the queen could agree to.

For all their sullenness, Elizabeth could not afford to alienate England's still-substantial population of conservative Christians, some of whom would remain steadfastly unconvinced by what they would call "the new religion" to the bitter end. Many, however, would prove to be open to persuasion – if the Church to which they were expected to convert did not feel, in tone and in action, radically different than the one in which they had grown up. And so the queen consistently tempered the Protestantism of her Church. Elizabeth seems, in fact, to have proceeded on the assumption that in matters of religious politics, her only truly troublesome subjects came in two easily identifiable cohorts: overenthusiastically Protestant clerics and grimly persistent Catholic subjects. These were noisy and trouble- some minorities to be sure, but in the end most of these puritans and papists depended upon Elizabeth's, or her Privy Council's, favor – if for very different reasons – too much to quit her.

A politic calculation, but one in which success would depend on matters largely out of the control of anything but the inscrutable designs of providence, which – or who – did seem to have favored Elizabeth. Against the received political wisdom of the day, the queen refused to marry and reigned alone for nearly fifty childless years. (Given the statistics for maternal death and maternity-related debility in the early modern period, these facts cannot be entirely unrelated.)

More than her practices of careful moderation, more even than the tireless work of the first well-educated parish clergy in the history of the English Church, it is undoubtedly the simple fact of Elizabeth I's longevity that accounts most for the success of Protestant religion in England. Between 1558 and 1603, Protestantism finally got the time – and all the cultural stability that a lengthy reign confers – to take root, hold on, and grow.

This extended period of relative stability may explain the array of English Bibles available in Elizabethan England. By 1562, the Geneva was being printed in London, occasionally by the queen's own printer, but it was never sanctioned by royal authority. Badly in need of a facelift, Henry's Great Bible was proving increasingly poor competition, and soon Elizabeth's Archbishop of Canterbury, Matthew Parker, was called upon to produce a newly authorized text for the queen's Church. It proved to be a poor competitor to any of the versions that had preceded it. Produced in 1568 by Richarde Jugge, printer to the Queen's Majesty, this lavish Bible, revised by Elizabeth I's bishops largely out of the "Great Bible," was an intriguing hybrid of Henry VIII's and the Geneva exiles' aims for the Bible. Like the Geneva Bible, *The. Holie. Bible. conteynyng the olde Testament and the Newe* offered textual helps, handy maps, and verse divisions; unlike the Geneva, it had no marginal commentary. It did feature a large number of lush woodcut pictures. Despite its visual beauty, and its placement by order in every cathedral and most of the parish churches of England, the so-called "Bishops' Bible" never achieved the popularity of the Geneva Bible. It was a hasty, half-hearted, and poorly executed revision, resembling the Geneva just enough to suffer by comparison. In an age hungry for user-friendly lay Bibles, the Geneva Bible simply did the job better.

At this time, another product of hybrid and contradictory impulses appeared on the scriptural scene. *The New Testament of Jesus Christ, translated faithfully into English, out of the authentical Latin . . . in the English College of Rhemes* (1582) was produced by members of the exiled English Catholic College in Douai, France. (Translating from the Vulgate, they completed the New Testament in Rheims when the college moved to that French city in 1578.) This Bible is evidence of two late sixteenth-century phenomena: the persistence of illegal Catholicism in Protestant countries, and the general appeal of vernacular Bibles. In the late sixteenth-century Roman Catholic Church, access to the Bible was restricted to the clergy, a rule effectively enforced by the concomitant rule that the text remain in Latin. In England, Roman Catholicism had itself been outlawed when Elizabeth I took the throne in 1558. Ownership of an English translation of the Vulgate Bible was an offense twice over – unlawful according to England's Protestant government, and antithetical to the doctrines of the Roman Catholic Church.

Why make one, then? Polemical necessity, for one thing. Post-Reformation England was often a bawling arena of public confessional confrontation. Hidden for the most part in plain sight, not so much underground as underfoot, outlaw Catholic priests now served as missionaries to a faithful and often powerfully connected remnant of English Catholics, many of whom came from old aristocratic families, as well as to congregations of foreign diplomats and court hangers-on. In this role, the priests were sometimes called upon to refute Protestants in surprisingly open debate. But Protestants invariably backed up their doctrinal points with scripture; bowing to the times, the priests accepted the rules of engagement. The debates were most often conducted in English; in the heat of conflict, mentally shifting from English to Latin to English could prove a bar to ready wit. An English translation of the Vulgate allowed these stalwart new defenders of England's old religion to proof-text without hesitation, which surely accounts for Rome's complicit wink at these doubly renegade Bibles.

Given its minority audience, this Englished Vulgate would have remained fairly obscure but for the efforts of one determined and outraged Protestant. *The Text of the Nevv Testament of Iesus Christ, translated out of the vulgar Latine by the papists of the traiterous Seminarie at Rhemes*, was printed in London in 1589, at the behest of the Puritan William Fulke. In order to best display its stubbornly heretical differences with the new Bible translations made by

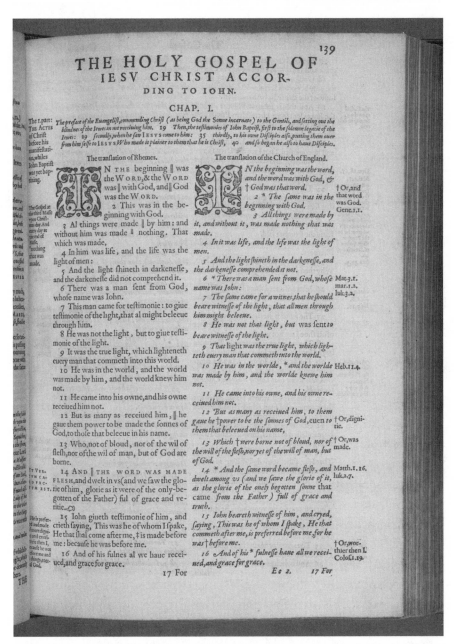

16 The puritan William Fulke inadvertently provides Protestant England with a full and accessible text of the Roman Catholic New Testament translated into English, 1589, along with a parallel text of the Bishops' Bible of 1568.

Protestants, Fulke printed the text of the Douai Bible in columns parallel to the text of the Bishops' Bible of 1568. He died the same year as his parallel Bible was published, and so did not live to witness one unintended result of his labors: Fulke's public exposure made the Douai–Rhemes much better known in England than it would have been otherwise.

This is probably why the vocabulary of this illicit, late sixteenth-century Bible can even be detected in the language of the impeccably legal, in fact "Authorized" (or "King James") version of the English scriptures. In 1604, James I (1566–1625; king of England from 1603) ordered into existence a Bible that, standing the test of time like none before it, became forever after associated with his name. *The Holy Bible, conteyning the Old Testament, and the New: newly translated out of the originall tongues: & with the former translations diligently compared and reuised, by his Maiesties speciall commandement*, printed by Robert Barker in 1611, is now considered a masterpiece of English prose. Its influence on English and American literature exceeds even that of the works of William Shakespeare, themselves products of the same golden age of English arts and letters (and which, we need to remember, antedated the Authorized Version (AV): given the years he was a working writer, Shakespeare must have been conversant with the Geneva Bible in order to mine the many biblical allusions that grace his texts). The Authorized Version has remained in continual use in English-speaking churches to the present day. Currently it is the best-known, best-selling, most published, most widely distributed – and, according to one recent book dealer's survey, the most frequently stolen – book in the English language.[21]

The clear market dominance of the Authorised Version makes it all the more interesting to recall that that this seemingly ageless and universally desirable Bible was, in its day, the product of a not particularly holy alliance of immediate political purpose and theological intent: to counteract the deeply Calvinist influence of the Geneva Bible on English Protestants – especially those uncompromising Protestants who were called "puritans" by their political enemies. Called "the godly" or "the hotter sort of protestants" by more sympathetic observers at the time, "puritans," as a recent author has observed, probably formed the "moral majority" in early modern England.[22] In any case, the puritans of *this* story were neither radical separatists on their way to Holland or America, nor were they the hypocritical figures of fun pilloried on the Elizabethan and Jacobean stage: they were simply disgruntled churchmen and laypeople who hoped that a new monarch might finally comprehend that their calls for further reform were not dangerously radical displays of disloyalty. Upon his accession to the English throne, then, King James I was almost immediately confronted with impetuous godly petitions, rudely importunate court sermons by novice preachers who didn't know any better, and the sneaking speculations and skepticism of a Parliament and councilors who saw the king as a Scottish foreigner first and an English king second.

Those who had been successfully keeping Puritanism at bay with the connivance of the queen were ecclesiastics of a more conservative stripe – conservative in this case meaning defenders of a Church defined as much, if not more, by the beauty and decorousness of traditional and inbred Prayer Book worship as by the edifying quality of its increasingly Calvinist preachers. The conservatives were probably best skilled in the art of raising alarums, however, as they detected in even innocuous demands for more doctrinal and liturgical reform an imminent takeover of the Church's beliefs and practices by radical forces. Here was a situation tailor-made for a new king who considered himself possessed of Solomonic wisdom and enjoyed proving it in public. Both sides of this unhappy and divided Church, James announced, would have their say and get their fair hearing.

But not one of the king's new English ministers and bishops, whether puritan or conservative, knew exactly what to expect from their canny new monarch. James, who had ruled Scotland as James VI since his mother's deposition in 1566, was the representative of a race as strange and unknowable as near-neighbors of the English could be. His mother was the infamously Catholic Mary, Queen of Scots; from infancy, however, his education had been presided over by Scottish Calvinists. As a result, James VI and I had surely learned more

Protestant theology, and just as surely learned to love that rigorous course of study, more than was usual – or even quite seemly – for a monarch. And so, all things considered, this king was better educated and, arguably, more politically astute and natively intelligent, than his Tudor predecessors.

The new Bible was conceived at the royal palace at Hampton Court, where in January 1604 James presided over an elaborately staged debate between the clergy of the increasingly divided and fractious Church he had inherited from his royal cousin Elizabeth. The evidence of his godly upbringing and *theophilia* probably encouraged the Godly to think their cause might actually get the fair hearing they had been promised. But the reports from the Hampton Court Conference reveal nothing less than a rout of the unfortunate ministers who served as the official puritan representatives to the conference. These coolest heads of the Hotter Sort had been chosen for their respectable standing in the established Church (one was Dean of Lincoln) and their ability to accept institutional compromise; their "puritanism" chiefly consisted in a principled refusal to disavow entirely the strict ideas about true doctrine and proper worship espoused by their less-politic brethren. Even so, the members of this "Puritan party" found themselves outmaneuvered, ridiculed, and bested at every turn until they finally advanced a petition that would have seemed a sure thing, even to them: that a new translation of the scriptures be made to replace the corrupter bits of the Bishops' Bible. In a rare burst of acquiescence, the king acceded to their request.

And in so doing, took game, set, and, eventually, match for the conservative wing of the Church of England. For what the king went on so enthusiastically and determinedly to sponsor was a version of the scriptures aimed at replacing, not the undistinguished and unlamented version commissioned by Elizabeth I, but the *Geneva* Bible, the best-selling English Bible of the era and the primary if unofficial sourcebook for English Puritanism.

James I's Bible was eventually drawn from several base texts, notable among these the discredited Bishops' Bible and even the Catholic Rheims New Testament. Still, the locutions of Tyndale continued to saturate the language of the new Bible's New Testament – and because of this, the radical spirits of the Geneva exiles and the Wycliffites can be detected hovering anxiously if faintly over the whole enterprise. In the end, though, the text to which this royally commissioned Bible was most indebted was the Church of England's own Book of Common Prayer.

Like the Protestant Church of England, this was a Bible also famously designed "by committee": forty-eight scholars assigned to six task groups (each with its own head, to make a total of fifty-four); Archbishop of Canterbury Richard Bancroft, an irascible hammer of puritans, overseeing the entire operation. To understand exactly how this process could produce a Bible designed to stamp out English Puritanism, we need know only three things: that Bancroft, operating in the king's interest, appointed a theologically diverse committee that ran the gamut from conservative to Puritan; that their labors were defined primarily by the king and his archbishop as "revision" rather than "translation"; and that, after all matters of translation and collation were copy- and proof-edited on the page, the entire text of the new version was read out loud in a final quality-control check.[23]

The broadly drawn composition of the committee might seem least conducive to the production of a religiously and socially conservative Bible, but it makes sense when understood as part of the king's overall policy of political containment. James was determined to achieve church unity and conformity – a strategy that was neither moderate nor tolerant in an age that felt no real admiration for religious moderation and evinced no cultural recognition of religious toleration. The puritans appointed to the committee were, like the contingent at Hampton Court, men known more for their allegiance to the king (despite his general coolness to their cause), and to the Church (despite her many lingering infirmities), than for their doctrinal or ceremonial radicalism. Those who could not contain their opinions of either king or Church had, of course, not been summoned to join the project in the first place. The opponents of the committee's puritans would not have felt the same need to make compromises.

This structure achieved a consensus-based conservatism that was underlined by King James's and Archbishop Bancroft's determination that, the claims of its title page notwithstanding, the 1611 Bible was not a "translation," a conversion into something new, but a "revision": mere amendment or improvement. The puritan complaints at Hampton Court about the translations of certain words in the Bishops' Bible were thus settled with the corporate decision to retain an institutionally oriented word like "Church" rather than replace it with the more populist word "congregation" as the Geneva had. The new Bible also lacked most of the maps, tables, and other edifying graphics that had been such a visible feature of both the Geneva and the Bishops' Bibles. Most significant, the margins of the so-called "Authorized Version" of 1611 – interestingly, it was never actually "authorized" but only "appointed to be read"; to this day, the only truly "authorized" English Bible remains Henry VIII's – were wiped clean of interpretation or commentary. The few side notes remaining dealt with matters of disputed Hebrew or Greek translation rather than theology or politics.

The argument from silence is the best evidence we have that the Authorized Version of 1611 was no politically neutral text, but one designed to arrest the seemingly unstoppable progress of a Bible meant primarily for individual edification and group study rather than corporate worship. With its ravishing flights of language and sonorous, rhythmic cadence, the King James Bible was and still is eminently suited to a liturgical rather than an educational life, auxiliary to the English Book of Common Prayer. The Prayer Book went on to become the primary religious text of the Church of England, providing it with a distinctively liturgical identity and a sacramentally oriented language of piety. The Authorized Version, now called the "King James Version," went on to provide these two gifts to the disparately Protestant churches of America. In the next chapter we will follow it across the Atlantic and into the northeastern regions of British America, tracing its uneasy progress towards independence.

Conclusion

In 1738, nearly two hundred years after England's first official Bible was printed in English, John Marsh published a book with the lengthy title *The New Testament of our Lord and Savior Jesus Christ translated out of the Latin Vulgat by John Wiclif . . . Prebendary of Aust in the Collegiate Church of Westbury, and Rector of Lutterworth, about 1378.* The title went on to advertise a "prefix" to this particular New Testament, a "history of the several translations of the H[oly] Bible and N[ew] Testament, etc., into English, both in M[anuscript] and Print, and of the most remarkable Editions of them since the invention of printing." This historical account was written by a man named John Lewis, whose mezzotint portrait in eighteenth-century clerical garb formed an elegant and pricey frontispiece to this, the first printed edition of England's best-known unofficial vernacular Bible. Unlike the illegal Wycliffite Bibles of the late fifteenth-century, Marsh's eighteenth-century edition was designed to be limited. The printer issued only 160 copies, which were subsequently sold in bookstalls on Tower Hill and the churchyard of St Paul's Cathedral at the relatively high price of one pound each.

In his day job, John Lewis held livings of several out of the way and uninteresting backwater churches and was personal chaplain to a very minor Irish grandee, Thomas, Lord Malton. Lewis's opening address to this worthy took the ingratiating tone typical of such prefaces, describing Malton as a man whose every action was informed by the "principles" of Holy Scripture. Malton's biography, while sketchy, nonetheless shows not the remotest evidence that he was one to seek scriptural counsel, and soon Lewis swiftly and wisely got out of the business of sycophancy and down to the business of his true prefatory intention, which was to use Malton's name to attract attention to a burning concern of his own.

Lewis was worried about the relaxation of Georgian Britain's position on Roman Catholicism, insinuating that two hundred years of accessible, official scriptures in English – and thereby nearly as many years of official Protestantism – had made the English soft, forgetful of the struggles that made their confessional conversion possible. "[W]hatever Arts have been used to soften the principles of the Romish Church and make them look more human than they did at the Reformation," Lewis wrote, "popery is still the same cruel, tyrannical imposition on the common faith and sense of Christians that ever it was."[24] Lewis wasn't, however, calling for the English to remember the Reformation. He was calling for the nation to recall its vernacular traditions that *predated* the Reformation.

As we saw in the Elizabethan Anglo-Saxon Bible that served as the introduction to this chapter, Lewis was not the first post-Reformation English churchman to invoke the pre-Reformation history of the Church of England in the preface to a "historical" Bible. The story of a vanity-press production of a late medieval manuscript Bible in English in 1731, two hundred years after the Wycliffites had ceased to wield any cultural force whatsoever, and the story of the official printing of an early medieval Bible in Anglo-Saxon at a time when readers of any Bible in English were still few and far between, both remind us that the relationship of the English language and the English Bible to the English Reformation is neither straightforward nor self-evident.

CHAPTER FOUR

MISSIONS AND MARKETS

The Bible in America, c. 1600–1800

The naturalization test for immigrants seeking US citizenship asks: *Why did the Pilgrims come to America?*[1]

The *Mayflower* first dropped anchor in America in the winter of 1620. On board were 102 English souls. Nearly half had spent time in Holland as religious refugees before making voyage; after a few false starts, they and the rest of the passengers finally boarded at Plymouth. Few people died in passage; the ship made port safely, near enough to its intended destination; altogether, it was an uneventful trip for an age routinely chastened by reports of the perils of sea travel. It wasn't the voyage that was remarkable, anyway; what made it memorable was the *reason* for the voyage. The Pilgrims sailed to America to reinvent their church.

The correct answer is: *for religious freedom.*[1]

To trace the progress of the American soul from the landing of the *Mayflower* to the new Ellis Islands of a myriad airport queues is to connect the dots between a set of dubious generalizations. To begin, the separatists who came ashore at Cape Cod and established a settlement they would name after Plymouth, Devon, were not in search of the kinds of religious freedom we would recognize as religious freedom today: they would never have advocated religious freedom for non-Christians, Roman Catholics – or, for that matter, most of their one-time co-religionists. The Pilgrims sought instead their own liberation: to be free to worship like the purer Christians of the New Testament, far away from the corrupt influence of the Church of England.

In any case, Pilgrims made up only a small fraction of the emigrant English of the New World. As the seventeenth century gave way to the eighteenth, America provided fertile, if not exactly virgin, ground for a wide variety of English religious opinion, from church loyalism to religious separatism – and all the hybridized beliefs in between. And then there were the native peoples who, standing freely on their own ground, met the Pilgrims and saw their world – and worldview – contested nearly out of existence.

It's far too qualified an answer to write on any examination, even one as important as the US naturalization test, and accordingly the American government has chosen to count the least subtle – and, indeed, the most controversial – response as the correct one. But this does not so much reflect a failure of political imagination as it does a long-standing historical bias toward, and mistaken ideas about, New England's best-known immigrants. By 1630, what scholars used to call the "errand into the wilderness" was no longer a bid by a few schismatic radicals to declare independence from a backward-glancing national Church. Other ships followed the *Mayflower*, other landings were made on the eastern seaboard, other settlements grew up beyond Plymouth, other errands occupied those who confronted the wilderness. The religious temperament that informed these endeavors was, in the main, not Pilgrim separatism but good old-fashioned English Puritanism.

A phenomenon with roots in British history and branches throwing shade on large swaths of American history, Puritanism is one of those maddening subjects that is either accurately defined using lots of precise terms and provisos, or tolerably defined using a few reductive terms and generalizations. Popular memory on either side of the Atlantic has made for two distinctly different approaches to this historical topic as well. The English have not been kind to their puritan forebears: understandable, perhaps, given the role Puritanism played in England's civil wars of the 1640s. As a consequence, English Puritanism has most often been explained there in terms of what it left behind, namely, the Church and State that expelled it for its antisocial and countercultural beliefs. U.S. Americans, on the other hand, have enshrined Puritanism as a foundational belief system for U.S. religious and political liberty. And so they have tended to define Puritanism in terms of the presumed object of its presumed search: *religious freedom.*

In order to redefine Puritanism, then – either villainously or heroically – both schools have been less open to what most scholars on both sides of the Atlantic would now have to say about the majority of English settlers in the American northeast: they were Puritans, not Pilgrims, and as such professed and professing members of the Church of England. So while we might call the Pilgrim separatists of 1620 Puritans, we cannot call all the Puritans who followed them in the subsequent decades separatists. In any case, the Pilgrims were not separatists simply because they came to America: there were separatists in England busily conducting clandestine services and private meetings throughout this period. Nor were the Pilgrims separatists simply because the Church of England maligned, examined, and prosecuted what it considered defiance of ecclesiastical authority: in the seventeenth century, this Protestant Church would malign, examine, and prosecute a good many people, Puritans and bishops alike, who had never considered themselves anything but its lawful and faithful members. The Pilgrims were separatists because they claimed a private and singular ecclesiastical authority. Their behavior thus constituted a particular and provocative form of rebellion, independent of geographical location, which both rejected the Church of England and made a radical claim to an entirely new social identity.

We find many professed heretics (of omission, commission, or both) over the course of early and medieval Christian history. But we find far fewer schismatics, people possessing the rigor of soul and heart required to break away openly from bred-in-the-bone cultural assumptions about the place of the Church in society. The Reformation only proved such a thing could be done, but by entire kingdoms: what it did not do was provide schism with doctrinal justification – which was why, as we have seen, opposing sides did not defend truths divided up into categories labeled "Protestant" and "Catholic" but instead taxed and arrested and incinerated one another over truth claims called "Christian."

Most Puritans were not, then, separatists: their seventeenth-century habits of thought, which took as given that Church and society would necessarily claim coterminous boundaries, were too deeply ingrained. In fact, as we saw in Chapter Three, Puritans earned their name precisely by *not* separating. Remaining in the English Church as long as they could demand change without intolerable consequences (that is to say, until the reign of Charles I and Archbishop William Laud), they importuned bishops and arch-bishops; they petitioned kings and queens; they harangued tradition-ally minded local communities and argued with the radical religious underground networks of London. By the early seventeenth century, they had importuned and petitioned and harangued and argued themselves right into their detestable nickname, as well as the polit-ical spotlight. The superheated atmosphere this generated clouded the fact that the issues that divided England's Protestants from England's Puritans were remarkably subtle: easy enough to detect but nearly impossible to prise apart.

What made the issues so polarizing was that, without exception, every one originated in devastating disagreement over the meaning and application of Holy Scripture. As we have seen, the Church of England's bishops and the majority of its clergy, along with the monarch who was their employer, taught that on issues whereupon the Bible was silent, Church and State were free in the interest of public decorum and uniformity of practice to make regulations: to require such things as the rote recitation of common prayers, for instance, or kneeling at communion, or making the sign of the cross, or giving rings in marriage. None of these practices appear in the Bible; they were socially enshrined practices retained from the long age of Catholic tradition. Neither spiritually nor doctrinally necessary, they were legally and ecclesiastically binding nonetheless.

Those called Puritans noisily balked and bit and chafed at these extra-biblical embellishments, denouncing them as hateful artefacts of an idolatrous Roman Catholic past. They especially deplored the state of English worship, which, as they saw it, had by the early seventeenth century become more devoted to the words in the Book of Common Prayer than the Word of God. About this, it must be said, the Puritans were correct. From the reign of Elizabeth I, the Church of England *had* increasingly advocated conservative interpretations of Protestant liturgical practice in its official documents, in its episcopal rulings, and in sermons preached in important public and courtly venues and subsequently broadcast through publication. The sacred jewel in the crown of King James's reign, the Authorized Version of the Bible first printed in 1611, simply provided symbolically definitive proof of the shift. This was a Bible more suited to public speaking than private understanding: not the successor to traditional liturgy but its adjuvant.

Those who reacted to this inhospitable and ultimately intolerable climate by making the Atlantic passage had courageously crossed a divide. The separation they effected, though, was geographical. What New England's Puritans sought to create was nothing new but something improved – the Church as once envisaged in the heady early days of the English Reformation: austere in its appearance, Calvinist in its theology – and no less hegemonic nor authoritative than the Church they left behind. Safely protesting their purity – and often, their loyalty – across an oceanic redoubt, far from the disciplinary eyes of their erstwhile bishops, the settlers of towns like Cambridge, Salem, and Boston set about establishing their churches anew: on freshly asserted biblical principles *and* familiar notions of ecclesiastical authority.

This is not to imply that the Pilgrims' more separatist motives in leaving the Old World behind took them beyond the beckoning call of the past. The almost visceral tug of the memory of repetitive behaviors, the way religious attitudes are bred into the bone of generations of practicing worshippers, may explain the curious fact that at least one of the Puritan-friendly Geneva Bibles that came over on the separatist-friendly *Mayflower* was bound together with a government-friendly English Book of Common Prayer. Currently held at the Harry Ransom Library at the University of Texas, Austin, the "Mayflower Bible" of 1588 symbolizes the hybrid and paradoxical desires of the early settlers of New England, both those who craved their own religious freedom but could not advocate religious liberty for others, and those who wanted their Church transformed but would not allow themselves to be accused of anything so radically unthinkable as schism.

The story of early American religion has a plot, then, that turns on the possibilities afforded by the length and depth of the Atlantic Ocean. New England's Puritans were Old England born and bred: disinclined, like most Christians even after the Reformation, to declare themselves in a state of open and belligerent schism. Far from home, though, they were able to exploit their lack of continuous and direct government supervision to worship differently than they had, eventually creating what we might call a condition of plausibly deniable *separateness* rather than *separatism*. Escaping the long reach of their State Church, the Puritans were intent upon founding a Church State, using their dashed hopes for England as a pattern and the Bible as a measuring tape.

Along the way their Bibles changed. In a few short decades, Geneva Bibles were replaced by Bibles in the Authorized Version. This did not reflect New World spiritual trends but old world print and shipping realities.[2] In the century and a half following the *Mayflower* landing, British America's dependence on British goods would necessarily coexist with America's *de facto* state of separateness. As production of the Geneva slowed after 1611, coming to a halt after the restoration of the British monarchy in 1660, what Americans would come to call the King James Version (KJV) was soon the only Bible crossing the Atlantic. America's demand for the Bible remained high; consequently, multiple editions of the AV were sent by the score to the New World over the next hundred and fifty years. There it was consulted by the descendants of the men and women who had once so successfully dodged the authority of King James. As Pilgrims and Puritans had once feared, England's Church remained forever after a national church centered on liturgy and obsessed with a prayer book; thanks to them and their bibliocentric ways, however, the King James Version, redolent of Anglican prayer and Shakespearean speech patterns, went on first to conquer and finally to divide Protestant America.

This chapter traces the origins of the KJV's irresistible colonization of the New World. We begin in the printing house of a colonial minister determined to convert the native populations of his new England: where the only American Bibles were printed in a stranger's tongue and when the Americans' Bible was an English import. We track the unusual and somewhat separate passage of the Psalms from the Church of England to the Puritan independent churches. And finally, we turn to the years before and after the declaration of independence, when American liberty worked against the production and distribution of a recognizably American Bible for nearly a century. The America we will consider will be, by and large, the northeast, for it was there that, once Americans quit buying their Bibles from England, the Bible was finally printed domestically in the early years of the Republic.

This is, in other words, a story about how the American biblical mission paved the way for the American biblical market.

Origins

But first a truer, or at least more complicated, account of origins using American Bibles as our guides. Even to speak of an "American Bible" makes it all too easy to think our way backward, forgetting that before 1776 what we usually call "early America" is better, if not entirely accurately, defined as "British America." As such it was neither independent nor united, nor was it made up of states; it was a foreign outpost with an alien and autonomous past, and it was eventually made up of colonies run by trade corporations and boards of governors based in the Mother Country. No revelations here. But stating the obvious underscores the fact that, in the beginning, American Bibles weren't all that American – depending, of course, on what we mean by the term.

In fact, they weren't even British. The first scripture typeset in the New World was not Protestant, was not printed in New England, and was not in the English language. In Mexico City, Juan Pablos was operating a printing press more than a century before his counterparts in the Massachusetts Bay Colony. One of Pablos's productions in 1548 was a book of Catholic sermons, *Dotrina christiana en lengua española y Mexicana*. It was printed in parallel columns of Spanish and Nahuatl, a dialect described in the title as the "language of Mexico."[3] One page contains *Dotrina*'s single complete scriptural text, Matthew 6: 9–13, the New Testament passage better known to Christians as the "Lord's Prayer." Unlike the others, this is printed in parallel columns of Latin and Nahuatl.

17 The Lord's Prayer in Latin and Nahuatl, 1548.

Dotrina christiana was created for Latin-reading, Spanish-speaking Dominican priests sent to the New World, who would have consulted this particular page in order to translate the *Pater Noster* (for its opening words in Latin: "Our Father") into the language of the region. No other substantial texts from the Vulgate Bible were printed in Nahuatl until 1833: this region was first evangelized not by Protestants but by Catholics, whose papal mandate expressly forbade lay reading of vernacular scriptures. The Dominicans' flock would have heard snippets of the scriptures in their own tongue, however, artfully woven throughout the texts of Catholic sermons, prayers, and catechisms. But while the Dominicans would first have composed these homelier pastorals in their own native language, they would have translated scripture directly out of the Vulgate, not bothering to pause at Spanish along the way. When they thought about scripture, whether Catholic or Protestant, sixteenth-century clerics first thought in Latin.

Nevertheless, from the period of the Reformation to the second half of the twentieth century, full-Bible translation was exclusively and controversially associated with the Protestant cause (sometimes, as we saw in Chapter Three, by governments less enthusiastically Protestant than the Bible-makers). The earliest edition of the first complete Bible translated into Spanish, in fact, was a book banned in both the Old World and the New. *La Biblia, que es, Los Sacros Libros Del Vieio y Nuevo Testamento* was originally printed in the Swiss Protestant city of Basel.[4] Translated by Casiodoro de Reina, a sixteenth-century monk turned Huguenot missionary, the text still forms the basis for the most popular Spanish-language Bible currently in print in the US, the "Reina-Valera."

But today's Reina-Valeras no longer come with the original title page reproduced; a pity, as the image was so famous in its day that the 1569 Bible was affectionately named after it – *The Bible of the Bear*. The cuddly-looking beast rummaging for the honey-pot is less important to the page's imagery, however, than are the bees that swarm instead around an opened Bible, recalling the maxim that the Word of God is "sweeter than honey" (Psalm 119). In the view of the Inquisition, it would seem, it was easier to catch readers this way: the publication and rapid spread of this tempting Bible finally provoked authorities into expressly banning Bible translation in 1562, declaring heretical the printing, owning, or distribution of any translated Bible. In a time when the governments of the Spanish-speaking world continued to profess religious loyalty to Rome, a Spanish-language Bible was forbidden fruit.

By the end of the seventeenth century, then, Bible translation and distribution had also become the defining acts of *Protestant* mission. The domestic missions of the sixteenth and early seventeenth centuries – a primary consequence of post-Reformation politics – had faded with the end of early modern wars of religion and the onset of Enlightenment. Now Christian missions sought new, native worlds to conquer. And while Catholic missionaries sought to teach new forms of devotion and prayer, inculcating the ways of the Church, Protestant missionaries sought first to teach the Bible, inculcating the way of the Word.

The motto on the seal of one English trade corporation chartered in 1628, the Massachusetts Bay Company, thus featured a bare-chested person clad in a crude skirt made of plant fronds, pleading "Come over and help us" – lines the imaginary unlettered heathen had apparently drawn from a close reading of Acts 16:9. This plangent image signposted all official correspondence of the company, broadcasting one great hope of the colonists sent to Massachusetts Bay in 1630 under the leadership of John Winthrop: not to establish their own religion – after all, it came over with them – but to convert the resident native population to Protestant Christianity, English-style.

The English had been schooled to investigate and embrace such a quest, not only by their ministers but also in their leisure reading. By the early seventeenth century, books on navigation, foreign exploration, and exotic lands and peoples had become extremely popular. While the marketable quality of these books attests to the literate audience's curiosity about the useful and interesting skills and observations they purveyed, many books aimed at more prurient interests.

LA BIBLIA,
QVE ES, LOS SA-
CROS LIBROS DEL
VIEIO Y NVEVO TE-
STAMENTO.

Trasladada en Español. *Wickham*

Por — Cassiodoro de Reyna *Calvinista*

רבר אלהינו יקומ׳ לעולם

La Palabra del Dios nuestro permanece para siempre. Isa. 40.

M. D. LXIX.

en Basilea.

18 *La Biblia*, better known as "The Bible of the Bear" (Basel, 1569), title page.

Wild depictions of native religious practices, many owing their style and tone to western medieval and Renaissance representations of Hell, were a staple of the lavishly illustrated, best-selling travel series of the day, a set of books about the New World illustrated by a Huguenot named Theodor de Bry.[5] Theodor's stated purpose was to persuade Protestants to challenge the undisputed primacy of Roman Catholic missions to the New World. His fabulous accounts and lurid portraits of strange worlds and "the Indian religion" sparked combustible dreams of mass conversion, but it also served the public appetite for armchair travel, produced a compellingly shivery *frisson* about the Other, and augmented contemporary and domestic speculations about witchcraft and demonology.

19 Theodor de Bry depicts the "religion of the Indians," 1613.

This, then, is the back-story to the emigration of John Eliot, who sailed to America in 1631, became the minister of Roxbury church in the Massachusetts colony the following year, and ushered in the first age of the "American Bible." In an era of foreign exploration, colonial expansion, and religious conversion, the Reverend Eliot still stands out as a missionary and educator of remarkable energies. He soon made a name for himself as the "propagator of the gospel to the Indians."[6] Eliot did not limit his evangelistic purview to a pulpit. Protestant doctrine stressed access to the scriptures through reading; for Eliot, literacy was essential to the Christianization of the New World. To that end, between 1647 and 1689 he founded what became known as the "Indian Library."

The Reverend did not work alone, but was aided by a purpose-built British support team called the Society for the Promoting and Propagating the Gospel of Jesus Christ in New England, a corporation formed in 1649 by an act of the Parliament that had also, in that same year, been responsible for the execution of King Charles I. The SPG sent over stores of paper and type, and provided English manpower in the form of an experienced printer named Marmaduke Johnson. Eliot put an experienced local pressman, Samuel Green, in charge of an operation that would often be employed in the production of books for the Indians of the region. Many of the press's title pages also credit a native with a Christian first name and a surname derived from his new profession – John Printer, whose birth name is lost to us. Printer's grasp of English was so competent that he was first employed as a teacher in the Indian Charity School in the Massachusetts Bay Colony. He went on to work for many years as a typesetter for Eliot's press at Cambridge, producing the dozens of religious books conjured into being by his indefatigable boss.

It was Printer who set into type what was quite possibly the best known, most arduous, and least read endeavor in the history of American print, *Upbiblum God*, popularly known as "Eliot's Indian Bible." The first complete Bible printed in the western hemisphere, this was also North America's first missionary Bible: 1,180 pages of the Word of God typeset by strangers for the native inhabitants of a strange land.[7] Its initial press run would have staggered the commercial imaginations of the men and women who printed Bibles in England. Perhaps as many as 2,000 – one Bible for every two and a half Christianized Indians in New England – were printed by Eliot's Cambridge press in 1663. The explanation for this market glut surely lies in the difference between supplying single Bibles to established churches and equipping individuals to distribute Bibles for missionary work. Their abundance at the time notwithstanding, they are exceedingly rare commodities today: most would be destroyed in King Philip's War of 1675–76.

This was no English Bible, but a translation of the scriptures into the Natick dialect of the Algonquin Indians of Massachusetts. Eliot's industry signals an important about-face in the history of Bible translation, which by the end of the seventeenth century had come to mean the movement of scripture out of familiar languages and into unfamiliar ones, the Word remade strange for the purpose of Christian mission. Eliot had learned native speech well enough to be able to converse with, preach to, and be instructed by the Massachuset – and then recast those sounds into the shape of English vowels and consonants. To line them up in orderly English sentences, moreover, he had to work out which words in Algonquian most closely approximated words in the English scriptures. This was nothing like the simple exchange of common terms. It was instead the act of translation twice removed: the replacement of exotic places, unpronounceable names, and miraculous deeds first conveyed in Hebrew and Greek by exotic places, unpronounceable names, and miraculous deeds conveyed in Algonquian.

So John Eliot aimed to teach the Massachuset how to read their own language – theirs, mind you, not his: admirable testimony to his staunchly precise conviction that the Bible should be conveyed in everyone's vernacular, a polyglot of vernaculars. He then had to wait to see if this led his new native congregations toward the conversion Puritans like Eliot believed in: a quickening of the heart prompted by a verbal comprehension of the Word of God, a faith coming in (as the New Testament's Paul would have it) by the ear.

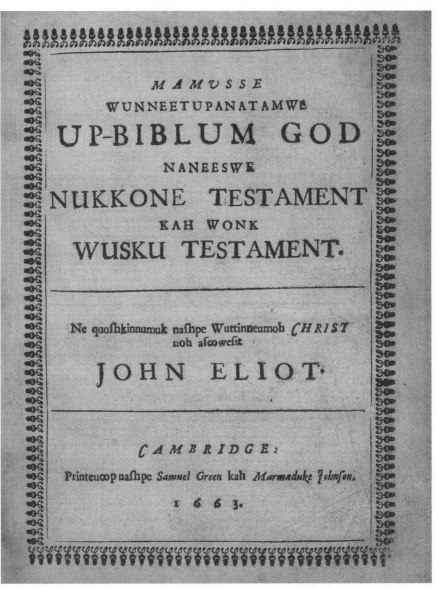

20 John Eliot's American Bible.

By 1674, it was estimated, nearly 30 percent of the converted Native Americans in Eliot's region could read their own language. Does this transformation of Algonquian from oral to written form represent an advance? Surely it did for Eliot and his English co-workers, who in the process learned the native tongue of their new land as well as mastering the skills required in setting unfamiliar type. (John Printer, we could argue, got to do the same.) The daily collaboration of words and skill must have produced threads of cross-cultural empathy, adding to the usual benefits of work in common. But whether the Reverend was successful in teaching natives how to comprehend not only the Christian message, but also its culturally idiosyncratic medium, is a question to ponder. Consider this sad observation, found penned in the margins of an Algonquian Bible: "I am forever a pitiful person in the world. I am not able clearly to read this, this book."[8] Written by a converted Native American living on Martha's Vineyard, it demonstrates both a heart-piercingly sharp understanding of the dynamics of Protestant salvation, as well as a bone-weary resignation to Protestantism's seemingly implacable requirement that faith must come through understanding the Word, even if translation had made what once was familiar newly and weirdly incomprehensible.

What makes this note particularly poignant is the social equation it suggests: if 30 percent of converted Native Americans could read the Eliot Bible (and surely this was a generous estimate), then 70 percent could not. Even remembering that it is virtually impossible to gauge the sincerity of any profession of religion (nor is it remotely possible to distinguish which is "best" of the many reasons, pragmatic or inspired, to embrace a faith introduced by interlopers), this highlights a core truth of evangelism. Many, if not most, souls are not converted by reading a book, but in acts of worship. Given its manifold interpretive challenges, its cultural mysteries, which it presented to all parties, English missionaries as well as native audiences, with a fine impartiality, the Bible may well have presented the greatest stumbling-block to successful Protestant mission.

Eliot's first acknowledgement that this may have been the case was expressed in a letter he sent back across the Atlantic to Richard

Baxter, a Kidderminster clergyman and a reliably best-selling Puritan author. "I am meditating what to do next for these Sons of this our Morning," Eliot wrote, describing Native Americans in brightly shining terms and asking Baxter for permission to publish one of his devotional books, *A Call to the Converted*, for them in their native tongue. Baxter agreed, for all the good it did. His *Call* was a clarion sounding to conversion and a heartfelt Protestant paean to reading: both of these acts originating in human desires – to be saved, and to be literate. *A Call to the Converted* is an astonishing book filled with assertions of the scripture's essential clarity and plain speaking, a text nakedly open to all who could read. It had been a hit in English. In Algonquian it fizzled: an easily ignored puzzlement to the natives, it was read less than even the Eliot Bible had been.[9]

Perhaps Eliot and company finally recognized that the Bible was not self-sufficient to the Native Americans' salvation. Forty years after the publication of the Eliot Bible and more than a century and a half after Pablos printed the double-columned, liturgically oriented *Dotrina Christiana* for Spanish-speaking Catholic missionaries in Mexico, they finally produced a liturgical text of the Psalms, translated into Massachuset. It featured Algonquian and English in parallel columns.[10] Building a new bridge across the Native American/British American divide, the dual-format Psalter may have been the one section of the Good Book capable of communicating its message with compelling beauty and resonance on both sides of that chasm. The British settlers had had *their* purpose-made copy of the Psalms since 1640, after all. The first Bible printed in North America may have been in the dialect of its natives, for instance, but the first book printed in North America was a new English edition of the Psalms.[11]

This makes sense. The Psalms are at one and the same time the most lushly alien and routinely accessible book of the Bible, which may well have made them the most relevant text for settlers facing the task of imprinting their religious culture on a beautifully strange and forbidding landscape. The *Bay Psalm Book* of 1640 thus offers an invaluable view into the developing spirituality of the English settlers of New England. Its impeccable Puritan credentials cover even the printing press on which it was produced, which came over on a ship from London in mid-1638. Its owner was one Jose[ph] Glover, a godly minister from Surrey who perished on the return passage later that same year. After Glover's will was probated in London, the machinery, left behind in Massachusetts, was taken up by an unprepossessing printer named Stephen Daye. Rumor had it Daye was practically illiterate, and couldn't set proper type to save his *own* soul. Despite these daunting drawbacks, he managed to use Glover's press to establish a printing house in Cambridge in 1639. The *Bay Psalm Book* was the first full-length text to emerge from the press.

At least four New England clerics contributed to the *Bay Psalm Book*. In addition to John Eliot (whose fingerprints are on nearly every press product issuing from early New England), the slate included a Mather (Richard, father of Increase and grandfather of Cotton) and the loquacious Puritan diarist Thomas Shepard. Making up the quartet was the English poet Francis Quarles, who in 1635 had written the verse captions for a popular emblem book (a collection of symbolic images with poetic explanations aimed at inculcating and making memorable, in this case, biblical ideas).[12] It is easy to see why such an impressive list of up-and-coming religious worthies, plus a well-known poet, would have wanted their names on the project. It offered an unparalleled opportunity to articulate and influence the established worship of the Massachusetts Bay community, which, while it already boasted lengthy extemporaneous ministerial prayers and an even longer ministerial sermon, lacked the proper script for collective hymn-singing.

Starting with the Psalms would have been, then, a given. Two thousand years after they were penned, they remain the least altered of any scriptural text, testimony to the settling effect of worship on what were once the words of an alien people, unfamiliar words and sentiments thoroughly domesticated through constant and ongoing use. Conventionally attributed to King David, these scriptures of the Hebrew Bible were central to Jewish and early Christian worship, and went on to form the heart of the liturgical offices of both the western and eastern Christian Churches for centuries.

Due to their scriptural origin, the translated Psalms also supplied Protestant worshippers with acceptable texts for hymnody: they were set to music by the irrepressibly music-loving Martin Luther and reprinted in their entirety in the English Book of Common Prayer. Playing a very different role than they had in Latin, in a Catholic Mass performed by priests and choristers, they became the most powerful expression of the communal nature of Protestant worship. And so, in 1645, after England's civil wars ushered in a period of religious and political radicalism – after the routing of the monarchy, the execution of the Archbishop of Canterbury, the collapse of the established Church, and the abolition of the Prayer Book – the parliament-issued *Directory of Public Worship* not only approved the singing of Psalms but even provided careful directions on how to sing them: with voices "tunably and gravely ordered."[13]

The Psalms' eminent suitability for worship of all sorts is surely related to the fact that their origins are poetic: emotionally expressive, piercingly humane, they are ingeniously and attractively cadenced in their original Hebrew. When translated into English, however, their rhythms become erratic; they cannot be set to music without restructuring. In the early years of the English Reformation, Thomas Sternhold, a government servant under Edward VI, had consequently set them in a standard, Englished, four-line rhyme scheme. Eager to reassure the strictest of the emergent "scripture-only" crowd, sixteenth-century Protestant scholars claimed that these metrical psalms captured the original intent of the Psalmist with more authenticity than could any other vernacular version.

A possibly disingenuous claim, given that Sternhold had set most of the English Psalter to the irresistible beat of a traditional ballad called "Chevy Chase," a tale of Anglo-Scottish border warfare that began "God prosper long our noble king/Our lives and safeties all/A woeful hunting once there did/In Chevy Chase befall": popular, yes; easily recalled, naturally; pious, not in the slightest.[14] Sternhold's Psalms may or may not have been more authentic than the rendition found in their contemporary, the Coverdale Bible (the version of the Psalms that remained in the Book of Common Prayer even after other versions of the English Bible had been issued), but they were certainly catchier. Compare the following doxologies, commonly known as "Old Hundredth" (Psalm 100), which in Coverdale reads, cheerfully enough: "O be joyful in God all ye lands; serve the Lord with gladness; come before his presence with joy." In its metrical version, however, Psalm 100 elevates scripted joy to lilting cadence: "All people that on earth do dwell/Sing to the Lord with cheerful voice/Him serve with fear, his praise forth tell/Come ye before him and rejoice."

By the early seventeenth century, Thomas Sternhold's Psalter, now with additional settings by a clergyman named John Hopkins, had become the third most printed book in England, coming in right after the Bible itself and the Book of Common Prayer. By the early seventeenth century, in fact, many Bibles were bound with the Prayer Book, which contained a full copy of the Coverdale Psalms, *and* a copy of Sternhold, which means that the folk who possessed a Bible "fully loaded" would own the Psalms in three forms: as scripture, as worship, and as song. The "Mayflower Bible," with its bound-in prayer book, was, then, not all that eccentric a combination – in fact, what might actually have made it unusual was that it did *not* include the Psalter.

It may be hard to understand at first why New England needed yet another version of the Psalms.[15] For the strictest of Protestants, Psalms were an acceptable – indeed the only acceptable – form of church music. For Puritans, though, "acceptable" never meant "uncontroversial": this persistently unsettled attitude was what made them Puritans rather than conformists. As they were by the Prayer Book, many godly men and women on both sides of the Atlantic were discomfited by the version of the Psalms proffered in Sternhold and Hopkins. Their concerns sound much like the ones that led certain of their representatives to ask James I for a new Bible in 1604: fears that many renditions of these scriptures were unfaithful to the original. Cotton Mather recalled these qualms, writing in 1702 that, while the colonists had been grateful to worship in the beginning with any available English version of the Psalms, Sternhold's version had rendered the scripture with "so many detractions from, so many additions to, and variations of, not only the text, but the very sense of the Psalmist," that the use of it had soon become intolerable.[16] Puritan wags even called the English Church's Psalter "Hopkins His Jigs" – which, given its reliance on the bouncing rhythms of "Chevy Chase," was a pretty fair assessment.

The *Bay Psalm Book* offered, then, an alternative to the standard, which Sternhold and Hopkins had so charmingly arranged that it posed a danger to Puritan consciences. The book's preface opens with an admission:

> The singing of Psalms, though it breathe forth nothing but holy harmony, and melody: yet such is the subtlety of the enemy, and the enmity of our nature against the Lord and his ways, that our hearts can find discord in this harmony and crochets of division in this holy melody.[17]

The lines betray an intimate knowledge of musical notation and the New England sensibility: "crochet" is both the English term for a quarter beat and, with the addition of a final "-y," a snappish way to say "querulous." But the lovely Latin-inflected flight "our *hearts* find dis*cord* in this *har*mony" reminds us that the Godly were not so much anti-sensualists as painfully aware ones. What aesthetic sensibilities Puritans possessed they surely absorbed from their rapt immersion in the exotica of biblical language. Obsessed with reading scripture, ravished by its aural effects, Puritans knew the somatic and imaginative possibilities offered up with every word of the Word: the immeasurable testament to divinity; the power mighty enough to shatter the tightly held illusions of the human will; the irresistible transformation wrought on hearts and souls. And so, in its opening lines, the *Bay Psalm Book* establishes the scriptural bona fides of psalm-singing, because it *has* to – and then admits that such seductive beauty will be both sought after *and* rejected for the wrong reasons.

It can, nonetheless, be hard to imagine anyone passionately loving the verses of the *Bay Psalm Book*, which even fall short of the standard of beauty set by the preface. Consider its version of "Old Hundredth":"Make ye a joyful sounding noise/unto Jehovah, all the earth/Serve ye Jehovah with gladness/before his presence come with mirth." Attending to the need for cadence while standing firmly against the influence of Hopkins's "Jigs," these lines may have rhythm but they do not dance. The words "ye" and "Jehovah" are repeated, making the inverted grammar awkward rather than mellifluous, the rhyme scheme feels begrudgingly stolid, and the third line scans only if the singer puts an unnatural stress on the second syllable of "gladness."

The practice of "lining-out," in which a song leader, usually the minister (who might not always have been possessed of a pleasing singing voice) flatly intoned each passage first with a pitch-imitative congregation following, became standard for New England psalm-singing. The practice must have emphasized even more the *Bay Psalm Book*'s metrical infelicities. But hardening into a style of collective lyric eccentricity, it surely must form one origin of the eerie, almost other-worldly beauty of a later form of American hymnody: sacred harp, or shape note, singing.

In any case, these pedestrian infelicities were energetically defended in the preface. "God's Altar needs not our polishings," protested the five translators, who claimed to "have attended Conscience rather than Elegance, fidelity rather than poetry": implying that, while *their* poetics may have been deficient, the competition's had been unscrupulous.[18] What else were they to do? After all, the *Bay Psalm* translators had assayed the impossible: to be purely faithful to the text and still render it in words that could be recited or sung. A poem by Shepard, sent to his collaborators at the Roxbury Church (Eliot, Thomas Welde) and Dorchester (Mather) outlined the task:

> you Roxburough poets take this in Time
> see that you make very good Rythme
> And eeke of Dorchester when you the verse lengthen
> see that you them with the words of the text doe strengthen[19]

That their efforts were successful, if not particularly sprightly (the final line of Shepard's doggerel presages the lumpish quality of many, many metrical lines to come from this crowd), is attested to by the number of British editions of the *Bay Psalm Book* printed between 1652 and 1759. These were, in all probability, not primarily made for the English market – which, with the exception of a few persistently godly souls, had already declared itself for Hopkins's jigs – but for export to the colonies. They were specially designed to be bound with the copies of the English Bible that were being shipped to the New World – a book which, we recall, was at this point exclusively produced in the Authorized Version.[20]

It would take a century's absence from the Mother Country, the resulting state of *de facto* separateness, and the subsequent creation of new forms for worship like the *Bay Psalm Book* finally to sever nearly all of the effective ties that bound the northeastern colonials to their Mother Church. One essential economic bind was the fact that affordable Bibles – any large books in English, in fact – still had to be obtained from England, which had large numbers of well-supplied and efficiently staffed printing houses.

More than fifty years after the Eliot Algonquian Bible, the next entire Bible to be printed in America (and the first Bible to be made for America's new settlers) was *Biblia, das ist: die Heilige Schrift Altes und Neues Testaments*. This American edition of the Bible translated by Martin Luther in the sixteenth century was printed in 1743 by Christopher Saur, a jack of many trades who finally found his life's vocation in Germantown, Pennsylvania, a borough founded sixty years earlier by German Pietists seeking the religious freedoms promised by William Penn.[21] After acquiring a printing press and establishing himself as a printer of works in German, Saur produced *Biblia*, which was aimed at the substantial cohort of German Lutheran émigrés living in Pennsylvania by 1720. Despite the crippling costs of producing such a large text, Saur priced his Bible more than fairly at eighteen shillings and gave away free copies to the poor. His son succeeded him in the business, thus ensuring that the age of the American Bible in Algonquian gave way to the age of

21 Christopher Saur's American Bible.

the American Bible in German: second and third editions of the Saurs' Bible were printed in 1763 and 1776, when talk of producing an American Bible in English was still an inconclusive discussion about import costs and trade embargoes. Before the 1780s, then, Algonquian and German were the languages of the North American Bible.

The American Bible in the English Language

The frontispiece from the *Self-Interpreting Bible* of 1792 portrays a classically styled woman presenting the scriptures to "America," a woman represented in Indian garb.[22] Another woman of classical mien, signifying "Liberty," leans on a tall cap-rack, benevolently observing the scene and apparently unconcerned about the economic effect that the declaration of American independence was having on the distribution of the scriptures in late eighteenth-century America. This depiction was one of twenty specially engraved plates added to *Brown's Family Bible*, a popular edition of the Authorized Version that had first been printed in Scotland in 1778. The Americanization of *Brown's Bible* fourteen years later – with the text now printed in America and supplied with a republican-themed frontispiece – reminds us that one task facing a newly independent nation was the production of its own Bibles. Returning to the pillar against which Miss America leans, we note it is inscribed with names. These were, in fact, a list of the first subscribers to the *Self-Interpreting Bible*; the roll is headed by George Washington.

The issues holding back the large-scale production of American Bibles were economic and political, unhappily entwined, as they especially tend to be in times of war. As relations broke down between the American colonies and England, Bibles became increasingly difficult to obtain. Bad became worse when, in 1775, the first Continental Congress finally banned the importation of goods, including books and Bibles, from England. One consequence of this declaration of commercial independence was, unsurprisingly, a Bible shortage, which was particularly unsettling in such a time of

22 Frontispiece, the *Self-Interpreting Bible*, 1792.

uncertainty and change. This 1777 petition from three clergymen in Philadelphia addresses the Continental Congress there resident, "humbly" demanding

> that under your care, and by your encouragement, a copy of the holy Bible may be printed, so as to be sold nearly as cheap as the common Bibles, formerly imported from Britain and Ireland, were sold . . .[23]

The problem is voiced in fiscal terms: books were "scarce," their price "dear." And this at a time when Bibles were needed "for . . . schools and families, and the public worship of God." Between every line, though, we discern an underlying fear: that this, of all times, was *no* time to be without the solace and direction of the scriptures.

Congress debated the problem for two months, after which it issued a public statement lamenting the fledgling nation's lack of paper, type, printers, and funds to produce its own Bibles. It proposed instead to import them from "Holland, Scotland, or elsewhere." This was a very costly, and, given the dangers of shipping in parlous times, risky proposition, which failed in the end.[24]

Their irresolution signaled a quandary more basic than wartime economics: what would an American Bible be, exactly? What would such a Bible look like, read like, sound like, *feel* like? What would it be called, now that the power that authorized the "Authorized Version" no longer wielded authority in this not-so-new world? There was neither pattern nor precedent for an "American Bible" – at least not one produced in the English language – in the year 1776. It might, in fact, seem that the sole impulse guiding the first American Congress in the matter of Holy Writ was anti-royalist and anti-monopolist. After a century and a half spent respecting Royal Copyright – as opposed to the licenses held by London's Stationers' Company, by which American printers were not bound – America had finally declared itself in a state of what we might call economic separatism: independent of the Crown's claim to have sole privilege of reproducing, printing, and selling the Word of God.

At the end of the Revolutionary War, having won a measure of independence, the Congress again took up the question of provisions for an American Bible. And for all their dedication to revolutionary action, the political and religious leaders of eighteenth-century America were decidedly non-partisan when it came to the scriptures. They did not call for a new translation or format, they formulated no new laws requiring or regulating Bible use, and, most significant, they refused to make financial provision for its domestic printing. Eventually they rejected any scheme for government-sponsored Bible publication.

And so the costs of producing Bibles were undertaken by the private sector. Robert Aitken was the first to rise to the challenge. Aitken had already published several very popular New Testaments – as did a number of other enterprising printers in the late 1770s – before he personally raised the wherewithal and took the risk of printing the entire Bible in 1781.[25]

Promptly, he lost his shirt. Aitken first asked Congress to authorize his Bible and distribute it under their auspices. It refused. Next, he asked Congress to help defray his by now considerable cost overruns, a request backed by the Congress's chaplains. It refused. Aitken then went, increasingly shabby cap in hand, to the Pennsylvania General Assembly. After several months it responded – with the insultingly paltry offer of a £150 loan, interest free for one year only.

Finally, with his Bible now printed in full, Aitken wrote Congress to ask for *post facto* approval of his Bible from the congressional chaplains and to inquire whether Congress might at the least consider purchasing copies for distribution in each of the new states of the Union. A government distracted by peace negotiations and a variety of secular start-up costs finally answered Aitken's pleas in September 1782 with high praise and a toothless statement "recommend[ing] this edition of the Bible to the inhabitants of the United States." In other words, they once again refused to offer any substantial support for Aitken's project.

Aitken's petitions to Congress in the early 1780s remind us that the notion that the Bible was a book with special claims to

S. J O H N.

unto you, while I was yet with you, that all things must be fulfilled which were written in the law of Moses, and in the prophets, and in the psalms concerning me.

45 Then opened he their understanding, that they might understand the scriptures,

46 And said unto them, Thus it is written, and thus it behoved Christ to suffer, and to rise from the dead the third day:

47 And that repentance and remission of sins should be preached in his name, among all nations, beginning at Jerusalem.

48 And ye are witnesses of these things.

49 ¶ And behold, I send the promise of my Father upon you: but tarry ye in the city of Jerusalem until ye be endued with power from on high.

50 ¶ And he led them out as far as to Bethany: and he lift up his hands, and blessed them.

51 And it came to pass, while he blessed them, he was parted from them, and carried up into heaven.

52 And they worshipped him, and returned to Jerusalem, with great joy:

53 And were continually in the temple, praising and blessing God. Amen.

¶ The Gospel according to S. JOHN.

C H A P. I.

IN the beginning was the Word, and the Word was with God, and the Word was God.

2 The same was in the beginning with God.

3 All things were made by him; and without him was not any thing made that was made.

4 In him was life, and the life was the light of men.

5 And the light shineth in darkness, and the darkness comprehended it not.

6 ¶ There was a man sent from God, whose name was John.

7 The same came for a witness, to bear witness of the light, that all men through him might believe.

8 He was not that light, but was sent to bear witness of that light.

9 That was the true light, which lighteth every man that cometh into the world.

10 He was in the world, and the world was made by him, and the world knew him not.

11 He came unto his own, and his own received him not.

12 But as many as received

him, to them gave he power to become the sons of God, even to them that believe on his name:

13 Which were born, not of blood, nor of the will of the flesh, nor of the will of man, but of God.

14 And the Word was made flesh, and dwelt among us (and we beheld his glory, the glory as of the only begotten of the Father) full of grace and truth.

15 ¶ John bare witness of him and cried, saying, This was he of whom I spake, He that cometh after me, is preferred before me; for he was before me.

16 And of his fulness have all we received, and grace for grace.

17 For the law was given by Moses, but grace and truth came by Jesus Christ.

18 No man hath seen God at any time; the only begotten Son, which is in the bosom of the Father, he hath declared him.

19 ¶ And this is the record of John, when the Jews sent priests and Levites from Jerusalem, to ask him, Who art thou?

20 And he confessed, and denied not; but confessed, I am not the Christ. 21

23 Robert Aitken's American Bible, 1782, was a very modest production.

governmental protection was another of the legacies – besides the words of the text itself, which remained resolutely that of the Authorized Version throughout this period – of America's British past. They also document the prohibitive costs of producing an entire Bible in the last decades of the eighteenth century, and paint a doleful picture of the near-ruin of a once resourceful man. (Aitken had done reasonably well as a printer of scripture prior to this for a very simple reason: the New Testament is a much shorter book than the Old.) At the end of the 1780s, his request for Congress to allow him a patent to print the Bible refused, Aitken finally gave up all petitioning. He was £3,000 in debt.

Poor Mr Aitken, he brought his troubles on himself. The smarter option in politically and economically uncertain times, and with a government that could not or would not publicly fund the printing and distribution of the Christian scriptures, was to offer Bible publication by "subscription," pledges of start-up money by private individuals. This is why George Washington's name headed the list of subscribers to the *Self-Interpreting Bible* in 1792.

The subscription method was best suited, however, to the servicing of "niche" markets: small but well-organized audiences that coalesced around specific needs. One such niche was the Catholic Bible market, very small but also very motivated: in this period, personal lay reading of the Bible was still strongly discouraged by Catholic authorities and the official Catholic Bible was still the Vulgate (a state of affairs that wouldn't really shift definitively until Vatican II). In a mostly Protestant and often militantly anti-Catholic America, English Catholics formed a distinct and concentrated minority in the only three states that had not outlawed them outright: in the state of Maryland, which had been established by Britain as a Catholic settlement in 1631 under the governorship of Lord Baltimore; in New York; and in the famously tolerant Pennsylvania. In 1785, the Archbishop of Baltimore, John Carroll, sent a report to Rome that contained his estimate of the Catholic population of America at the end of the eighteenth century: of the quarter-million Catholics he reckoned were in the

United States, nearly sixteen thousand lived in Maryland, with most of the balance residing in Pennsylvania and only a few thousand in New York.[26]

Infinitesimal, but enough to make a market: the first edition of the first Catholic Bible printed in the United States came quickly on the heels of Aitken's Bible, in 1790.[27] The printer Matthew Carey, another Philadelphian (possibly instructed by Aitken's example and definitely worried about the cost of such a risky endeavor), promised to print an American edition of the Rheims-Douai Bible only if he could persuade 400 subscribers to underwrite the cost. He collected 491 signatures, and produced one Bible for each signatory. Carey published several editions of Catholic Bibles in the early nineteenth century, but his press also produced over sixty editions of the King James Version during the same period in order to remain financially viable.

Conclusion

By 1825, Carey had parlayed his financial success and intrinsic marketing savvy into building the largest Bible publishing house in America. The success of the subscription method had taught him the importance of establishing his market before making his product, a lesson the unfortunate Aitken had learned the hard way. It also demonstrated the advantage of asking for money over time, a ploy that allowed Carey to sell Bibles at comparatively high prices – this at a time when, finally, the costs of printing in America were dropping precipitously – by loading them with new gimcracks. This canny piece of marketing was the suggestion of his man in the trenches, a colorful, hyperbolic traveling salesman named Parson (Christian name, not clerical title) Weems, a man now known only for his biography of President Washington (the first to include the colorful myth of young George and an ill-fated, candor-inspiring cherry tree). People who would never purchase a twenty dollar Bible when one could be had for four turned out to be surprisingly persuadable when that four dollars left their pockets each time over five installments – and the aggregate amount finally purchased a Morocco-bound set of the scriptures complete with maps, indices, and instructive add-ons like *A Clergyman's Address to Married Persons at the Altar*. It is to the success of these and other "niche" marketing strategies that we will turn next.

CHAPTER FIVE

ON NOT UNDERSTANDING
THE BIBLE

"There are many writings for beginners," St John of the Cross advised Ana de Jesus, Mother Superior to the sixteenth-century Carmelites of St Joseph's in Granada, Spain: the Bible, however, was not one of these. It was instead a trap for the unwary (especially those who were so foolish as to think themselves intelligent), who would find in its pages, John promised, "absurdity rather than reasonable utterances." Best to understand it mystically, in a spirit of ravishing love as John was wont to do (especially with the piercingly erotic Song of Solomon, the text that most gripped him over a lifetime of spiritual longing), and keep it out of the wrong hands.

It is time once again to make an observation that too often goes unacknowledged in books about the Bible: the Bible is hard. Like life itself, it is complex and complicated, and it can be deeply strange. Neither self-evident nor straightforward in the least, it is the slipperiest text around, its stories seemingly "wrapped in wrinkles," as Hugh Latimer candidly acknowledged in a 1537 sermon to fellow clerics warily facing up to the possibility of a reformation in the Church of England. This chapter takes up, then, a subject essential to any candid assessment of the Bible, which is: *not* understanding the Bible.

Having the Bible in translation should have been liberating, but in the reformation era liberties were not on general offer. In addition to demanding access to scripture for all, Protestantism taught that the Bible remained sacrosanct. Some pleasant, traditional paths to scriptural understanding that had flourished in the Middle Ages, like images and playacting, thus were now closed. New ways of biblical knowing, like reading, were yet to be widely inculcated. And the notion that the Bible could be generative of more than one legitimate reading was simply not a part of the early modern worldview.

But the powerful misgivings of newly Protestant authorities could not prevent newly Protestantized Bible readers from grasping at scripture in ways that were unprecedented and sometimes wildly imaginative. Readers aired their ideas on the biblical page, between lines and in margins. They created graphic depictions of biblical ideas that managed to bypass restrictions on illustration and warnings about idolatry. Their strategies and solutions were not always doctrinally orthodox, nor were they always particularly rational, and so they did not always please local clergy and government officials. But in the process of puzzling through the Bible, newly energized and inspired readers created new forms and expressions of learning. And so it was that, in a curious and exhilarating way, biblical *unknowing* became one of the great early modern engines of intellectual ambition, educational creativity, and, finally, radical political imagination.

Hugh Latimer would go on to resign his bishopric and, in time, sacrifice his life for a faith that was based on the belief that true Christianity was built from the unerring and authoritative words of the Bible, rather than fifteen hundred years of church precept. We might wonder if he made the right choice, rejecting orderly and articulate centuries of tradition in favor of a book whose pages, as Catholic opponents like St John might have pointed out to him, mystified nearly as often as they enlightened. But for Latimer, the convoluted, paradoxical nature of the Bible was exactly what gave its accounts the "face and similitude of . . . thing[s] done in deed . . . like a history." Scripture's very eccentricities, then, made it ring truest – made it human, entirely relevant to lived experience. And so its words called out to be studied into action: "[i]f ye diligently roll [them] in your minds," Latimer declared, "[y]e shall perceive that God by this example shaketh us by the noses and pulleth us by the ears."[1]

Ouch. If we are honest, our own encounters with this book may have bred a certain familiarity with the state Latimer described, one made up of equal parts vexed confusion, rapt fascination, and rattled recognition. This seems always to have been the case, no matter how theologically adept or inept the reader. Latimer spoke as he did to remind his ecclesiastical colleagues that the Bible – the perplexing, confounding book the Church had reserved the privilege to interpret for so many centuries – was more often than not most perplexing and most confounding to its official interpreters. And if not, Latimer implied, it *should* have been. In an age of rampant anti-clericalism, new humanist translations, and a very noisy Martin Luther, it was time priests admitted the humbling truth.

Latimer was suggesting, and not all that subtly, that the priesthood of a reformed future would need to start immediately upon a course of remedial and revisionist learning. At the beginning of the sixteenth century, many otherwise well-educated clerics, in a demonstration of St John's accuracy as well as his candor, did *not* know their Bible well – and in an age destined to fight over the meaning and authority of the Bible, surely never well enough. John Wycliffe's much-repeated remark that ploughboys would know the scripture better than priests if he had *his* way was as much a slap at local clergy, after all, as it was a plug for local farmhands. Martin Luther's obsession with scripture might have reflected a uniquely passionate religious temperament but also, surely, the demanding and unusual nature of his university duties: his appointment in 1511 as the first Professor of Biblical Exegesis at the University of Wittenberg predated his conversion to a theology of salvation by grace alone by at least five years, indicating that the regular task of lecturing on the subject of the scriptures to priests-in-training may have been what prepared Luther's mind and heart for conversion in the first place.

Monks working in eleventh-century scriptoria, scholars attending lectures at European universities in the 1400s and 1500s, Lollards hidden in plain sight in the towns of late medieval England, John Eliot's native neighbors, John of the Cross, Mother Ana, Hugh Latimer, Martin Luther: readers brave enough to take up the scriptures labored long and hard to understand what, exactly, this book was that they were reading.

After all, the Bible is not only hard but surpassingly strange. Translated into any language, it remains full of unique words (mostly place names and people's names) impossible to pronounce: *Ched-or-la-omer*; *A-bi-asaph*; *Thy-a-ti-ra*.[2] It brims with archaic cultural references even scholars don't always understand: cubits; talents; *selah*. Its most vivid stories can seem morally dubious at best and downright terrifying at worst: Jesus' cursing of the fig tree in Mark 11 or the rape of Tamar in 2 Samuel 13 have so frustrated centuries of trained exegetes that they have avoided discussing them in sermons or have merely glanced over them with far-ranging and even farther-fetched analogical explanations in biblical commentaries.[3] Educated as well as uneducated Bible readers alike took up the struggle to comprehend this most exotic and arcane text in the western canon as soon as its pages were opened to them. This chapter, then, recognizes their engaged confusion and imaginative persistence as a necessary aspect of the Christian Bible's remarkable cultural potency and appeal.

Considered in terms of theology only, Protestantism was neither particularly radical nor particularly conservative. (Protestants themselves, of course, could be either, and rather spectacularly at times.) But it did propose one extreme, revolutionary idea. This was the notion of *sola scriptura* ("the Bible alone"), which averred that the Bible, not the Church, was the authoritative structure underpinning Christianity. As the perfect Word of God, scripture carried its own authority and guaranteed its own, even literal, transparency. Seemingly opaque passages would always eventually be understood through recourse to other, more immediately lucid, biblical passages. The Bible, which *could* be made clear to any rational Christian reader, was thus to be considered sufficient to anyone's right understanding of Christian belief and practice.

Sola scriptura originated in radical reaction: to a Church that had always reserved the right to read and interpret the Bible to an educated and trained clergy. And as it dovetailed with the project to translate the Bible into the language of everyday life, the range of scripture's authority began to encompass truly unknown territory. Christians of any rank and education – or possessing neither to speak of – now began to hear that the Bible alone was the basis for their religion, and that they themselves had the capacity to understand and interpret it.[4]

Not even priests, though, had ever been able to delve into this particular text alone and unequipped. The Bible had never been a stand-alone book; its educated readers had always tackled the job with an array of textual tools. By the arduous nature of their own formal study, Protestant reformers knew as well as their Catholic opponents – who *had*, after all, written many of the biblical commentaries the reformers still consulted – the undeniable fact that scripture abounded with perilously dark passages. The doctrine of *sola scriptura* could do nothing to lighten this gloomy truth.

It is intriguing, then, to consider why *any* biblically literate reformer would actually want to throw open scripture's stores to *all* men and women. This is a question rarely, if ever, asked by historians of a faith so seemingly bound up with the translated Bible that it has become a basic assumption that Protestantism equals Biblical Access. But stop and think about it. Insisting that all Protestants become intimate with scripture made another part of their reforming program – for a faith based upon hearing that Word with legitimate, accountable understanding – not only dauntingly ambitious but also potentially off-putting.

Which is exactly why the reformers insisted upon it. The Geneva Bible editors, as we've seen, did not design a reader-friendly, graphically enhanced, densely annotated text in the sixteenth century because they thought the Bible was easy to understand, or because the editors were satisfied that most people would want to work hard to understand it. They knew that easy was the one thing the Bible was not and they harbored few illusions about its potential audience. What drove their task could not have been, then, a desire to make the Bible easier. The vernacular scriptures actually made things harder – for they now played to a larger, more demanding, more diverse and differentiated crowd in terms of education, social class, and desire to learn. What drove the reformers were the bracing imperatives of their primary religious mission: salvation. And salvation, as they taught it, did not come easy, nor did it come to all.

By its very insistence that the words of the Bible were entirely accessible to anyone, should be made accessible to all, and nonetheless would require hard work and study, the doctrine of *sola scriptura* not only provided a convenient way to separate the wheat from the chaff on the threshing floors of hundreds of newly Protestant churches. It also created a boom market in scriptural aids. Faced with the vernacular Bible's apparent inaccuracies, contradictions, and confusions, clerical and lay readers alike demanded new forms of expert assistance in order to gain a sense of mastery over the contents of this profoundly difficult work. The rise in vernacular Bible production in the sixteenth and seventeenth centuries thus came accompanied by a concurrent rise in production of a wide variety of Bible aids: so many early modern versions of *The Bible for Dummies* creating the first age of How-To Christianity since the apostolic era.

This chapter considers, then, a number of different, mostly reformation-era, biblical how-to's, poring over them in search of the ambitious but puzzled seekers who turned their pages in search of answers and explanation, recognizing that intellectual engagement often led to spiritual enlightenment. We need only peer into the pages of scripture to find evidence of their quest in abundance, for, as anyone who owns a family Bible or has thumbed through an old one in a bookstore, auction, or yard sale can confirm, people write in them. (As the editor of the *Cambridge Dictionary of the Bible*, S.L. Greenslade, once remarked, old Bibles are truly *used* books.[5]) Readers have cudgeled their brains and worked out their confusions in margins, between lines, and between pages of their Bibles, penning brief clarifications, lengthy digressions, abrupt check-marks, or neatly drawn pointing fingers – all keyed to significant words, verses, or passages. These notes refer to other texts: often biblical, sometimes not. They compare and contrast strangely poetic, archaic biblical passages to plain old everyday realities.

And they lodge complaints. We find many inky proofs that even the most serious and sober readers responded emotionally as well as intellectually to their Bibles, spelling out their delight or frustration – most often, it seems, the latter. One sixteenth-century Huntington Library edition of the New Testament, otherwise unremarkable, shows many simple notes in an early modern hand, most of these cross-references to other passages of scripture.[6] But at Ephesians 6:4, "Fathers, provoke not your children to wrath but bring them up in instruction and information of the Lord," a note in the margin headed EDUCATION states, darkly: "[h]ere the universities & common schools with all their profane arts & sciences are exempted."[7] It would seem our reader had little faith in the educational systems of his day, at least where matters of faith were concerned.

Once every Protestant had been told to read scripture for him- or herself, "Bible scholar" started to become a pretty capacious term, with familiarity breeding an interesting kind of contempt. Taking exception to an author's lofty contention that "the Heart must pray with knowledge," the poet William Blake reacted to R.J. Thornton's 1827 revision of the Lord's Prayer (Matthew 6: 9–13) with this blunt response in its margins: "Christ & his Apostles were Illiterate Men/Caiphas Pilate & Herod were learned."[8] Granted, Thornton's revision of scripture was not one for the ages: it was tedious, self-important, and pedantic, all grave sins in Blake's universe. But Blake was expressing more than boredom or offense, and his sly aside allies his reaction to that of our earlier reader who had apparently decided that the English university curriculum was seriously deficient where matters of the soul were concerned. This nineteenth-century artist and the anonymous reader from the late sixteenth were not simply dismissive of claims by highly educated men to understand the Word of God better than the less-lettered; they argued that the Bible was

BISHOP HORNE *on the Lord's Prayer.*

The LORD'S PRAYER is twice introduced in our New Testament; first, as an *Example* for other Prayers, Matthew, Chap. vi. verse 9, "After THIS MANNER pray ye:"—and secondly by ST. LUKE, Chap. xi. verse 2, as a *form* of prayer to be used precisely in the *words given*, being introduced by these words, "when ye pray, say, *Father*, &c."

The LORD'S PRAYER is *nine times* repeated in our church service. Nor can it be too often repeated: for, to use the language of a fine writer, BISHOP HORNE, "The fairest productions of human genius, like gathered flowers, by *frequent repetition* pall upon the sense: but *this divine* composition becomes, in the using still *more and more beautiful*. New charms are found in it, and *fresh sweets* are gathered for the mind. HE who tastes *its excellencies* will desire to *taste them again*; and he who enjoys them *the oftenest*, will relish them *the most*. Grateful as the MANNA that descended from *heaven*, and *pleased every palate*, it suits every individual, and has been the *admiration of every age and country.*"

DOCTOR JOHNSON *on the Bible.*

The BIBLE is the *most difficult* book in the world to comprehend, nor can it be understood at all by the *unlearned*, except through the aid of CRITICAL and EXPLANATORY *notes*. He therefore who labours to enable the *ignorant* to comprehend it,—to persuade the *careless* to examine it,—and to awaken and stimulate the *formalist* to feel it, certainly undertakes a very useful task, and deserves great commendation. He does honour to the church, by exemplifying its *excellencies*: and confers an important benefit upon *mankind* at large, by furnishing them with the means of increasing both the RATIONALITY and SPIRITUALITY of their DEVOTION."

KING *on the present Translation of the* LORD'S PRAYER.

"If a boy at school were to translate THE MOST DIVINE OF ALL COMPOSITIONS, The LORD'S PRAYER, as it appears at present in our BIBLES, and PRAYER BOOKS, for a certainty he would be *very much blamed* by his master." From KING's "Criticisms tending to illustrate some few passages in the Holy Scripture. Dedicated with permission to the Right Rev. the Lord BISHOP OF LONDON."

LORD BYRON *on the Ethics of* CHRIST.

"In my mind the *highest* of all Poetry is *Ethical*, or *Sacred* Poetry, as the highest of all earthly objects must be *moral truth*, and hence MILTON is *the first of Poets*, whose genius alone could reach it. What made SOCRATES *the greatest of men?* His *moral truths—his ethics*. What proved JESUS CHRIST to be the SON OF GOD, HARDLY LESS than his *miracles* did? His *moral precepts*. And if *ethics* have made a *philosopher* the first of men, and have not been *disdained* as an adjunct to HIS *Gospel*, by the DEITY HIMSELF, are we then to be told, that *Ethical Poetry*, whose object is to make men BETTER and WISER, is not the very *first* or der

of POETRY?" THE RIGHT HON. LORD BYRON's published Letter to the REV. MR. BOWLES.

EDWARDS *on* DR. THORNTON'S *New Translation of the Lord's Prayer, in a Letter to a Friend.*

"No one *at all conversant* with THE GREEK, would have thought of translating in the LORD'S PRAYER, the word ἐπιούσιον by our English word "*daily*," which is rendered by old JEROME, who wrote the LATIN VULGATE, "*superstantialem*," "*supersubstantial bread*," and by the very erudite and elegant CASTALIO, "*victum nostrum alimentarium*," "*our alimentary food*:" but with more propriety and force, are the same words translated by DR. THORNTON, "both *spiritual and corporeal food*;" the Greek adjective, ἐπιούσιον, is certainly "*spiritual*," and as applied to ἄρτον means a grant, or request of *food equally for the mind as body*.—I agree with DR. THORNTON in his Translation of this PRAYER throughout: πάντες ἡμῶν, means, rendering it literally, "*Father of us* ALL," ὁ ἐν τοῖς οὐρανοῖς," "*He in the Heavens*," in the plural, so rendered by every translator, except our own: *en cieux*, in FRENCH; *en los cielos*, SPANISH: ἡ βασιλεία σου, *thy Reign*, and not *kingdom*, as in the French, "*ton Règne vienne*" and not "*Royaume*, kingdom; μὴ εἰσενέγκῃς ἡμᾶς, is properly translated by the learned DR. CAMPBELL, and DR. THORNTON, "*abandon us not*," instead of "*lead us not*," and we find the same expression in the *French* Testaments, "ne nous *abandonne point*," also "ne nous *laisser pas succomber*:" τοῦ Πονηροῦ, means, *the evil one*, or SATAN, in French "LE MALIN," the DEVIL; "o MALIGNO," Spanish, and in our Catechism," our GHOSTLY ENEMY." The *true* rendering of the *Greek* is to be found in DR. THORNTON'S *New Translation of the Lord's Prayer*, in a language appropriate to the subject, (without the *errors* of the former translation,) and such as impresses a *proper* understanding of the words we offer up to GOD,—not as a *lip service*, but with *real devotion*. DR. THORNTON'S notes are not less learned, than they are *edifying*, and prove the *imperative necessity* there was, in *this enlightened period*, for a NEW TRANSLATION of the LORD'S PRAYER, undertaken as it was, by the learned Doctor, not in the *Spirit of controversy*, but of *truth*." T. W. C. EDWARDS, M. A.

*** This Gentleman is the well known Translator of the "Greek Drama," Author of the "First Principles of Algebra," Editor of the "Eton Latin and Greek Grammars with the *Quantities* and *Notes*," Translator of the Works of "Virgil" and "Homer," Author of "a Latin" and also of "a Greek Delectus," &c. &c.

REV. DR MOSELEY'S *Opinion.*

"DR. THORNTON'S *New Translation* of the LORD'S PRAYER is equally *correct*, *elegant*, and *sublime*; and ought to be *printed* in LETTERS OF GOLD." REV. DR. MOSELEY, of Sidney Sussex College, Cambridge, a learned Greek scholar, Master of Goodenough House Academy at Ealing, and Author of a "Dictionary of Latin Quantities," "Exempla Graeca Minora," &c.

FLEETWOOD in his "Life of Christ," says "we are commanded to address GOD as "our FATHER," to put us in mind, that we are all *brethren*, the *children* of one common parent, and that we ought to *love one another* with sincerity; and we PRAY not for OURSELVES only, but for ALL THE HUMAN RACE." The LORD'S PRAYER is then an *Universal Prayer.*

"FATHER OF ALL, in every age adored!" POPE.

[handwritten marginalia, left margin:] Christ & his Apostles were Illiterate Men Caiphas Pilate & Herod were Learned

[handwritten marginalia, lower left:] If Morality was Christianity Socrates was The Saviour

[handwritten note at foot:] The Beauty of the Bible is that the most Ignorant & Simple Minds Understand it Best — Was Johnson hired to Pretend to Religious Terrors while he was an Infidel or how was it

24 William Blake's handwritten commentary on R.J. Thornton's formal commentary on the Lord's Prayer (1827). Also note Blake's additional remarks at the foot of the page.

best served when academics left it well alone. In backing their claims so vigorously, directly, and – well – rudely, they took up the art of authentic, if amateur, biblical commentary.

Their work depended not only on a certain amount of vernacular confidence but also on just feeling free to scrawl in books. In time, though, this attitude began to look less like essential interaction and more like defacement to book producers, who began to provide spaces, formally blocked off from the text itself, for people to write in more decorously. By the nineteenth century, when it sometimes seems that *everybody* was out to revise, bowdlerize, and domesticate the scriptures right off their pages, Bible publishers were providing purpose-built family trees, empty-lined genealogical charts, and special spaces to insert photographs in the middle of Family Bibles. "Student Bibles" were designed with narrow texts and large lined margins for note-taking: removing the reader's problem – or, perhaps, the unmediated pleasure – of choosing their own spaces in which to scribble.[9]

Such unauthorized incursions onto the page were not only acceptable, however, but often encouraged in earlier Bible readers.[10] Medieval and reformation Bibles designed for workaday reading can resemble today's used college textbooks, sporting the historic equivalent of yellow highlighted passages, anxious question marks, and jejune comments. This should not surprise us. In the Middle Ages and the reformation era, after all, scripture was considered to be the premier carrier of similarly essential and comprehensive knowledge, and so its pages became personalized landscapes of learning, marking, retention, and recall.

And frustration: a certain twelfth-century Bible manuscript tells a very short story: once upon a time, somebody reading Paul's letter to the Galatians wrote on one of its vellum pages, in red, *eheu!* (Latin: alas!).

The end? Not *quite* yet. This faded exclamation lends a certain piquancy to and brief diversion from our own study of these Pauline Epistles. Perhaps we are also students of the twelfth-century biblical scholar Anselm of Laon (this particular commentary of his, *Pro*

25 A twelfth-century Bible, opened to Paul's letter to the Galatians, with formal commentary by Anselm of Laon in the margins and informal commentary (anonymous) at bottom left, in red.

altercatione, is a well-known piece of medieval scriptural analysis); or we may be students of eleventh-century religious educators (this particular Anselm was the teacher of the far more famous Peter Abelard); or we may be interested in twelfth-century biblical manuscripts in general (this is a nicely penned one). But no matter our original interest, odds are we'll end up pausing here, momentarily captivated by this wee bit of evidence left by an unknown reader, wondering what the sigh was about. Perhaps the underlined passage was difficult or controversial, and we are curious why, when it seems neither of those things to us now. Perhaps it was a long, late night in a cold and badly lit study and a student finally became eyesore and exhausted.[11] Maybe the poor guy was just plain lonely. We smile, perhaps a bit wanly, and a sympathetic and evanescent link to the past is abandoned so we can get back to *our* work.

The scribbled *eheu!*, marking momentary irritation as informal commentary, draws our eyes to another, more formal, aspect of this page: the words of Anselm of Laon's *Pro altercatione*, skillfully and purposefully inserted on its pages around the words of Paul's letter to the Galatians. The academic art of marginal commentary, like so many other book-practices originating in personal, informal interaction, eventually became standardized, first nudged into place, interestingly enough, by the Irish and English scribes who began leaving spaces between words in their manuscripts in the seventh and eighth centuries. We have already seen how their innovation made way for the practice of silent reading, but here we see that the spaces between words also ceded room on the page for more formal interlineations, leading to a host of orderly looking (and thus official-looking) explanations of scripture. Such annotation or *glossing*, whether on the sides or between the lines, provided analytical or explanatory notes for a text *in* the text, thus making additional and immediate scholarly content dependent on the physical reformatting of a book's words on the page. Glossing shaped reading in the same way as it shaped the page: authoritatively directing the eye between original passage and comment, which meant that the book and its explanatory materials could be accessed at the same time. It could also imply by its look of regularity that here, additional explanation was as important as the original text.[12]

Formal annotations can be found in the earliest Bible manuscripts – indeed they were a feature of classical manuscripts of all sorts – but the glossing of scripture reached new heights of visual and intellectual sophistication in the medieval era, when appearance as well as content became an essential part of the educational process. The formats of glossed texts provided visual lessons in the art of relating disparate concepts and setting them down neatly and helpfully on the page, thus teaching far more than scriptural meaning. A manuscript of the well-known and highly popular biblical commentary eventually dubbed "Ambrosiaster" – it had circulated for centuries under a misattribution to St Ambrose[13] – shows regular, small curved marks down the center of its right-hand pages: a manuscript style of quotation mark that distinguished citations from the Bible from commentary on the text. The left-hand pages feature synopses of the contents of the Pauline epistle, chapter by chapter, beautifully picked out in green, red, or purple ink. The words rest on "dry point" or "blind" rules, raised lines in the vellum, which originally laid out the page and defined the areas for writing.[14] One couldn't ask for a better physical model of a medieval-style notebook, ledger, or steno pad.

Protestant Bibles drew upon these existing models of scriptural teaching and pedagogical formatting, but in England the first attempts to create study Bibles were fairly short-lived. We have already seen how the Geneva Bible of 1560, following the daring example of William Tyndale, provided such pungently political material alongside its more conventionally exegetical marginal commentary that James I decided to replace it. The age of the popular how-to Bible might seem, then, to have ended with the ascendance of the Authorized Version and its terse, strictly scriptural citations.

By the end of the seventeenth century, the printed art of biblical annotation had become so stylized and circumscribed it could surely be thought redundant, and it was, in fact, a cynical strategy to circumvent the rules of copyright in England. Bible production in England had long been restricted to the Royal Printer and the universities of

26 Along with its biblical commentary, the Ambrosiaster provided an excellent secretarial model.

Oxford and Cambridge. Shut out of the most lucrative book market in Britain, certain resourceful printers finally figured out how to dodge the rules of copyright by carefully interpreting the word "Bible" to mean chapter and verse only. Bibles with footnotes could, by this clever reckoning, be legally produced without license. And so some printers printed their Bibles with commentary confined to footnotes so that the notes – vapid, useless, and conveniently crammed into the very bottom margins of the page – could simply be cut away by an owner before taking it on to the binder's.

This bit of trivia about a tiny class of renegade printers and their Bibles demonstrates something not at all trivial, something, in fact, essential: that after nearly two hundred years of access to it in English, the Bible, while not really a stand-alone text in terms of literate understanding, was nevertheless considered a book physically, and thus ultimately, separable from all forms of extraneous interpretation. Additions to the pages of scripture could thus change with the prevailing culture, with concepts of orthodoxy, with political trends, or with the educational needs of readers. The interpretive voice could even be officially silenced, as in the Authorized Version. When that voice re-emerged, it issued from the university in the eighteenth century. The margins of ordinary laypersons' Authorized (or King James) Versions did not reflect these new findings until later and after a good deal of watering-down, culturally speaking.[15]

The Christian conviction of the Bible's essential textual stability, combined with the Protestant notion of its literal integrity, however, could not by mere assertion and repetition resolve scripture's narrative tensions and narrative incompatibilities – not, at least, to the curious and determined reader. The harshest challenge to the dictate "by scripture alone" was the uncomfortable fact that the words of the Bible can be very contradictory: especially and most alarmingly, for Christian readers, in the accounts of Jesus' life and Passion as recorded in the synoptic books of Matthew, Mark, and Luke. (The Book of John, with its vivid philosophizing and general disregard for detailed or accurate chronology, had long been absolved of the responsibility to recount Jesus' history with any clarity of time and place.)

But if the Bible provided its own – and served as its only – authority, the gaps in the synoptic Gospels demanded even more urgent explanation. In the two centuries following the Reformation, gospel "Harmonies," long a staple of elite ecclesiastical instruction in the medieval era, began to make their appearance in the vernacular. Major Protestant writers set out boldly to reconcile the evangelists' silences and contradictions.

First, they rejected what had been the traditional explanation, which they considered a corrupt interpretation based upon an already corrupted version of scripture. Jerome's fourth-century commentary had proposed that the gospel writers had drawn on each others' work, a plausible enough reason why, with each retelling, the story of Jesus' life and Passion gained in theological depth what it lost in narrative cohesion. Jerome's explanation for the disparities in the gospel accounts could also be seen, then, as a metaphor for his Church's authority: one that had been built out of successive statements by leaders entrusted with the transmission of God's Word. For Jerome and his medieval successors in the West, ecclesiastical tradition, not textual perfection, was the ultimate source of Christian authority.

Twelve centuries later, the Protestant reformer John Calvin stated resolutely that Mark had not consulted Matthew's work, nor had Luke Mark's; the evangelists had, instead, come up with similar recordings of Jesus' life based upon their own, individual, similar, but singular experiences of Jesus:

[W]hen they all determined truly and faithfully to set forth those things which they had thoroughly known and approved, every one of them followed what order he thought best him self. And like as this came to pass, not by blind chance or fortune, but by the divine providence of God: even so, *the holy ghost ministered unto them a marvelous consent under a contrary form and style of writing. The which harmony itself were sufficient to confirm their credit.*[16]

Calvin's advocacy of such "marvelous consent" captured nonetheless in "contrary form[s] and style[s]" explained away scripture's discrepancies as inessential matters. This ingenious description allied him more closely to Jerome than he might have intended, however. For Calvin's gospel, too, was built from a model drawn from Calvin's world. Underneath his preservation of the essential unity of the seemingly disordered New Testament, we find a plea for the diversity of European Protestantism, which was proving itself resistant to a single form of worship in Protestant countries or a single doctrine of grace in Germany and Switzerland.

Calvin also set his Harmony into a persuasive physical format for the edification of those readers who might not be convinced by the verbal bravura of an argument like "marvelous consent":

> [N]one of the three evangelists can be truly and rightly inter-preted unless he be conferred with the two other . . . But since that *mean wits* cannot easily confer the Evangelists together, whilst they turn and return from the one to the other, I thought this brief method might be profitable, if by a continual process or discourse, like as it were in one table, the three histories were joined together: wherein the readers may see and discern at once, what is dissonant and agreeable to them all.[17]

On the page, Calvin's Harmony was rendered in similar passages of Matthew, Mark, and Luke lined up side by side. None were left out. Empty space on a page indicated one evangelist's silence, set over from, and against, other written accounts. Contradictory accounts of the same event could now be detected immediately.

Introducing its theologically sophisticated analysis to a broader readership in 1584, Calvin's translator, Eusebius Paget, called this Harmony the "profitablest work for the Church" he could imagine. And while it may seem strange to indoctrinate laypeople into the doctrine of the perfection of scripture by so graphically pointing up its apparent mistakes, what Calvin and Paget relied in large part upon was the essential veracity granted diagrammatic presentation in this era: the way that format could impart an almost scientific look of truth to any page. In the late sixteenth century, even as Protestants

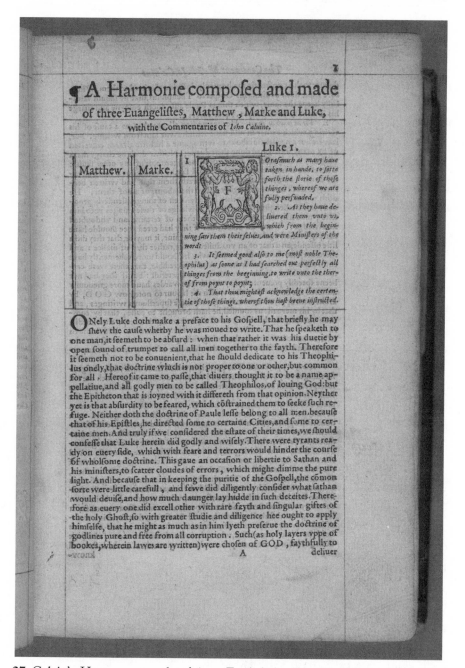

¶ A Harmonie compoſed and made

of three Euangeliſtes, Matthew, Marke and Luke,

with the Commentaries of *Iohn Caluine.*

Luke 1.

Matthew.	Marke.

Oraſmuch as many haue taken in hande, to ſette forth the ſtorie of thoſe thinges, whereof we are fully perſwaded,

2. As they haue deliuered them vnto vs, which from the beginning ſaw them their ſelues, and were Miniſters of the word:

3. It ſeemed good alſo to me (moſt noble Theophilus) as ſoone as I had ſearched out perfectly all thinges from the beeginning, to write vnto the therof from poynt to poynt;

4. That thou mighteſt acknowledge the certentie of thoſe things, whereof thou haſt beene inſtructed.

ONely Luke doth make a preface to his Goſpell, that briefly he may ſhew the cauſe wherby he was moued to write. That he ſpeaketh to one man, it ſeemeth to be abſurd: when that rather it was his duetie by open ſound of trumpet to call all men together to the fayth. Therefore it ſeemeth not to be conuenient, that he ſhould dedicate to his Theophilus onely, that doctrine which is not proper to one or other, but common for all. Hereof it came to paſſe, that diuers thought it to be a name appellatiue, and all godly men to be called Theophilos, of louing God: but the Epitheton that is ioyned with it differeth from that opinion. Neyther yet is that abſurdity to be feared, which côſtrained them to ſeeke ſuch refuge. Neither doth the doctrine of Paule leſſe belong to all men, becauſe that of his Epiſtles, he directed ſome to certaine Cities, and ſome to certaine men. And truly if we conſidered the eſtate of their times, we ſhould confeſſe that Luke herein did godly and wiſely. There were tyrants ready on euery ſide, which with feare and terrors would hinder the courſe of wholſome doctrine. This gaue an occaſion or libertie to Sathan and his miniſters, to ſcatter cloudes of errors, which might dimme the pure light. And becauſe that in keeping the puritie of the Goſpell, the cômon ſorte were little carefull, and ſewe did diligently conſider what ſathan would deuiſe, and how much daunger lay hidde in ſuch deceites. Therefore as euery one did excell other with rare fayth and ſingular giftes of the holy Ghoſt, ſo with greater ſtudie and diligence hee ought to apply himſelfe, that he might as much as in him lyeth preſerue the doctrine of godlines pure and free from all corruption. Such (as holy layers vppe of bookes, wherein lawes are wyritten) were choſen of GOD, faythfully to

A   deliuer

27 Calvin's Harmony, translated into English by Eusebius Paget, 1584. The empty spaces on the upper left-hand side of the page show that the preface provided by the Gospel of Luke was not part of the Gospels of Matthew or Mark.

rejected religious images, many of their strategies of biblical interpretation aimed at a popular audience – the majority of whom were not literate – depended upon some kind of *visual* instruction. Like reformation teachers everywhere, Calvin had figured out that "scripture alone" was a precept that required visual aids if Bible reading and comprehension were to become widespread.

As his many rewrites of his landmark *Institutes of Christian Religion* between the 1530s and the 1550s suggest, Calvin had become adept at sizing up the new Protestant lay book market. The most difficult and exotic text on offer in early modern England now shared a market with other vernacular books, some of which purported to deliver once unobtainable knowledge and skills to all with the ambition to read and learn – and the shillings and pence to purchase. The primary intent of these early modern how-to books, whether secular or sacred, was the sparking of lay ambitions of all kinds: persuading amateurs that, yes, even they could progress to expertise given enough time and the right instructive book.

The assertion that anyone who could read their own language could also master other once inaccessible cultural skills was as common in sixteenth- and seventeenth-century how-to books as they are in the *You Name It . . . for Dummies* books of today. That a reader could become a successful surveyor, a crack astronomer, or a dependable navigator of a large seagoing vessel simply by reading a book or two was more than a bit far-fetched, but these bold claims paled next to the fulsome promises made in early modern biblical how-to books. The title page of Francis Roberts's *The Key of the Bible* stated, for example, that it was designed "for the help of the weakest capacity in the understanding of the whole Bible."[18] And while the intricate scheme of note-taking and passage organization Roberts advocated to his readers would seem to present intellectual weaklings with an alarmingly difficult basic training program, Roberts's book is just one of many in the seventeenth century that aimed at the inculcation of basic cognitive skills using the Bible.

Key was designed to help readers with memorizing information, a task that we might think had been rendered unnecessary in an age of humanist learning. In the early modern period as well as the medieval, though, memorization was still considered a premier aid to learning. Today critics of education often regard learning by rote as mere "busy-work," but that expression would have made no sense in an age when education was rare, paper was a valuable commodity not to be thrown away carelessly, and work was, well, *work*, rather than a euphemism for "time-serving." Consequently early modern students, like their medieval counterparts, were taught intricate and captivating methods for retention and recall with the same seriousness of intent with which they were taught the contents of the theological and philosophical texts they were enjoined to commit to memory.

Prior to the enshrining of originality as a mark of genius, an idea not commonplace until the nineteenth century, to be able to memorize well was in fact to perform a creative act. Medieval and early modern diaries describe firsthand what would seem to us now as inexplicably thorough feats of memorization; these remembered accounts of sermons or books or speeches can be extraordinarily accurate when we compare them against the texts of sermon, book, or speech. Much of this proficiency had to do with how memorization was taught in earlier times: meticulously and skillfully. Students were enjoined to construct elaborate visualizations and develop characteristic habits of thought to assist them in remembering the lines of books or sermons. They were instructed to create mental scaffolds on which they could hang memorable representations of the ideas they heard or read. No wonder, then, that the books written to help people read and recall the Bible presented themselves as more than mere containers of words. Their contents were literally designed to impress the patterns of scriptural ideas onto the already purpose-built and orderly minds. Such books were tools made for the skillful appropriation of ideas. This work demanded that intellectual activity be considered as new forms of physical labor.

Rhyme schemes were a time-honored way to retain ideas swiftly, reminding us that, then as now, brevity forms the heart of memory. Simon Wastell called his 1629 rendition of scripture *Microbiblion*: an "epitome," or summary, of the Bible rendered in rhyming verse,

A good help for weak Memories:
Or, the
CONTENTS
Of every CHAPTER
In the Bible
In Alphabetical Dyſticks.

Being very profitable for ſuch as de-
ſire to repeat Books, or find out divers places
in the Scriptures, eſpecially in the Hiſtorical
BOOKS.

Whereunto is added the Order of
Times wherein the Propheſies and New
TESTAMENT were penned,
As alſo
A CHRONOLOGY from ADAM
to the deſtruction of Jeruſalem by Titus Veſpaſian.
With other Scriptural Paſſages made eaſie to be re-
membred.

LONDON,
Printed for Thomas Helder, at the Sign of the Angel
in Little Britain. 1671.

28 John Lloyd's contribution to the art of scriptural mnemonics, 1671.

arranged in alphabetical order to aid memorization. John Lloyd's 1671 *A Good Help for Weak Memories* billed itself as "the contents of every chapter in the Bible in alphabetical dysticks," and William Samuel stressed that his *Abridgement of Goddes Statutes* was in meter. These books reset the ideas of the Bible into doggerel verse, arranged these lines in alphabetical order, and concluded with two-line stanzas summarizing each chapter. Copies of the 1646 broadside (single-sheet publication) of another, less ambitious poetic synopsis (this time simply of the Book of Genesis), "The Creation of the World," was designed to be hung on the walls of a home, a parish church, or even the local pub – thereby proving another adage, that ready proximity (if not always a night at the pub) is Recall's handmaiden.[19]

Other more complex methods seem doomed to failure, even accounting for our own poor memory skills today. According to its preface, the purpose of E. Beecher's *The Christian School, or Scripture's Anatomy* was to enable students of the Bible to "be able at any time to declare the chief subject of a Chapter or Psalm, or, hearing its passages, to recollect . . . to what Chapter or Psalm they belong, sooner and more certainly than any shall find them by a concordance." Mastering Beecher's elaborate system, which combined scripture keyword memorization with a numbered organizational scheme, would have required laborious study and an inexhaustible delight in performing mental gymnastics.[20] It seems likely that the effort, rather than the success of the effort, was the true goal of this intricate little Bible game.

So "by the Bible," as the seventeenth-century poet Alexander Ross claimed, "the world [was] instructed": a comment that in its wide-ranging optimism should now seem to us at least plausible.[21] Protestant commentary on the Bible invariably stressed that scripture instructed the world in ways that were as complex or as plainspoken as its educationally diverse audience needed them to be. Better yet, with application and inspiration, many of seemingly lesser capacity and education could eventually progress to greater understanding.

Ross was expressing a cultural truism – not so much about the Bible as about his world's dependence on the Bible as an all-around instructional tool. Bible books were increasingly designed to teach things other than scripture by means of scripture by the end of the seventeenth century. Many early modern books used biblical passages to teach languages, for example – though none, perhaps, so determinedly as Elisha Cole's *Nolens Volens*, a children's language primer with the vaguely threatening subtitle *You shall make Latin whether you will or no*.[22] *Nolens Volens* featured biblical extracts and distinctive icons that turned verses of the Bible into a source for Latin instruction. Scriptural passages set out in English alongside their Latin translations allowed the learner to connect foreign words and phrases with those made familiar by long acquaintance and repetition. The subjects of those passages ("vomit," a word that appears ten times in the Bible, inspired one particularly graphic example) appeared on the page in small pictures. The emblematic figures formed a "visible Bible" that assisted the memory by the technique of visual association.

29 The letter V, in Latin, English, and pictures, from *Nolens Volens*, 1682.

Nolens Volens was designed to force-feed schoolchildren their Latin, but William Robertson's Hebrew coursebook *Sha'ar ha Rivshon 'o Petach Hechivson 'el L'Shon Hakodesh: The First Gate, or the Outward Door to the Holy Tongue* (which had been commissioned by a committee of radical London ministers during the Protectorate of Oliver Cromwell) was written to counteract instruction in the language used by the Roman Catholic Church – and the English university. Here, though, Hebraic learning took a second seat to political purpose: *First Gate* proposed a radical theory of cultural, not educational reform.[23] Even after the establishment of scripture in the vernacular, Latin remained the base language of higher learning in England, a fact that grated upon those Protestants whose radical anti-Catholicism went so far as to include forms of classical learning. The elimination of Latin as a base instructional language was, in effect, a rejection of one of the powerful vestiges of pre-Reformation culture: a dependence on scholarship refracted through the language of the university.

The "first gate" of the title referred to Robertson's basic premise: that in order to learn biblical languages, it was not necessary first to learn Latin, which formerly had been the "only door by which men were let into the knowledge of the Hebrew and Greek." Hebrew-language translation, in other words, had always been taught from a Latin, not an English, base text. This meant that anyone without Latin could not be taught to read the Bible in its original languages of Greek and Hebrew. Robertson claimed that translating Hebrew directly would allow "any Christian of ordinary understanding" to attain an "immediate access" to the "language and Spirit of God," a claim bolstered by the book's Hebrew title, sounded out and shaped into the form of English letters.

Robertson also insisted upon a direct line to the divine as articulated in the original scriptural Word, an idea that was radical in a world where men's educations, if not their souls, were considered to be as unequal as their stations in life. His work reflected, then, one powerful aspect of the political dilemma of the 1640s. By the middle of the seventeenth century, England's reformation, seemingly secured for good if not for perfect in the long reign of Elizabeth I, was proving as divisive as it had been under Henry VIII, albeit in a very different way. What had once been a fierce struggle over the nature and form of England's Christianity had become a fierce internal struggle over the nature and form of Britain's Protestantism. The culmination of these internecine battles between king, Parliament and Church over forms of worship and doctrine was a set of very real and bloody battles in the mid-seventeenth century: Britain's own civil wars of religion, which devastated not only England but also its kingdoms of Scotland and Ireland.

The issues dividing Church and State were many and deep-seated, set into motion by the Reformation. Chief among these were questions of just how faithful to the word of scripture, and unfaithful to its Catholic past, England's Church was supposed to be. Radically inclined writers, captivated and inspired by the unfamiliar and unmanageable in scripture, delivered fervent and fearsome prophecies of England's downfall if she did not reform every vestige of ecclesiastical tradition, expressing extreme fears couched in the language of the one English book with which they were intimately familiar. Perhaps *too* familiar: responding to the richly emotional, exotic, and violent imagery provided on every page of scripture, these authors applied the Bible's phrases to their own political concerns, often with a fine disregard for originality of expression or, indeed, rationality of discourse.

Hugh Broughton, an elegant translator of Hebrew but a maniacally overenthusiastic interpreter of biblical texts, was one such author of Protestant propaganda, producing admonitory interpretations of the Bible that sounded more like fever-dreams than exegesis. With meticulous numbered charts and intricate symbolism, Broughton's own take on the Harmony genre, *A Concent of Scripture* (1590), not only claimed to harmonize contradictory scriptural accounts, but also to establish the true chronology of the events described in the Bible and correct the chronologies of classical histories. In his efforts, then, if not their effects, he anticipated the work of later scholars like James Ussher. (Partly in response to a world seemingly gone mad with civil war and regicide, Ussher wrote the more sober-sided *Annales Veteris et Novi Testamenti* over the decade of the 1650s, an ambitious and academically well-regarded work of scriptural dating that thereafter appeared with some regularity in the margins of the Authorized Version until the nineteenth century.)

Significant here, though, is Broughton's innovative and vivid use of graphic design and pull-out charts, another demonstration of some early modern biblical writers' delight in designing visible, "scientific" proof to accompany their arguments. *Concent*'s illustrations depict the "Babylonian captivity" and the mass deportation of the population of Judah by the cruel King of Babylon, Nebuchadnezzar (II Kings 24: 14–16) in the late sixth century BCE, matching these to prophecies contained in the Books of Ezekiel and Revelation. The connection made clean visual order and elegant linear coherence out of what was otherwise a rambling and overheated narrative argument. It also allowed for the making of swift visual connections between difficult ideas. These gave Broughton's conjectures immediate traction in the late sixteenth century, when the anxiety of the English over the militant intentions of European Catholicism was at its height, as they contemplated the death of an aging and childless queen who, in refusing to name an heir, was seemingly determined to plunge the kingdom into a succession crisis.

Admittedly, Broughton was the kind of writer who would have found dire conspiracies in the steadiest of times. His combative prose style and unconventional ideas were soon satirized by the playwright Ben Jonson – never one to avoid a slap at a contemporary – in *Volpone* and *The Alchemist*. But no matter how wild and weird it was – or, probably because it was so *very* wild and weird – Broughton's book found popular favor in a culture still picking its way through the political and religious wreckage of the Reformation. Soon Broughton was lecturing from *A Concent of Scripture* to audiences so large he was forced to change the venue several times for safety's sake.[24] This pursuit of notoriety finally caught up with him. The intemperate, eccentric, and now broadly cast opinions expressed in *Concent* kept

30 Explanatory illustration in Hugh Broughton's *Concent of Scripture*, 1590.

him off the slate of translators for King James I's new version of the Bible – an oversight, and a translation, about which Broughton (who, despite his defects of personality, was acknowledged by his contemporaries as one of the finest Hebrew scholars of his day) noisily complained for the rest of his life.

Other authors managed these intemperate times a bit more skillfully – or perhaps it is better to say the times managed *them*. Several years and a few monarchs later Joseph Mede (1568–1638), a lecturer in Greek at Christ's College Cambridge, produced *Clavis Apocalyptica*, a commentary on the Book of Revelation, in 1627, in the waning days of political and religious stability in England. Arcane, elegant, and in Latin, Mede's publication perished in the bookstalls of London. But in 1643, with the Church of England dismantled, the king armed against his Parliament, and fears of civil war at apocalyptic pitch, once-overlooked theories on Revelation suddenly took on uncanny popular resonance. Richard More's English translation of Mede, *The Key of the Revelation*, was revived and ordered into print by the House of Commons's Committee for Printing and Publishing Books, whose opinion was that a translation of this work on Revelation would shed "much light for the understanding of many obscure passages in that sweet and comfortable prophecie."[25] The prophecy on display in the table insert designed to supplement the book seems more forbidding than any sweet and comfortable prophecy should have required, but its purpose was again to demonstrate, in a style that suggested arithmetical and geometric proofs, the orderly, visible relationship between the symbolic language of the Book of Revelation and the experiences of a nation violently divided, politically and religiously.

When that violent and divisive time ended with the restoration of the Stuarts in 1660 and a consequent imposition of stern laws against religious radicalism and nonconformity, John Bunyan, a man who did not let his lack of formal education stand in the way of his literary and theological ambition, lay in prison: locked up by Charles II's government for refusing to stop preaching without

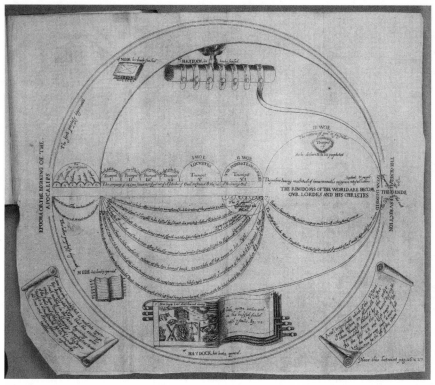

31 Joseph Mede's graphic key to the Book of Revelation, translated and reprinted in 1643.

ecclesiastical license. While incarcerated, he began to write a story of Christian fortitude, an allegory of the human quest for salvation. His manuscript would eventually become a book entitled *The Pilgrim's Progress*, which became a literary and religious best-seller almost immediately upon its first publication in 1678, and continues to be to this day.

Bunyan's busy epic, teeming with archetypical figures with names like Christian, Mr Worldly-Wiseman, Mr Save-all, Despair, and Patience, would seem to follow the tradition of medieval mystery plays – which were, after all, simply biblical epics played out on the streets. (He may also have been acquainted with popular versions of epic, and allegorical poems like Edmund Spenser's *Faerie Queene*.)

The Pilgrim's Progress owes its structure to the Calvinist doctrines of predestination, conversion, and salvation. Bunyan's ambition to write it, however, came straight from his epic personal struggle to read and understand the Bible. In a poetic prologue that heads the book, Bunyan speaks to his own hard pilgrimage through the pages of scripture:

> Am I afraid to say that Holy Writ,
> Which for its style and praise puts down all wit,
> Is everywhere so full of all these things,
> (Dark figures, allegories), yet there springs
> From that same book that lustre and those rays
> Of light that turns our darkest night to days.[26]

Bunyan's wrestlings with the Book that he possessed only sufficient education to interpret had been mighty and arduous over all his adult years. His Opponent could be slippery, changeable. "I have sometimes seen more in a line of the Bible than I could well tell how to stand under," he wrote, "and yet at another time the whole Bible hath been to me as dry as a stick." The stubborn opacity of scripture had even led Bunyan at times to think the Bible was a mere "think-so" that he had conjured from a personal imagination so desperately desirous of understanding that he was reading *his* thoughts rather than *its* meanings. Nonetheless he continued to "look it all over," becoming in the process a skillful negotiator of the Protestant vernacular (just look again at his phrase "think-so" and try to make up an apter term for that particular worry), sounding the depths of his own soul while working to save others'.

Conclusion

In post-Reformation, English-speaking society the Bible became exactly the cultural powerhouse its proponents had envisaged: the only essential book for Christians at a time when their religious identity, if not their way of expressing it, was still a non-negotiable matter. The reformers had advocated universal access to a book which was at one and the same time eccentric and essential, bewildering and bewitching. The play of paradox created between its textual inaccessibility and its textual availability invested it with new, powerful meanings, even when these turned out to be obscure or disturbing. And if its readers first applied themselves to its pages out of a sense of Christian duty, most who kept on reading did so to fulfill desires sparked into flame by the mysterious and exotic nature of this required text.

For translation into the language of everyday life in the sixteenth century merely brought the teeming mysteries and cloudy ideas of scripture up to an equally murky surface. Constructed out of several languages, reflecting the values of Jews and Christians from very different societies, written by a myriad authors over many centuries, transmitted from generation to generation (and by hand for the first fifteen centuries of its existence as a Christian book) without provision made for well-lit workspaces, intellectual property rights, or rigorous copy-editing, the Bible often posed an insuperable intellectual challenge to the very Christians who wrought the age of *sola scriptura* – even more so the ordinary lay readers for whom they labored.

But no reader compelled by desire or necessity to read the Bible or consult any form of Bible "help" was anything less than highly ambitious, no matter his or her educational level or theological aptitude. What drove the early modern market for "how-to" textbooks, those reassuring works offering skilled and tactical assistance to beginners, was the same thing that drives it these days: the simple fact that "dummies" neither need nor want them. Dull people aren't interested in reading difficult, absorbing books, and this characteristic of cognitive ambition was as true of early modern Bible readers as it is today.

As was their dependence on visual information to negotiate and order the more difficult ideas contained on the pages of scripture. The sheer number of inventions and interventions – books, graphs, charts, images – that people used to comprehend and even re-tailor scripture is evidence that the Christian Bible was something quite unusual: sacred words, yet liable to all sorts of manipulations and transformations. How far these mechanics could proceed without dislodging the essentially sacrosanct nature of the Bible is the subject of my next chapter.

CHAPTER SIX

EXTRA-ILLUSTRATING
THE BIBLE

What happens when the human impulse to make the Bible accessible extends even more radically, even to the altering of the material shape and form of the scriptures? The scriptures have been interactive since early Christians decided to keep reading their Hebrew Bibles and simply add new material to them, but the books featured here take scriptural interactivity into new territory. And so we will begin our exploration with what many of us consider an unthinkable practice indeed: the willful destruction of books, or *biblioclasm*.

In this enlightened age, we treat books with respect – and a bit too much hands-off respect, perhaps, considering the dire reports issuing daily on post-modern illiteracy. My students highlight their assigned texts with garishly colored abandon, but outside the university classroom, it seems, few people dare do more than inscribe their name on the flyleaf of a book. And if the book in question happens to be a library book, such behavior is called "defacement" and is subject to fines.

The marking-up of books, in any case, may seem relatively benign when compared to the *cutting-up* of books. "I have a friend who collects leaves from medieval manuscripts," a Ms Eleanor Pachaud of Kirkland, Washington fretted to Randy Cohen, a weekly columnist who solves problems in everyday ethics for readers of the *New York Times*. "I feel that this encourages cutting apart codices[1] . . . which, if studied as a whole, would yield more information about the history of bookmaking." Her page-collecting friend's defense was, apparently, that he not only collected these single pages but also bound them into volumes to preserve them – which was more than he could say for the dealers who had sold him the leaves to begin with.

Stumped by the Solomonic nature of the problem, and unfamiliar with the ways of bibliography, Cohen consulted a rare books dealer, who replied that the common notion that a book was a more or less rectangular object made up of serial pages, bound and specifically designed to fit together "as a whole," was misguided. Not everything between two covers was necessarily a book "in the manner we conceive of contemporary books"; it could be something that only "looks to us like a book." These days booksellers sell already-assembled collections of single pages or pages long dismantled; generally speaking, they do not themselves cut up books. And so, as the collector had obtained his single leaves from non-books and then went on to make them into new non-books, he destroyed nothing that had been any *thing* to start with, at least in this exchange.

Satisfied, the Sunday Morning Ethicist pronounced the behavior in question "innocuous," if piratical. He then took the opportunity to instruct his general readership that, come to think of it, even "real" books were not always to be considered inviolable simply because they were books. "Some," Cohen declared, peremptorily wresting a large, general principle out of a small, particular issue, ". . . are worth preserving; others are not."[2]

This may well be so, but we only have to search out entries for single leaves or cropped illuminated capitals in any prestigious library's catalogue of manuscripts to find that books of quality have often been considered only worth preserving in pieces. "Cut missal up in evening – hard work," the Victorian essayist and art critic John Ruskin wrote in his diary, a remark that is often quoted but rarely contextualized.[3] Historians and librarians love to cite Ruskin's entry for 3 January 1854, and it is easy to see why: what fun to remind their bibliophile audiences that in the not so distant past precious manuscripts were routinely rifled and dismantled for purposes, as Christopher De Hamel writes, of "pleasure and profit."[4] This is true for printed books as well. Single leaves of the Gutenberg Bible can still appear at auction. (This does not explain why many library copies of the Gutenberg, the Huntington's included, lack them. Most of these separate pages probably came instead from the infamous "Noble Fragment," a damaged copy dismantled and sold by bookseller Gideon Wells in 1922.[5]) In any case, orphaned leaves, avidly pursued by private collectors and library curators alike, attest to the fact that there has always been an open and thriving market for bits of books.[6]

The ethical dilemma documented in the *Times* in 2004, and the untoward notice taken of an ordinary journal entry in 1854, are reminders: not only that *what makes a book a book?* is a more difficult question than we might think, but also that the related query *what can a person do to a book?* might yield some astonishing answers. And so I begin this chapter with the reminder that all kinds of books are subject to acts of violence. (Or, to say it less harshly, if more theoretically, they are susceptible to physical as well as critical acts of de- and reconstruction.) It is tempting to wonder if any of the leaves collected by Ms Pachaud's buccaneering friend were razored out of a book by John Ruskin and now making the rounds of the rare book trade. In fairness to our nineteenth-century diarist, however, Ruskin's behavior should be considered as simply part of the documented daily round of collecting, inscribing, preserving, and cataloguing that constituted the human heart of Victorian industry. What is of most interest is not that Ruskin dismembered books of a winter's evening; it is that Ruskin's acts of literary destruction appear to have been directed exclusively towards religious texts.

We do not know if, in addition to Catholic mass books, Ruskin also cut up Bibles. If he did, he did not confide it to his diary. But what we surely know is that Ruskin's contemporaries and their forebears did. No matter its sacred status – in fact, precisely *because* of its sacred status – the Bible has been one of the books most often dealt with in such incisive fashion. And by now this may strike us as an extremely sensible way to deal with that set of quandaries between two covers commonly called The Bible. Not "a book" at all, but a collection of books placed (arguably) into false proximity and (inarguably) uneasy relation by the restraining structure of religious narratives, the Bible practically begs for dismantling and reassembly. As we have seen, readers have been quick to come to its rescue, generating commentaries, concordances, and Harmonies to undertake the formidable task of making scripture not only comprehensive but also comprehensible.

Once printed books had become so available as to be deemed materially expendable, some redactors did that work with literal as well as theological or philosophical scissors. In Little Gidding, a private home near Huntingdon in England, members of the extended family of Nicholas Ferrar, a deacon in the early seventeenth-century Church of England, lived communally by intention for more than twenty years. Ferrar's Anglican "nunnery"[7] lived as if under monastic rule, albeit with variations reflecting its essentially Protestant nature. They marked the passage of the day by performing the liturgical offices of the Book of Common Prayer, in English. They heard sermons regularly. And they recited from the Bible, copied out its passages, and composed scriptural paraphrases in their spare hours.

The routine would have been familiar to any member of a Roman Catholic monastery. But the inhabitants of Ferrar's cloister – which, despite the popular if pejorative label, was actually a familial community of men, women, and children – rang one remarkable change on the traditions of a medieval scriptorium. In dual pursuit of good works and good book-making, the female members of the community spent many hours under Ferrar's direction, carefully snipping the passages of all four Gospels out of Renaissance Bibles. They then glued these scraps of scripture onto clean sheets of paper in order to create one continuous, coherent gospel narrative out of the four versions presented in the New Testament.[8] A description of their labors suggests that the continuity at which they aimed was as visual as it was historical:

> When they had first cut out those pieces with their knives or scissors, then they did neatly and exactly fit each verse that was so cut out, to be pasted down on pieces of paper; and so *artificially* they performed it, that it looked like a new kind of printing, when it was finished; so finely were all the pieces joined together, and with great presses for that purpose, pressed down on the white sheets of paper.[9]

Here "artificial," following seventeenth-century usage, does not mean "fake" but its opposite: such perfect execution as to make a spliced-together page look original and whole rather than Frankensteinian. The visual appearance of the page thus itself conveyed the message that the rough places of contradictory gospel accounts could be made plain.

That the makers of these books could create an unbroken gospel narrative, either physically or theologically, without eliminating a single passage from Matthew, Mark, Luke, or John might strike us as incredible. But indeed, Ferrar could not advocate discarding even a single word of the evangelists; Protestant teaching regarding the sufficiency of the scriptures forbade such selective inattention. On the other hand, Ferrar felt no compunction to keep to any one of the evangelists' timelines. He intercalated all four gospel narratives into a master copy, ironing out their discrepancies along the way by extracting from them 150 subjects: "John's beheading," "The five loaves," and "Jesus walking on the sea," to name a very few.[10] Marks placed in the margins identified each passage's provenance: "A" for Matthew, and so on. He then arranged these topic headings into a newly integrated chronology that eventually accounted for every episodic detail in every Gospel.

Illustrations pasted onto every page of the Little Gidding gospel books helped to reinforce both the method and the message of the Little Gidding Harmonies. Ferrar had traveled extensively on

32 Little Gidding concordance, seventeenth century.

the continent in the 1610s and returned to England with a large number of woodcuts and engravings acquired in countries less iconophobic than post-Reformation England. These prints were dismantled as deftly as had been the pages of the Gospels. The book-makers of Little Gidding dissected them, creating skillful and imaginative page layouts designed to provide visual cues to, and non-verbal commentary on, the page's pasted text. The title pages of the Harmonies state explicitly that the images were added simply to "[express] either the facts themselves or their types and figures." The claim was self-protective rather than disingenuous. In an image-suspicious age, religious texts were rarely illustrated.[11] The vocal segment of the seventeenth-century English public who found the notion of a Protestant monastery an abominable contradiction in terms would undoubtedly consider a decorated scripture book nothing better than blasphemy in leather bindings. Better, perhaps, to deflect Puritan disapproval up front.

Hand-cut and handmade, every Harmony was unique – despite the fact that it took many mass-produced, printed books to construct it. These were composite texts, wherein picture and scripture worked together to educate as well as to delight. Examples of this paste-up team-teaching abound: one page of the British Library copy includes the verse "It were better for him, that a millstone were hanged around his neck, and he cast into the sea, th[a]n that he offend one of these little ones."[12] The central image on the page appears to have been selected for both its memorable visual impact and its ability to explain the symbolic meaning of Jesus' words with shocking economy. It depicts neither millstone nor ocean, for this is not a verse about drowning, but about consignment to fathoms far deeper: eternal damnation. The top half of the page features a lurid engraving of a man prodded by demons into a distinctly earthy and bestial Hell-mouth; underneath, between two columns of print, three smaller imps (individually cut from separate illustrations) launch their own malign attack. Towards the central illustration they flap, long, tapering fingers stretching up to point to the Hell-mouth and clawed feet pointing directly down to the relevant verse.[13]

In their day, Little Gidding's Harmonies made the community famous – or notorious, depending on how contemporaries felt about such Catholic-looking experiments in Protestant living. Their fame, or infamy, was assured on that day in 1635 when the community presented a nearly completed copy to King Charles I, who apparently liked its pictures best of all.[14] But until very recently, the Harmonies have attracted relatively little notice, probably because they fall through the cracks of reformation and literary scholarship (like the polymorphous community that created them, they provide neither an impeccably Protestant nor a spectacularly illicit Catholic perspective on the English Bible) as well as library curatorship (they are generally listed as both rare books and collections of mutilated prints, and no one ever seems to know exactly which research division is in charge of them).[15]

We understand the Harmonies best, however, when we remember their primary purpose, which was didactic, not decorative. While the composite books created at Little Gidding have commonly been called "Harmonies," their arrangement by subject heading and their structure as an unbroken collated narrative suggests that they are actually best classified as illustrated amalgams of two distinct styles of Bible workbook: the Gospel Harmony and the Topical Concordance. In this form, organized and orderly, the Harmonies were teaching texts *par excellence*. Ferrar used the books to catechize the community's children, who were required to read through a Harmony in its entirety every month. By this scheme Ferrar's nieces and nephews must have been drilled five times daily, a chore that could swiftly have become tedious in the extreme. Leading restless children through Bible drill would require more than a strong-minded uncle; the children would also benefit from a teaching method based on the fact that pasted-in visual cues would make for easier memorization. The physical work of creating a seamless gospel narrative would also have served to instruct the children's mothers and aunts: the members of the community who actually did the work of cutting, matching, arranging, and pasting these scriptures and their illustrative images onto every new page.

Singular as they are, the Little Gidding Harmonies were not the only books to deal with the confusions of gospel narrative by way of the cut-and-paste method. In a famous example of 1795, Thomas Jefferson forwarded a bold proposal to the English radical clergyman and expatriate scientist Joseph Priestley, whom Jefferson admired for the rationality of his theological sentiments. Inspired by Priestley's treatise *Socrates and Jesus Christ*, Jefferson outlined an ambitious plan he had once sketched out with the Philadelphia physician Benjamin Rush: to write an account comparing the "moral precepts" of Jesus to those of the ancient philosophers. Jefferson noted that such a work would need to begin with a precise distillation of Jesus' ideas, drawn out of the sprawling and often contradictory apostolic accounts recorded in the New Testament. Only then could the philosophical message of the Christian religion be weighed against the words of the ancients in credible fashion.[16]

Priestley's death two years later forced Jefferson to undertake this work on his own. Several years of careful study of the New Testament had convinced him that "fragments only" of the "genuine" teachings of Jesus had been transmitted to posterity, and even those few words had been, as he wrote, "mutilated, misstated, and often unintelligible." By 1813, his methodical response to this discovery had followed philosophical judgment in exactingly literal fashion:

> I have made a wee little book, which I call the Philosophy of Jesus. It is a *paradigma* of his doctrines, made by cutting the texts out of the book, and arranging them on the pages of a blank book, in a certain order of time or subject. A more beautiful morsel of ethics I have never seen.[17]

Jefferson's morsel, eventually titled *The Moral Teachings of Jesus Christ*, reconciled the often conflicting accounts of the evangelists by setting corresponding texts against each other, demonstrating truth by affinity, in large part by displaying passages in proximity. But Jefferson made his case for the authenticity of the Gospels in another way, going well beyond the opportunities presented by page

S. MA THEW.

10 ¶ And behold, there wa a man which had *his* hand w thered : and they afked hin felf, and they enter in and dwell there : and the laſt ſtate of that man is worſe than the firſt. Even ſo ſhall it be alſo unto this wicked generation.

46 ¶ While he yet talked to the people, behold, his mother and his brethren ſtood without defiring to ſpeak with him.

47 Then one ſaid unto him, Behold thy mother and thy bre- thren ſtand without, defiring to ſpeak with thee.

68 But he anſwered and ſaid unto him that told him, Who is my mother ? and who are my brethren ?

49 And he ſtretched forth his hand towards his diſciples, and ſaid, Behold my mother, and my brethren.

50 For whoſoever ſhall do the will of my Father which is in heaven, the ſame is my bro- ther, and ſiſter, and mother.

CHAP. XIII.

THE ſame day went Jeſus out of the houſe, and ſat by the ſea-ſide.

2 And great multitudes were gathered together unto him, ſo that he went into a ſhip, and ſat, and the whole multitude ſtood on the ſhore.

3 And he ſpake many things unto them in parables, ſaying, Behold, a ſower went forth to ſow

4 And when he ſowed, ſome *ſeeds* fell by the way-ſide, and

the fowls came and devoured them up.

5 Some fell upon ſtony pla- ces, where they had not much earth : and forthwith they ſprung up, becauſe they had no deepneſs of earth :

6 And when the ſun was up, they were ſcorched, and be- cauſe they had not root, they withered away.

7 And ſome fell among thorns : and the thorns ſprung up and choked them.

8 But other fell into good ground, and brought forth fruit, ſome an hundred-fold, ſome ſixty-fold, ſome thirty-fold.

9 Who hath ears to hear, let him hear.

10 And the diſciples came, and ſaid unto him, Why ſpeak- devils.

25 And Jeſus knew their thoughts, and ſaid unto them, Every kingdom divided againſt itſelf, is brought to deſolation: and every city or houſe divided againſt itſelf, ſhall not ſtand.

26 And if Satan caſt out Sa- tan, he is divided againſt him- ſelf : how ſhall then his king- dom ſtand ?

27 And if I by Beelzebub caſt out devils, by whom do your children caſt *them* out ? therefore they ſhall be your judges.

28 But if I caſt out devils by the Spirit of God, then the kingdom of God is come unto you.

29 Or

33 Thomas Jefferson, *The Life and Morals of Jesus of Nazareth*, 1791.

layout. He simply discarded those parts of the gospel accounts that did not correspond, either to each other or to his own sense – an instinct honed by his close training in classical philosophy – of what constituted respectable moral teaching.

Jefferson's cavalier treatment of the less conformable words of the Gospels surely made the Gospels easier to harmonize; it would just as surely have shocked the denizens of Little Gidding. What unites the Ferrarians' and Jefferson's very different approaches to the work of scriptural interpretation, however, is the fact that both employed the method of cutting and pasting to create a new work out of excised pieces of Bibles. At first, their choice may seem mystifying. There is little reason to think Ferrar's followers or Thomas Jefferson could not have used a printing press to achieve their aims. The need for secrecy would not have been a major consideration. Nor would financial exigency. The question then becomes: given that their works could have been easily produced by typical means, why did the Little Gidding community and Thomas Jefferson choose scissors and glue?

Our sensible suspicion might well be that the texts created at Little Gidding and Monticello were little more than scriptural scrapbooks, fiddly pastimes designed to keep intelligent, orderly minds and careful hands occupied on long winter evenings. But we can consider instead how the focused, intimate acts of cutting and pasting and reassembling and rebinding were intended themselves to be essential, physically instantiated elements of the statements these books were purposefully designed to communicate.

And that consideration can lead us to some intriguing suppositions.

To begin on a practical note, it is important to remember that readers had been encouraged to cut things out and paste things into all kinds of printed books since the early sixteenth century. This was particularly true of a genre best described as "how-to" books. As we saw in Chapter Five, these works were remarkably popular by the end of the sixteenth century, trading on the notion of the printed book's accessibility to tout their capacity to teach any reader all kinds of useful trades and skills: surveying, mathematics, shorthand, navigation, and the like. Befitting their intentions to teach skills and "artes," these innovative works could also be splendidly manipulable: once authors and printers figured out that books were potentially interactive, the only limits they observed were those of cost and imagination. The 1560 English edition of Euclid's *Geometry* featured cut and paste strips with meticulous instructions for readers who wished to construct three-dimensional objects in order to study solid geometry; early modern surveying manuals often included tools for linear and angular measurement that could be cut from the page and taken into the field; in a kind of parody of verisimilitude, one pamphlet warning of plots against the State actually featured an extractable *paper* knife (this last suggesting that, if unchecked, print could also facilitate the dangerous notion that Anyone Could Learn Armed Rebellion).[18] And so, since biblical workbooks like Harmonies and concordances constituted a subset of the popular "how-to" book trade, we can also see how Bible readers might be encouraged and inspired to commit acts of daring (re)creation on Holy Writ itself.

In their material construction, therefore, these works embodied the very distinctive – and disparate – minds and hearts of their makers. The Little Gidding Harmonies testify to a singular community's unique relationship to scripture. Attempting to create a Protestant monastic community with only medieval Roman Catholic models to emulate, Nicholas Ferrar and his family structured their idiosyncratic *opus dei* around a variety of intense engagements with the Bible. This organizational strategy, generally speaking, was nearly the same as could be found in any pre-Reformation residential monastic community, wherein scripture-reading and psalm-singing traditionally marked the passing of the hours. But Little Gidding was a mixed, lay community; its common work made not only Ferrar, a priest in the Church of England, but also every other of its members – man, woman, and child – into a Bible reader and a biblical commentator. Their communal manipulation of the Bible then, not only, demonstrated the reformed doctrine of the priesthood of all believers; it also very literally embodied the Protestant ideal of unfettered access to the scriptures.

Jefferson's approach may have been less pious than the Ferrarians', but his intense engagement with the doctrines of Jesus also led him to interact with the Bible in an intensely physical fashion. In cutting, discarding, comparing, and pasting, Jefferson performed a ritual that was only partly secular: one symbolizing his own very personal, serious, and ongoing philosophical argument with Christian orthodoxy. Gluing the fragments of authoritative moral truth he could acknowledge onto clean pages, throwing out the passages he simply could not countenance, Jefferson reclaimed the New Testament by – literally – removing and re-*placing* it.

There is little to ally the devout community at Little Gidding with the deist third President of the United States besides the fact that both created Harmonies in an attempt to make sense of the contradictory accounts of Jesus' life and teachings as recorded in four very different Gospels. More important, however, is that both used the same physical method to do so. Their spiritual and intellectual aims may have been disparate, but the Little Gidding community and Thomas Jefferson both treated the Bible as a material object – a physical repository of detachable notions, filled with ideas that could be cut apart, cut up, or cut into. Cut-and-paste Harmonies thus represent one significant aspect of biblioclasm – *scripturo-clasm*. This physical and instrumental approach to biblical commentary and analysis introduces another, related version of interactive scriptural interpretation: the *extra-illustrated* Bible.

Extra-illustration

The bibliophilic and biblioclastic pastime called "extra-illustration" flourished in Britain and America between the mid-eighteenth and the early twentieth centuries. At first, extra-illustration allowed fashionable people to showcase their private collections of print portraiture. Starting with a book on a topic of interest, the hobbyist would collect separate prints, engravings, drawings, and paintings that might serve to illustrate it. He – and until the latter years of this craze it was invariably a "he" – mounted these illustrations on uniformly sized sheets for insertion at appropriate places. The extra-illustrator also removed the original book from its binding and remounted its now separated pages on sheets that conformed to the size of the collected and mounted artworks. In this manner, his foundational text grew, often to several volumes, transformed into a different and unique set compiled and constructed out of the work of other writers and artists. Reflecting the status of what had become a new work, the extra-illustrator's name replaced that of the original's author or editor on the title page. This was serious book-play indeed.[19]

By the end of the nineteenth century, the art of extra-illustration was often called "grangerizing" after its first advocate, the Reverend James Granger, an eighteenth-century English cleric and collector of published portraits of famous, and not so famous, people. In 1769, Thomas Davies published Granger's four-volume *Biographical History of England from Egbert the Great to the Revolution . . . Adapted to a Methodological Catalogue of Engraved British Heads*. To call this a work of "history" is somewhat misleading. Granger did not write a typical narrative of the past; instead, he compiled an exhaustive checklist of portrait engravings, attaching under each "head" a brief biographical sketch that ran to anecdote and character analysis.[20]

This was History as Biography, to a certain degree. But it was more notably History as Inventory. Or, perhaps best put, History as Treasure Hunt. The "engraved British heads" listed by Granger were to be acquired by individual owners of the *Biographical History*, thereby making every collector his own historian, and every collector's Granger a unique artefact reflecting the extent of his aesthetic interest and personal industry. Declaring his intention in this new style of history to "reduce . . . biography to system," Granger organized portraits by chronology, from Anglo-Saxon England to the English Revolution, and class, from monarchs to the lowliest of subjects. In the staid and stuffy world of eighteenth-century history-writing, Granger's method was truly novel. But a simple innovation in his book's material construction allowed his readers to act more creatively than Granger had envisioned. Granger left the left-hand pages of the first edition of his *Biographical History* blank in order to provide space for the book's purchaser to list any relevant items from his own catalogue of collected portraits or jot down bibliographic details Granger might have missed. Readers discovered, however, that they could simply glue their own engravings directly onto the blank pages. While Granger never directly encouraged the latter practice, this apparently is what most of the people who bought Granger's *History* actually did.[21]

Collecting, like all hobbies, walks a thin line between gentle pastime and fierce obsession. As the popularity of extra-illustration grew, the print stalls and trading networks of eighteenth-century London struggled to keep up with demand. The prices of engravings rose steeply, and would-be grangerizers began to look to other venues for print acquisition. Ambitious and insatiable collectors began raiding illustrated books to add to their collections. The price of illustrated books rose accordingly.

Aspiring extra-illustrators soon cast their restless eyes toward the possibilities afforded by such lively texts as travel accounts, Shakespeare's works (which quickly became popular texts to extra-illustrate) – and, inevitably, the Bible. As a result, the demand for illustrations soon encompassed a broader range of print genres: depictions of foreign lands, famous characters of the stage, and religious imagery. And so the system Granger once described as "reduction" actually inspired a number of significant *expansions*: of the market for engraved portraits, of the price of prints altogether, of the number of illustrated books bought for the sole purpose of cutting apart, and, eventually, of the size and weight of any work containing extra-illustrations.

Based as it was on the idea that a book could become a vehicle for the acquisition, preservation, and storage of a large and ever-increasing collection, Granger's historical method was necessarily built upon principles of organization, classification, and retrieval. Given its orderly nature and acquisitive appeal, it is perhaps unsurprising that what once had been a genteel amateur hobby was soon redeployed to commercial purpose. Grangerizing captured the fancy of print sellers, who recognized its potential for organizing and presenting reproductions, paintings, and drawings of subjects ranging well beyond portrait heads. The shopkeeper's embrace of what we might think the most crassly material aspect of extra-illustration – its ability to turn a literary work into a display cabinet – might finally lead us to think that, in becoming repositories for collections of prints and engravings, grangerized works somehow ceased being books altogether.

Many did, but this is not always the case. From this businesslike turn in the history of a literary pastime emerged the set known as the Kitto Bible. Arguably the largest Bible in the world, the Kitto was compiled in the mid-nineteenth century by a London print seller and bookbinder named James Gibbs.[22] Gibbs built his sixty-six-volume project from an entirely unremarkable two-volume base. Despite its long-standing association with Gibbs, to this day "The Kitto Bible" has retained the title of its original text: an ordinary nineteenth-century Bible, Authorized Version, originally published with extensive footnotes written by a clergyman named John Kitto.

Like Victorian ottomans and Victorian curiosity cabinets, Victorian Bibles tend to be overstuffed: with illustrations of the flora and fauna of the Middle East; with drawings of the ancient pottery and farming implements of the Mediterranean; with reproductions of well-known, if not always well-executed, art; with extraordinarily learned, if distractingly tangential, notes citing the work of nineteenth-century archeologists, biblical commentators, and historians; and, finally, with seemingly no end of elegant references to things extra-biblical: the poetry of Alexander Pope, the essays of Jonathan Swift. The original *Kitto Bible* (when referring to the original work I will italicize its title to distinguish it from what it became) contained just such a surfeit of dubious riches. To what might already be considered an obsessively supplemented original text was added the fruits of enthusiastic collecting. Eventually, this Bible expanded to hold more than *thirty thousand* added prints, engravings, and drawings, as well as hundreds of excised leaves from many other printed Bibles.

THE

HOLY BIBLE.

ILLUSTRATED BY J. GIBBS.

VOL. XXII.

LONDON.
1836.

34 J. Gibbs's title page for volume 22 of his Kitto Bible.

The extra-illustrated Kitto Bible is housed in large folio volumes, 22.5 by 15.25 inches, which currently take up an impressive amount of shelf space in the Huntington Library's rare book vault. Each volume contains approximately two hundred folio sheets and has a separate title page inscribed with the same information (only the volume number changing): *The Holy Bible. Illustrated by J. Gibbs . . . London. 1836.* The plainspoken approach ends here, though, for every title page introduces a remarkable hodgepodge – not only all those tipped-in sheets of mounted art and pages from rare old Bibles in several languages, but also notes made by (we must presume) the extra-illustrator, curious snippets of illustrations, and, intermittently but predictably, the pages from the original *Kitto Bible* (for none were discarded) in perfect order, often with passages or footnotes underlined in red or black keying illustrations to specific moments in the original biblical text.

The art contained between the covers of every volume of the Kitto is impressive, not least because there is so much of it. Most pieces, from the most massive engraving to the tiniest woodcut scrap, have been meticulously mounted. (The largest artworks, which run to two to three times the size of the folio volume, however, were instead folded and tipped directly into the volume between its regular pages.) The smallest images are glued directly onto the folio sheets, generally several to a page; most are carefully outlined with red or black ink. Single additions of quarto size or larger have also been pasted directly onto the page; many, however, have been inlaid into an excised window, allowing the reader to see not only the front (or recto), but also the back (or verso), of the page. While this is nearly always the case with pages in which both sides are printed or illustrated, many one-sided prints are also inlaid, allowing the viewer to examine the blank overleaf of an engraving or woodcut. On some pages, the leaves are mounted three or four deep. These methods of display can allow the reader to treat the volume as a kind of pop-up book – with all the kinetic and tactile satisfaction playing with books invariably affords. Weighty it is, but the Kitto is an immensely pleasurable set to handle.

35 Some volumes of the Kitto Bible, shelved.

The art displayed in the Kitto Bible falls into two general categories. First, and most significant, are the thirty thousand or so prints,
which have yet to be completely catalogued by the Huntington
Library. But even on a less formal reckoning, the Kitto Bible has
still been called "one of the most comprehensive collections of early
European prints in America." It has appeared to more than one
dazzled observer to contain nearly every visual image of biblically
inspired topics that could have been made available to an obsessively
ambitious nineteenth-century collector. The prints are either woodcuts or engravings; the latter are far better represented. They represent
every major school of art from the fifteenth through the nineteenth
century.[23]

By far the largest number of Kitto prints depict typical biblical
characters and subjects: "The prodigal son," "Job in despair," "Herod
in his rage," "Noah's ark," "The empty tomb," and the like. Judging
by sheer numbers alone, it would seem that Gibbs included every
single version of each topic he could find, which he then grouped
first by schools and then by date. Prints of the most popular subjects
– "Eve tempting Adam" or "The expulsion from Paradise," for
example – can run to forty or fifty versions, and in each grouping we
observe how famous artists influenced not only each other but also
the lesser artists who made their living producing copies of famous
works. Turning page after page of the same depiction thus provides
a crash course in the patterns and fashions of religious iconography.
And to view all the prints keyed to a particular passage, in chronological sequence, can feel more than a bit like leafing through a
family album of scriptural symbolism.

The Kitto also contains complete print series on broader themes
inspired by the Bible. These are not grouped together as a rule; they
can be found tipped in throughout the Kitto, keyed to the specific
scriptural citations they illustrate. We find many velvety mezzotints
by John Martin, the superb nineteenth-century depicter of the
darker and stormier episodes in the Old Testament. Another series,
by William Blake, conspicuously – and, as we will see, significantly
– retells twenty-one events in the Book of Job.

36 A typically dark and stormy night in the life of a prophet as imagined by the mezzotint artist John Martin. (Extra-illustration, volume 22, the Kitto Bible.)

In addition to the Martin series, and the Blake series (which will be described at length below), the Kitto contains most, perhaps all, of the fascinating plates from an ambitious visual encyclopedia created by an eighteenth-century Swiss physician, Johann Jakob Scheuchzer. Scheuchzer spent four years cataloguing the fossils and other artefacts held by the Public Library of Zurich, creating in the process a system designed to make scientific knowledge available to the public, demonstrate rational proof for the existence of God, and explicate the natural history underpinning Protestant doctrine. The printed culmination of his life's work was the *Physica Sacra*, a series of more than 750 prints illustrating scriptural passages in both the Old Testament and the New.

Physica Sacra provides us with a remarkable view into early modern beliefs regarding the relationship of science and religion. One striking plate illustrates Genesis 1:26, which begins, "Then God said: 'Let us make man in our own image' . . ." The Latin tag

37 Jakob Scheuchzer reconciles theology and science in *Physica Sacra* (extra-illustration from the Kitto Bible).

reads: "Human [made] from earth." The German inscription reads: "The Creation and Procreation of Humankind." The scientific purpose of this print, displayed around the border, is to illustrate the stages of gestation. Its theological purpose, however, is to contrast the physical stages of human development with the single divine act that created humankind. The consequences of that act are summed up at the upper left by a skeleton holding the fatal apple in its right hand and, in its left, a pawnbroker's symbol, which intersects with a beam of light streaming upon Adam. The confluence represents redemption, the ransom paid by Christ's death for the sins of the world. In this and the other entries in this set of beautifully executed engravings, we see clearly that for Scheuchzer science served Christian doctrine, giving Enlightenment a Protestant gloss and lending Protestantism an elegant look of truth.

There are also approximately two hundred original drawings mounted or inlaid in the Kitto. These too give us a flavor of the art market of nineteenth-century London, but here the wares are not quite so impressive. (This notwithstanding, the Huntington Library exhibited a selection of fifty drawings from the Kitto in 1969 and another six in 2004.) The one serious painting in the Kitto, a water-color by William Blake entitled *The Conversion of Saul*, is the only such work with a claim to fame. Or, at least, a clear and full record of provenance: it was painted by Blake for Thomas Butts, for whom the artist produced over eighty watercolors on biblical themes; it was sold at Sotheby's in 1852 for nineteen shillings and again in 1876 for a little less than nine pounds. Some time after that date it was inserted into volume 56 of the Kitto, probably by the Kitto's second owner, Theodore Irwin, who after purchasing the set from Gibbs had added some artworks of his own. After its acquisition by Henry E. Huntington it was removed from the Kitto and placed into the curatorial hands of the Huntington Art Gallery. It has been placed on exhibition at least three times, once in New York City.[24]

Not only printed art, but the art of the printed page is on rich display. The Kitto holds many single leaves, and possibly entire Bibles, dating from the second half of the fifteenth century, some in

38 William Blake's *Conversion of Saul.*

first edition. These are printed in Hebrew, Greek, Latin, French, German, Italian, and Dutch. In addition, every one of the English Bibles discussed in Chapter Three of this book is showcased, making the Kitto not only an unparalleled collection of religious art, but also a richly documented material history of the printed Bible.

One person's industry, then, turned an ordinary Bible into an extraordinarily comprehensive collection of scriptural arts and letters, but what we may never know is exactly *why*. We know very little about the man listed on its title pages. James Gibbs appears to have been an enthusiastic collector as well as a tradesman, and the Kitto Bible probably reflects the passionate interest of both the amateur collector and the professional bookseller. Gibbs may well have crafted all sixty-six volumes to serve as devices to display prints for the purpose of sale. (If this is so, however, it is a notable case of commercial overkill.) But even if it would be most thrilling to imagine Gibbs as some pious privateer of the print stall, driven by a passion for biblical scenery he simply could not deny, what, truly, would we lose if we discovered that Gibbs was no more than a buyer working to serve someone else's obsessive desires, or no less than a craftsman especially skilled in the art of extra-illustrated inlay? Purchased by the Huntington Library in 1919, the Kitto has – in part because it has found a home in a research library – taken its place as a book, albeit one with an identity we can be hard pressed to define. In its size, comprehensiveness, and singularity the Kitto transcends the notion of the commercial or the acquisitive. True to the very method of extra-illustration, it has become something different and distinct from its original – original book *and* original purpose.

Finding The Bible in the Kitto Bible

So perhaps we should not be so swift to reduce the Kitto Bible to a curiosity cabinet or a European art gallery between sixty-plus sets of hard covers. To this day, however, the Kitto Bible has been considered a repository of religious imagery first and foremost. The bounty of religious art and scriptural letters in the Kitto certainly testify to the eighteenth- and nineteenth-century mania for collecting, collating, and classifying that we saw documented in John Ruskin's diary. But if we allow ourselves to be overly impressed with the sheer, crazy abundance of it all, we may overlook its discernible message. Whatever his reason, the one thing Mr Gibbs surely did not do was simply cram an enormous number of pictures into a dismembered book. If we look with care, we can detect the mind behind the work.

Scholars have, admittedly, been very slow to analyse *any* grangerized text as a book in its own right.[25] And so, contemplating what the Kitto might be, let us return to the question raised at the beginning of this chapter: *what makes a book a book?* After twenty or so pages about cutting and pasting, we may be inclined to agree with our rare books dealer that the one thing a book is *not* is a pristine object with a set number of pages and a DO NOT DISTURB sign posted implicitly on its title page. After thinking on his warning that everything that looks like a book might not be a book, we might be content to move on to the second query: *what can a person do to a book?* And, after spending time with the Gospels as remade by Nicholas Ferrar's followers and Thomas Jefferson, we might offer this experienced reply: *well, you can cut it up and reset it and throw some of it away and illustrate it and...*

Fair enough. But, in the end, Little Gidding and Thomas Jefferson left us coherent gospel narratives. The Kitto, however, with its two little volumes of quarto Bible locked away in sixty-six folios, each roughly the height (and seemingly the weight) of a home safe, may have taken this notion of playing with books to an extreme. And so it tempts us to ask a very old-fashioned question: *Can we read it?*

The best place to find out the answer would be the Kitto's Book of Job. To begin with, this book has good bones. The text is well structured and seemingly self-contained. Memorable enough to have circulated orally for more than a century before it was finally written down, Job has a tidy plot and plenty of narrative drive. Its language is lushly poetic, filled with evocative images. It is structured as any good story ought to be, with a beginning, a middle, and an end: a prologue that features a conversation between God and Satan that sets a tale spinning into motion; a set of attention-grabbing, heart-wrenching reports of the destruction of all Job holds dear that advances the plot; a series of accelerating and ultimately unsatisfying debates between Job and his friends over the reason for Job's suffering that raises the tension level to unbearable heights – and then a daring, impassioned challenge to God by Job that leads to a sweeping denouement: God's breathtaking declaration of Divine power and justice.

The End.

Again, not quite. In the Kitto's Job, these bones have been beautifully fleshed out. Amidst the plethora of pages from other Bibles (and what is, quite possibly, the largest grouped collection of depictions of Job being harangued by his wife in the history of engraved art), the volume is regularly and frequently punctuated by two famous print series. It contains many entries from Scheuchzer's scientific-theological series, the majority of which can be found interleaved with the final chapters of Job. Scheuchzer appears to have been beguiled by the opportunity to depict every meteorological and zoological phenomenon God claims as evidence of His majesty in chapters 38–42.

Another notable set of engravings in the Kitto Job takes a very different, though no less spiritual, view. *Illustrations to the Book of Job Invented & Engraved by William Blake* (1826), arguably Blake's most powerful artistic achievement, is a series of twenty-one scenes from this most compelling of the tales told in the Hebrew Bible. The swirling lineaments that fuse the figure of God, the forms of angels, and the human players in this visual drama find their refrain in the arcing words, extracted from the scriptural text, that frame each image. The effect is neither rational nor natural: Blake's faith required no explanation and no proof. His religion was a religion of art – and his art was an art of magnificently, eccentrically realized imagination.[26]

The inclusion of the series by both Scheuchzer and Blake creates, then, a visual analogue to the storyline that stretches across the whole of the volume and provides a narrative "spine" for the story. But we have further evidence of the extra-illustrator's intent. Like all grangerized works, the Kitto is organized, sometimes quite loosely, around the narrative device of its original book. Unusually for an extra-illustrated book, the Kitto also contains a more focused plot within its narrative, one made up of underlined passages on the pages of the original Bible around which the vast collection associated with Gibbs was dispersed. And so, what follows below is the story of Job as extracted from the Kitto volume's underlined verses:

> While he was yet speaking, there came also another, and said, The Chaldeans made out three bands and fell upon the camels, and have carried them away, yea, and slain the servants with the edge of the sword, and I only am escaped alone to tell thee.[27]

> So went Satan forth from the presence of the Lord.[28]

> The thing which I greatly feared is come upon me.[29]

> Though he slay me yet will I trust in him.[30]

> For I know that my redeemer liveth, and that he shall stand at the latter day upon the earth. And though after my skins worms destroy this body, yet in my flesh I will see God. Whom I shall see for myself and mine eyes shall behold and not another; though my reins be consumed within me.[31]

> Who is this that darkeneth counsel with words without knowledge?[32]

> Canst thou draw out leviathan with an hook? Or his tongue with a cord which thou lettest down?[33]

Not the most embellished of tales, perhaps, but a tale nonetheless.[34] Note that the essential elements of the Book of Job remain – as do, if very sketchily, the most pertinent turns of its plot: disaster strikes; Satan departs the story, leaving the washing-up to others; Job acknowledges his fate; defends his God once and his faith twice; and then is put in his place by the One whose works transcend any human ability to praise or justify or explain.

It seems clear enough that our extra-illustrator was moving about his task intentionally, but on further examination it also seems his choices reflect the fact that he was in actuality tracking the intentions of another, more famous biblical analyst: William Blake.[35] For with only one exception, every underlined page in the Kitto Job faces or is sandwiched between engravings from the Blake series.[36] So it may be that the extra-illustrator's intent was simply to highlight the aspects of the story already given prominence in this well-known collection of prints. In short, the underlinings may be nothing more than a set of abbreviated signposts to Blake's eccentric and well-known visual interpretations of the Book of Job.

Does this return us to the commercial argument for the Kitto's existence? Possibly. Does this mean the primary purpose of the Kitto was to house interesting arts and letters? Who cares? A measure of the Kitto's greatness as a print collection is that one can find between its covers – often bound next to each other as if in passionate and contentious conversation – the rational works of a Jakob Scheuchzer and the mystical works of a William Blake. At the very least, the Kitto stands as an incomparable testament to the manifold complexities of the Victorian religious temperament. But it also reflects the range of voices – historical and current, competing and complementary – that are read into the Bible, including our own.

Which is just the problem. We *can* read it, but its overall message remains elusive and contested. One Book of Job does not a Bible make, and therein lies an elegant if frustrating paradox. The Bible is not *a* book, but it is *one* book. It may be held uneasily together by the restraining structure of religious narrative, but we are stuck with the whole library. This is something that Nicholas Ferrar knew because he believed every word of scripture and Thomas Jefferson knew because he could not. And, I think, it is also something the maker of the Kitto Bible also knew, and that is why he was determined to reduce the Bible to system – by expanding it and contracting it all at the same time.

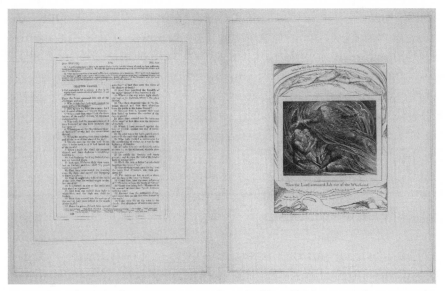

39 William Blake's illustration, inserted in the Kitto Bible, extra-illustrating the underlined verse from Job at left.

And so we can make the case for the Kitto, not only as a book but as a Bible because, unlike most books meant for our reading, the Bible is neither single-minded nor straightforwardly narrative in its unfolding. We need to recall the Kitto's material and literary origins in Granger's first *History*, and remember how the Bible, like history, invariably presents its readers with special narrative problems, problems that require snipping and relocating and adding and subtracting and a constant process of reassessment. As we have seen, the only way to read the Bible is not exactly from first page to last, but, in a sense, sideways: moving back and forth between lines, applying judgments, forming palimpsests – we have to engage in some serious play indeed in order to trace the story it tells. So we begin this last investigation of the Kitto bearing one aspect of biblical reading firmly in mind: the need for the reader's ongoing, intentional acts of interpretation – or *redaction*.

To see the Kitto redactor's mind at work, we need go no farther than two-page episodes found on hundreds of facing pages in nearly all sixty-six of the Kitto's volumes. In volume 58, for example, we come across an underlined passage from Romans 16:16: "Salute one another with an holy kiss . . ." Paul's description of the nature of Christian fellowship is extra-illustrated on the facing page, as well as above and below the inlaid page 349 of the original *Kitto Bible*, with three prints of Elizabeth, mother-to-be of John the Baptist, and Mary, mother-to-be of Jesus, embracing each other.[37] The print on folio page 10556 verso is a copy of a famous woodcut by Albrecht Dürer; its central image is reproduced in a small print at the top of folio page 10557 recto. Another rendition of the exchange between Mary and Elizabeth graces the bottom center portion of the same folio page.

This is why art historians love the Kitto: not only for its comprehensiveness, but also for its scheme of organization, which allows anyone to follow the path of an iconic representation as it makes its way through a variety of formats and uses. (Dürer, whose work is liberally represented in the Kitto, was both a creator of images that subsequently took on iconic status, and a skillful reinterpreter of older iconic images.) But as we have seen, the principle that repetition not only breeds familiarity but also signals a message in itself is also a common narrative strategy – *especially* in the Bible. An image, after all, can be verbal or visual. But in either case, if a particular image shows up time and again in a story, you can be certain it holds an important – if not the important – key to that story's meaning. A repeated image tells us, in other words, how to read the story properly, to its fullest extent.

Now, Romans 16:16 is not the first place Dürer's woodcut print of Elizabeth and Mary appears in the Kitto Bible. It also, rather unsurprisingly, illustrates the passage in the Book of Luke that describes the first meeting of Elizabeth and her cousin Mary after Mary has miraculously conceived.[38] Tipped in at Luke 1:39–56, the Dürer woodcut would seem simply to depict the event the evangelist describes. And so, we view the scene: as her own unborn child, the future John the Baptist, leaps to testify *in utero*, Elizabeth becomes the first person in the Gospels to recognize and declare Mary as uniquely blessed by

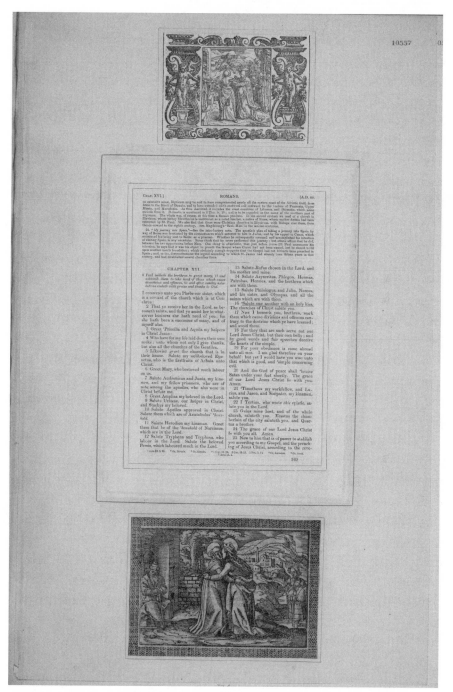

40 A page from the Kitto Bible, vol. 58, extra-illustration of Romans 16:16.

God. Coming across the same portrayal a second time, cut and pasted into the context of Paul's concluding command for the members of the Church at Rome to "salute one another with an holy kiss," we see that the Dürer woodcut goes beyond its primary illustrative role in Luke to become something more complex: a visual medium for scriptural commentary, a clue that the scene in Luke and the passage in Romans are somehow related.

Consider, however, the "salute" that constitutes the central act in both passages. In no place in the Luke passage are Mary and Elizabeth described as actually "kissing," or even touching, one another. (In fact, Luke 1:44, ". . . as soon as the voice of thy salutation sounded in mine ears, the babe in my womb jumped for joy," explicitly defines their "salute" as auditory.[39]) Romans 16:16, on the other hand, provides us with the first description of a Christian liturgical act, the so-called "kiss of peace." And so our minds return to Luke, and we realize that Mary and Elizabeth were the first persons depicted greeting each other as fellow Christians – if by Christians we mean, simply, "people mutually and joyfully anticipating the arrival of Jesus" – which remains, after all, a pretty accurate description of Christians even now. The Kitto redactor retro-fitted Paul's idea of a salute as a "holy kiss" back onto the Luke text, and so the flash of joyful recognition that animated Mary and Elizabeth becomes the original model for the quasi-familial, affective ties that bound the early Christian community. The practice, poignantly necessary in an age of persecution, was eventually reified into an act of Christian worship that features in the liturgy to this day.

At this point, we realize that the maker of the Kitto was not only extra-illustrating a passage but also illustrating one of the basic principles of Bible-reading we examined in Chapter Five. The relationship between any two scriptural passages can never be straightforwardly linear. The verses are intricately bound up in one another, but their interaction moves in both directions. We glimpse a complexly plotted relationship. The Bible is a text that has been read into a peculiar narrative existence by centuries and communities of very disparate readers – all of whom had to forge connections between disparate passages, books, and testaments in order to make sense of it for their own beliefs and practices.

And so, while the Kitto is not only a picture gallery, it is also not only a book (even for those of us who, like Alice, prefer our books to have pictures). Like many excerpted Bibles – children's Bibles, schoolboys' Bibles, and women's Bibles – the Kitto is a specifically narrated Bible, built out of selections and extractions and additions, reflective of its moment in time. And so it requires its readers to be willing not only to read it closely, but also, as Adam Gopnik writes, to read *past* it, looking beyond, reaching around, or making relevant its obscure references and archaic practices.[40]

Conclusion

Maybe Gibbs was a print-seller who happened on a nifty way to display his wares – by scriptural classification. Or maybe Gibbs was just an obsessive collector who happened to corner the market in religious prints. Or maybe he was both. Whoever he was, there is method in his Bible – a "reduction to system" that had to deal with the expectations of narrative unity generations of believers have placed on a narratively impaired Bible. Whatever else it is, the Kitto Bible is surely a Bible like no other. Its volumes tell many tales: of the eighteenth-century impulse toward classification, of the nineteenth-century passion for art collecting, of the twentieth-century pursuit of a world-class library – and now, on these few pages, of the twenty-first-century search for what makes such a Bible biblical. Unusual as it is, the Kitto Bible stretches but does not break our notion of what makes a Bible a Bible – or what makes the Bible a book in the first place. In fact, it may well be the best answer to the question *what makes a Bible a Bible?* that we have. For the Bible, like the Kitto, has always both escaped – and required – the confining expectations readers place on it. Perhaps that is the secret of a sacred text.

CHAPTER SEVEN

TRAVELING COMPANION

THE BIBLE IN THE NINETEENTH CENTURY

The nineteenth-century Methodist clergyman William Taylor described his work among the "forty-niners" of northern California in classic up-by-the-bootstraps style:

> I went into Sonora at nine o'clock one Saturday night, not knowing a man in the place; and finding the streets crowded with miners, who had gathered in from all parts of the surrounding mountains, I felt a desire to . . . preach the Gospel to them, so I asked a brother whom I chanced to meet to roll a dry-goods box into the street nearly in front of a large crowded gambling house . . . my congregation packed the street from side to side. Profound attention prevailed while the truth, in the most uncompromising terms, was being proclaimed.[1]

Taylor's uncompromising truth was drawn directly from the Bible he pounded while balanced on that dry-goods box, set amidst gamblers, drunks, and other homesick sinners. Everybody in that street had come to Sonora from somewhere else, and it's a good bet many of them wished they had never left home in pursuit of destinies that stubbornly refused to manifest. Not so Taylor. In

1848, sent west by the Methodist General Conference, the Virginia native packed up his scriptures and other books and sailed to the golden, godless frontier. Also along for the trip were his wife, his children, and a 24 by 36 foot portable chapel, stowed in the passengers' hold of the *Andalusia*.[2]

Like Taylor and his disreputable audience, the Bible had come a long way from the settled homes and churches of Old and New England. In this chapter we will follow the Bible on a few of these journeys, accompanied by itinerant preachers, door-to-door salesmen, and philanthropists. Like these travelers, we will find ourselves increasingly drawn away from the comfortable and familiar to the vibrant, restless, and expanding Bible cultures of nineteenth- and early twentieth-century America.

Family Bibles

Every journey, however, begins from home, while "home" remains tucked away safely in the imagination. The engraved frontispiece to one popular Bible, *The Comprehensive Bible* of 1860, shows an idealized portrait of family Bible instruction, a cozy image that was many times reproduced, purchased, and displayed on the better walls of Britain and America.[3] Novels of the period abound with references to family practices of Bible reading, in offhand, unelaborated remarks that suggest its ubiquity in real life. These are often idealized portraits of decency and goodness: Marmee leading nightly worship for daughters playing out their own versions of *Pilgrim's Progress* in Louisa May Alcott's *Little Women*; George Eliot's sharply observant portrait of the Bible's shifting effect on Adam Bede: "[h]e held one hand thrust between his waistcoat buttons, and the other ready to turn the pages; and in the course of the morning you would have seen many changes in his face."[4]

But other authors offered sly insights into luxurious hypocrisy, placing family Bibles in spiritually impoverished settings. After she mercilessly lambastes her husband for mismanaging a potentially ruinous ecclesiastical scandal (and wins the argument that ensues),

41 Family Bible instruction, portrayed in a frontispiece to *The Comprehensive Bible*, 1860.

Anthony Trollope's Mrs Grantly "descend[s] to family worship, the pattern of a good and prudent wife." Still feeling the sting of her rebukes, the archdeacon gathers his wits about him like a chasuble and follows her into the bosom of his unpleasant family, who sit surrounded by clotted food and thick furnishings. "With imperious brow," Grantly reasserts what's left of his moral authority by "command[ing] silence from the large circle of visitors, children, and servants who came together in the morning to hear him read the word of God."[5]

At the heart of these fictional as well as many actual scenes of domestic piety was a very real "Family Bible." This Authorized, or King James, Version of the scriptures kept the standard content and the minimalist marginal notes of its 1611 incarnation, but now also contained a vast array of instructive illustrations, extensive foot- and endnotes, and additional commentaries: features the publishers touted as designed to encourage family reading and assist parental, usually paternal, instruction.

Curious about what the family in the frontispiece might be learning from Papa, we need look no further than a title page: Family Bibles claimed not only to assist in the inculcation of familial piety but also to educate. They extended, then, the promise of scriptural learning made in the seventeenth century, but in a different direction than university scholars would eventually take. By the end of the eighteenth century, in Protestant universities in Germany, Britain and, finally, even America, the historic and cultural origins of the Bible were subjects of humanistic, not pietistic, academic study. These facts of origin could make laypeople uncomfortable. But still the very historic and cultural diversities and disparities of the Bible were what made it a fascinating *book*, replete with accounts of natural disasters; long, tongue-twisting genealogies; ancient facts and figures; exotic flora and fauna. Popular nineteenth-century Bibles were billed not only as sacred but also and at the same time as informative: historical and, best of all, encyclopedic.

For the Victorians the Bible was no longer simply a master text from which to learn scriptural history or classical languages; it had become a master class, a cabinet of curiosities, purveying a marvelous range of useful knowledge and eccentric trivia, much of this secular, to Christian families.[6] Notes on the text assumed an importance and prominence they hadn't enjoyed since their heady days in the margins of the Geneva Bible. But Family Bibles resembled the Geneva only insofar as both were designed to instill lay knowledge. In an age of religious tolerance, few obvious politics sullied the marginal universe of the Family Bible – save, perhaps, the wishful politics of the Victorian family, wherein fathers ruled with benevolent despotism, mothers were gentle domestic guardians, and children were seen and not heard.

Father read this Bible to his gathered family, but Mother took care of it, ministering angel to both the book and the room it inhabited, the family parlor. The culture of the middle-class home in Victorian America and Britain was very much a culture of *things*, with the Bible heading the list of proud possessions. Recall the Grantlys' archidiaconal home, with its "air of heaviness" and its "silver forks . . . so heavy as to be disagreeable to the hand," or the depiction of static Canadian-Gothic interiors in Robertson Davies's *Salterton Trilogy*.[7] Here massive furniture and wrist-spraining cutlery represent the sheer suffocating weight of lately acquired wealth: the heavy responsibilities felt by substantial middle-class families to earn a place alongside people who, from generation to generation, had inherited their homes and furnishings.

With their heavy, carved façades, and bright gilt edges, Victorian folio Bibles could easily be mistaken for ponderous pieces of Victorian furniture in themselves. The busy, lavish covers of most Family Bibles imitated two older, and historically incompatible, styles of finer bookbinding. (Designed to look like hand-carved wood, these were in fact constructed out of machine-stamped printer's board; their leather overlays would never have been found on a medieval wood cover.) These Bibles were not designed to be pushed into bookcases. They were meant for special, singular view, left out and left open: displayed, like the great manuscript gift Bibles of medieval times they evoked so inexpertly, on specially designed lecterns or

THE
PICTORIAL HOME BIBLE,
DEVOTIONAL AND EXPLANATORY:
CONTAINING THE
OLD AND NEW TESTAMENTS,
APOCRYPHA AND CONCORDANCE,

With nearly One Hundred Thousand Marginal References and Readings. The Text conformable to the Standard of the American Bible Society. Translated out of the Original Tongues, and with the former Translations Diligently Compared and Revised.

WITH

COMPANION ARTICLES written expressly for THIS EDITION, by M. LAIRD SIMONS, Esq., and founded on the Standard Evangelical Authorities; the Whole forming a POPULAR CYCLOPEDIA Explanatory of the Scriptures. A Careful Examination will convince you of the Vast Practical Value, Interest and Importance of this UNEQUALLED EDITION OF THE HOLY BIBLE FOR THE FAMILY. Its Talented and Accomplished Editor, whose PEOPLE'S EDITION OF D'AUBIGNE'S HISTORY OF THE GREAT REFORMATION has been so Favorably Received, has made its Preparation a Labor of Conscience and Christian Love.

GENERAL CONTENTS OF THE PICTORIAL HOME BIBLE:

1. THE APOCRYPHA of the Old Testament—those books of the Hebrews not forming a part of Inspired Scripture, but all written prior to the birth of the Lord Jesus Christ, and hence of assistance in explaining Jewish thought, manners, and life.

2. A CONCORDANCE, by which the leading words of Scripture can be traced through all the passages in which they are employed, and any text desired can be found by means of its chief terms.

3. MARGINAL REFERENCES, about One Hundred Thousand in number, exact and carefully verified, by which the parallel parts of the sacred writings explain and comment upon each other.

4. ILLUSTRATIVE ENGRAVINGS, on Steel, Wood, and in Colors, more than Three Hundred in number. None of these are mere pictures, but all tend to illustrate the letter or spirit of the sacred text. Many are engraved from photographs made in the East by travellers and Missionaries, while others are but original designs drawn at great expense by the best native and foreign artists.

5. COMPANION ARTICLES, an original series of more than twenty, vivid and absorbing in description, yet all strictly in accordance with the best Evangelical authorities, explanatory of the HOLY BIBLE, and forming together a Popular Cyclopedia of Biblical subjects, viz:—

6. THE HOLY BIBLE AND ITS HISTORY, an account of the evidences of its Divine authority, the preservation of its Texts in purity, formation of the Canon, Ancient Manuscripts and Versions, English Translations, etc.

7. ANALYSIS OF THE BIBLE, comprising 11 quarto pages, wherein is grouped together for devout reading its own teachings about God; Man; Jesus Christ; the Holy Spirit; the Holy Scriptures; Providence of God; the Christian Life; the Sabbath; the Church, and its Ministry; Family Life; Time and Eternity—Life, Death, Resurrection, Last Judgment, Heaven, Hell.

8. BOOKS OF THE OLD AND NEW TESTAMENTS, with Apocrypha, giving a separate history of each book and writer, with analysis, comment, and a comparative Table of the Kings of Judah and Israel. Table of probable occasion of each Psalm. Chronological Table of the Prophecies. Chronological Table of each of the Prophecies. Table of the Harmony of the Four Gospels. Table of Sacred Quotations. Tables of Parables, Miracles, and Discourses, as recorded in Scripture. Tables of Titles of Jesus Christ and the Holy Spirit; Prayers; Origin of Nations. Interspersed with eloquent extracts from eminent Divines.

9. ANIMALS OF THE HOLY BIBLE, a description of every creature mentioned in the Inspired writings, with their individual characteristics, showing the peculiar appropriateness of the Scriptural allusions thereto.

10. TREES, PLANTS, FLOWERS, AND FRUITS, OF THE HOLY SCRIPTURES, likewise a popular but accurate article on the past and present vegetation of the Holy Land, profusely and choicely illustrated.

11. EASTERN MANNERS AND CUSTOMS, a vivid explanation of many obscure parts of Scripture, by reference of travellers to the present mode of life in the East.

12. THE FORTY YEARS WANDERINGS, a survey and confirmation of Israel's march in the wilderness, in the light of recent travels.

13. JEWISH WORSHIP: ITS TYPES EXPLAINED, an illustration of the spiritual and perfect harmony of its Divine law as successively revealed in the Old and New Testaments.

14. IDOLS AND IDOLATRY OF THE ANCIENTS, in Egypt, Canaan, Phœnicia, Babylon, Assyria, Greece, and Rome.

15. COUNTRIES AND NATIONS OF THE BIBLE, a brief geographical and historical outline of Egypt, etc., Shinar or Babylonia, Media, Persia, Asia Minor, Greece, etc.

16. THE HOLY LAND: its mountains, hills, lakes, valleys, streams, and towns, an exhibit of its appropriateness to be the sanctuary of the Lord, and the scene of the life ministry of the Saviour of mankind.

17. THE CITY AND ENVIRONS OF JERUSALEM, its past glory and present wretchedness, in accordance with the latest scientific explorations in Palestine.

18. HISTORICAL CONNECTION OF THE OLD AND NEW TESTAMENTS, tracing the history of Judea from the reformation by Nehemiah, as a Persian province, through its conquest by Alexander the Great, oppression by the fierce Antiochian Epiphanes, independence achieved by the Maccabees, partial conquest by the Romans, and final iron rule by Herod the Great, who slew the babes at Bethlehem.

19. BIBLE PROPHECIES AND THEIR FULFILMENTS, as already manifested in the life of our Lord; Israel as a nation; Egypt; Arabia; Sheni, Elam, and Japheth; the cities of Sidon, Tyre, Nineveh, Babylon, and Damascus; the Amalekites, Ammonites, Edomites, and Moabites; the Assyrian, Persian, Grecian, and Roman empires.

20. IMMANUEL, OUR LORD JESUS CHRIST, the person, office, and life-work of the God-Man, —the Word that was made flesh and dwelt among men.

21. THE MISSIONARY JOURNEYS OF THE APOSTLE PAUL, chronologically arranged and harmonized with the Epistles as respectively written.

22. THE BIBLE IN HISTORICAL ORDER, by which every chapter is arranged so as to be read as a consecutive narrative, founded upon Townsend's Harmony of the Old Testament, Archbishop Thomson's Harmony of the Gospels, Conybeare and Howson's Life of St. Paul, etc.

23. THE SYMBOLICAL LANGUAGE OF SCRIPTURE, a guide to the Prophetic Books, exhibiting the figurative symbols employed and their generally recognized interpretations.

24. CHRONOLOGICAL INDEX TO THE HOLY BIBLE, with the principal events in profane history, according to the computation of Abp. Usher, compared with the labors of the latest Christian chronologists.

25. KEY TO THE ANTIQUATED WORDS OF SCRIPTURE, defining not merely those which are obsolete, but also those not now used in their ancient significations.

26. THE PROPER NAMES OF SCRIPTURE, with the etymological meaning in English of the original Hebrew and Greek Terms.

27. JEWISH WEIGHTS AND MEASURES.

28. A TABLE OF OFFICES AND CONDITIONS OF MEN.

29. BIBLE AIDS FOR SOCIAL AND PRIVATE PRAYER.

30. TABLES OF SCRIPTURAL COINS AND MONEY TERMS, with their values expressed in the money of the United States.

31. HOW TO READ THE BIBLE THROUGH IN A YEAR.

32. BOOKS, CHAPTERS, VERSES, WORDS AND LETTERS OF HOLY SCRIPTURE, showing their authors, arrangements and peculiarities.

A beautiful Lithographic Family Record of Marriages, Births and Deaths, a very unique Marriage Certificate, and a Photographic Album for Sixteen Portraits.

The Introduction of the Adjustable Photographic Album is a new and interesting feature. It relieves the book from all strain and breakage, as in the old method of binding. It comprises four highly ornamented quarto pages, with openings for 16 card pictures, inserted in a recess in the lid or cover of the Bible, and can be removed at pleasure. The inestimable value and great satisfaction of preserving for generations the portraits of beloved members of the family circle is apparent to all; and this home-like feature alone is a strong inducement for the head of a family to give his order to an agent for a copy of the best Family Bible published in America.

The Publishers have spared no expense, and its Edition so labor in his power, to make the PICTORIAL HOME BIBLE a standard and cheap edition of the HOLY BIBLE for the family. Its preparation has been a labor of love and of conscience. Each copy also represents the outlay of many thousands of dollars. It is submitted with confidence to the approbation and verdict of the Christian homes of this free and enlightened land.

CONDITIONS:

The Pictorial Home Bible is printed from large, clear and handsome type, on beautiful white paper, manufactured expressly for this work, and bound in the most substantial manner from entirely new dies, the designs of which are a study in themselves; containing over Eleven Hundred Pages, and over Five Hundred Illustrations on steel, wood and in colors, and will be furnished to subscribers at the following prices, payable on delivery:

No. A, *American Morocco, Marbled Edges*,	$7 50
No. B, *American Morocco, Marbled Edges, Gilt Centre Stamp*,	9 00
No. C, *American Morocco, Gilt Edges, Gilt Centre Stamp*,	10 00
No. D, *French Morocco, Antique and Gold, Gilt Edges, and Edges of the Cover rolled Full Gilt*,	14 00
No. E, *French Morocco, Panelled Sides, Full Gilt, with Clasp, Edges of the Cover rolled Full Gilt*,	16 00
No. F, *American Russia Leather, Panelled Sides, Full Gilt, Edges of the Covers rolled Full Gilt*,	15 00

No. A is bound in the same beautiful style as No. B, it is without the Commandments and Tabernacle in the Wilderness, and the Centre Stamp in Gold. It contains (200) Illustrations (Twelve of which are Steel Plates), with Photograph Album for Sixteen Portraits, it is printed on paper of lighter weight than the other styles. The No. A is not printed in the German language; all the other styles are.

This Bible cannot possibly be obtained except by subscription and through our duly authorized and commissioned agents. Subscribers will not be obliged to take the work unless it corresponds with the description in every particular.

42 The contents of a typical family Bible as described on its title page.

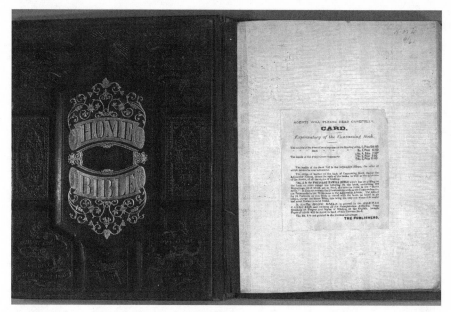

43 Sample binding and salesmen's instructions on prices and versions of the Home Bible, nineteenth century.

tables. Book and prop came together to form what the historian Colleen McDannell has termed a "protestant altar."[8]

McDannell's phrase is no paradox, for by the late eighteenth century the Protestant stricture on fancy Bibles and their Romish associations had all but faded away, proof of the power of the combined forces of market innovation and consumer desire to effect cultural change more efficiently, and with less fuss, than religious doctrine. In an age when Protestant qualms about idolatry and blasphemy could still emerge in public discussions of Catholic emancipation, and laws banned the playing of biblical characters on the British stage, Bible editors were able to claim more than educational purpose for Bible pictures. If their images managed to delight along the way, well, so much the better for a thriving market.

The Bible's reputation as the one book no home could do without made it a perfect product upon which to base innovative schemes of production and distribution. The astoundingly popular *Illuminated and New Pictorial Bible* was sold by Harper & Brothers in fifty-four separate parts (each costing 25 cents), at a total cost to the buyer of $13.50, which included complimentary binding.[9] The prospectus advertisement promised, in addition to scriptural contents "drawn from the standard copy of the American Bible Society," "SIXTEEN HUNDRED HISTORICAL ENGRAVINGS . . . MORE THAN FOURTEEN HUNDRED OF WHICH ARE FROM ORIG-INAL DESIGNS," as well as a presentation plate and ornamental borders.[10] At additional cost, the buyer's name and a picture of his or her church could even be stamped in gilt on the cover. This marketing strategy eventually garnered fifty thousand original subscribers, attracted no doubt to the beauties of its pages, the thrill of having one's name in gold on the front cover, and the budgetary convenience of paying by installment. Subsequently printed as a single volume in 1846, 1859, and 1866, Harper's *Illuminated Bible* made its originator and engraver, Joseph Adams, a very wealthy man.

We have seen one consequence of this loosening of strictures in Chapter Six: many images in the Kitto and other extra-illustrated Bibles were snipped out of Bibles like Harper's *Illuminated* or the *Universal Family Bible*, taking their place alongside more conventionally obtained engravings and watercolors. But the best known, most widely distributed, and, undoubtedly, most snipped of the biblical illustrations were those by the French illustrator Gustave Doré, whose mysterious, exotic – and, to be as frank as his pictures were – openly erotic black and white engravings of scriptural scenes defined his career and filled out many an extra-illustrated book. Doré's 1866 *Holy Bible*, made up of 250 elaborate woodcuts in two folio volumes, inspired a spin-off, *The Bible Gallery*, published in London in 1880. The *Gallery* featured one hundred selections from Doré's larger work, and was designed to be a moderately priced alternative with popular appeal. Doré's dark and stormy style was a good match for the Bible's narrative tensions and the moody, senti-mental temperament of an age captivated by the Gothic. But an equally significant aspect of a Doré Bible's appeal must have been its capacity to capture the sexual imagination of the Victorians.[11]

In any case, buyers of Doré's cut-rate *Bible Gallery* got value for money: carefully erudite explanations along with the illustrations, a variation on the user-friendly public lectures on academic subjects so popular in this age of literary clubs, dramatic associations, lending libraries, and the adult and family summer schools called Chautauquas. The *Bible Gallery* was undoubtedly called a "gallery" to tout its resemblance to an educational trip to the art museum.[12] Or Sunday School: the words as well as the woodcut were designed to provide, in the words of the editor, "a useful companion to God's holy word." Doré's horrifying depiction of the Flood, for example, was accompanied in the *Gallery* by a brisk and simple disquisition on comparative religion, a smattering of archeology, and a poignant (if hair-raising) moral reflection upon the story told in Genesis 7.

"While the Holy Bible is in the largest and truest sense a book for all," stated the editor of *The Child's Bible* of *c.* 1870, "there are some parts of it that are as milk for babes, and some as strong meat for men."[13] But Doré for children, while popular, could be more than a bit meaty, especially considering the milky sentiments professed in the children's books of this era. In the *Child's Bible*, smudgy reproductions from the *Bible Gallery* accompanied simple versions of biblical stories, all concluding with morals "drawn from the actual sayings of childhood." Actually reading them, a painful task for anyone who's ever known a *real* child, makes it clear that these words emerged instead from the saccharine imagination of Victorian adults. The story of the Flood, for example, concludes in another cheaply derivative production, *Bible Talks with Children*: "Whenever my little readers look upon the [rain]bow, remember God is looking upon it too . . . God is very good and kind."

The illustration adjoining stands as luridly mute testimony that, whilst (as children's book scholar Ruth Bottigheimer has discovered) "God's anger was gradually edited out of children's Bibles" in the previous century, the consequence of divine wrath surely wasn't edited out of their images.[14] The accompanying picture is an exact, if very poor, copy of the Flood portrait in Doré's *Bible Gallery*: the naked and the dead flung over unforgiving rocks; still

44 A bad copy of Doré, depicting the Flood in *Bible Talks with Children*, 1889.

others, not waving but drowning, sinking in the roiling waves; tiny children abandoned and imperiled, every mouth open in final, shrieking despair. The reproduction's irredeemably cheesy quality (the besetting sin of most nineteenth-century Bible books for children) somehow manages to render the scene even more terrifying.

In all these modes, elegant and not so elegant, we see the Bible gaudily repackaged to appeal to a broader audience: an imitation of luxury goods at lower cost. That the model was successful in the extreme can be deduced from even the briefest consideration of the vast numbers of Victorian "heirloom" Bibles currently on offer to rare books dealers, the curatorial staffs of research libraries, and the overworked assistant producers of television's *Antiques Road Show*. People who have never handled a medieval illuminated manuscript Bible or a first edition of the King James *are* likely to have encountered one of these characteristic books. True to its name, the Victorian Family Bible makes a "familiar" impression: it is the book we picture to ourselves when we hear the word Bible. We think *old*, *weighty*, and, consequently, *valuable*. Sad to say, most of these Bibles are – at least in today's book market, if not in family sentiment – not rare at all but a dime a dozen.

Packing the Bible

The Bibles of Britain and New England were destined, however, to leave the comfortable environs of well-settled churches and homes, following human migratory impulses both secular and sacred. Those who carried scripture to new places were, then, often doing so to establish new Protestant churches. (At this time, Roman Catholic missionaries would still have carried and distributed devotionals to new devotees.) One consequence of the Reformation, as we have seen, was the inexhaustible capacity of Protestants to disagree, often violently, not only with Catholics but also with each other. Steadfastly maintaining all the while that they had left the Roman Catholic Church because it was false, they found themselves unable to form a single, unified Church of their own. By the middle of the eighteenth century in Britain, however, Protestant acts of separation from the State Church were, in general, no longer viewed by the authorities as insufferable political resistance. The idea of a State Church had been declared unconstitutional in late eighteenth-century America, after the fiery preaching of men like Jonathan Edwards had led to an outpouring of public piety and private conversion experiences in the colonies. The most notable effect of this newly roused religious fervor, or "great awakening," was the splintering of long-established American churches into new, individual churches and staid congregations of Protestants into hotly professing individual sects. Confessing mild variations on Protestant doctrine, small groups of like-minded Protestants in both countries increasingly felt free to band together, put down new roots, and work out distinctive forms of governance, eventually becoming the subgroups we now call "denominations."

Arguably the most distinctive, characteristic, and successful of all the emergent Protestant denominations began life as an evangelical tendency in the Church of England, teetering around its narrower edges of respectability before finally falling away. Methodism's first half-century in the Mother Church had been marked – like all adolescent reforming movements – by dogged reluctance to endorse its enthusiasms by the leaders of the Church and by a corresponding reluctance to leave that Church by the leader of the movement. And so it was that John Wesley, the Father of Methodism, died in communion with the Church of England in 1791, a charitable act which ensured that, having already declared their doctrinal dependence on his *Notes on the New Testament*, his followers would finally be able to declare *their* independence.

British Methodism then made an administrative virtue out of necessity, organizing what had once been a scattered movement into a system whereby no clergyman was tied to a particular parish – the Church of England held a monopoly on the parish system, anyway; instead clergy ministered to what became known as a "circuit" of regional churches. In this we could say that Methodists were natural successors of the Dominicans and Franciscans, who had also taken their Bibles on the road and into the rapidly developing and under-served settlements of Europe in an earlier age. This time, the territory with most promise for expansion, both geographical and ecclesiastical, was in the New World. Men like John Asbury had already begun traversing America in the second half of the eighteenth century, where the Methodist system of clerical itinerancy eventually found a natural home in the restless, frontier-obsessed, and onward-bound nature of American lives. Looking back to aspects of Anglican tradition that were expressed in its commitment to biblical education, yet looking ever onward to lives of scripturally inspired immediacy, Methodism took fast root in America and soon became its most successful denomination.[15]

In America, "circuit rider" was a synonym for "Methodist clergyman," for, unlike his condition in Britain, the path he rode followed the farther-flung and more scattered patterns of American settlement. Moving first south and then west across the North American continent, the "circuit riders" became known as "saddlebag preachers," so-named for their distinctive travel cases, big enough to carry a Bible, if not much else. The scriptures had been sized to hand for several centuries by now, but the size of the antique saddlebags and waterproof carrying cases designed for Methodist horseback preachers suggests that these ministers of the Gospel carried impressively sized Bibles: ones that could, in effect, create a church wherever they were taken up and laid out. William Taylor had set out for California, recall, intending to throw "a Gospel hot shot right through the masses of every saloon" he passed in nineteenth-century America. Bibles were Tabernacles carried into a new Promised Land, available whenever a preaching opportunity presented itself.

Bibles Door to Door

The Salesmen

Any consideration of the impressive contents of a Victorian parlor or an itinerant preacher's saddlebag might seem, however, to overlook

45 A Methodist Bible and its metal box, protection for the journey.

just how cheap, plain, and (to speak only of page format and bindings) undistinguished the Bible had become by the beginning of the nineteenth century. In the Industrial Age, improved print technologies made it possible for publishers to produce the scriptures at remarkably low cost. This abundance of cheap goods, along with an evangelical fervor for saving souls, inspired the American Bible Society, the American Tract Society, and the American Sunday School Union to join forces in the 1820s and announce a "general supply": a plan to distribute Bibles and other religious literature to every person in the United States, either gratis or priced on a sliding scale.[16] By the 1840s, a complete Bible could be purchased for a half-dollar; a New Testament cost six cents. And by mid-century, the American Bible Society alone was either selling or giving away a million copies of the Bible every year; the British Foreign and Missionary Society was distributing as many if not more.[17] The Bible had become, in other words, an ordinary, workaday commodity: easy to produce in bulk and distributed in large numbers by missionaries and Sunday School teachers to their respective captive audiences.

Cheap Victorian Bibles explain, rather than explain away, a market for pricier versions, then: they could not serve the needs of a Gilding Age wherein what glistered often had to count for gold. The trick, then, was how to make the Bible more expensive, and how to sell it in larger numbers to more people. So, along with their actual wares, American Bible salesmen carried promises of a new and improved product. They sold the big, gaudy Bibles that graced so many Victorian parlors: the old familiar King James, but now with bright additions, inside and out, to pique the interest and pry open the wallets of a wide variety of customers. In the nineteenth century a fifty-cent King James Bible could be customized upward to cost anywhere between $7.50 and $15.00, a significant sum at the time. The extra dollars bought "fine" leather covers (like Webster's Dictionary, "Morocco-bound") and "lavish" page marking, although neither usually as fine or lavish as a salesman's claims.

The innovative instincts of Bible publishers and sellers followed domestic tastes, but then, as in all successful marketing campaigns, they went on to shape them. The Bible salesman's obligation was to erase older cultural stereotypes of shabby peddlers and traveling tinkers, those rootless purveyors of shoddy materials. One nineteenth-century catalogue described their new task in glowing terms: "It carries a dignity with it that is found in very few other lines of business, and that makes the work very pleasant, for a Bible representative is welcome everywhere." Jokes about farmers' daughters notwithstanding (or perhaps even more to be expected), door-to-door sales of Bibles presented one of the more "respectable" pretexts for allowing a stranger into the home.

Bible salesmanship depended on the grassroots relationship between schools and Protestant churches. We see this civic connection in publishing-company-issued books containing tips, both inspiring and practical, for Bible canvassers, or potential canvassers. These sprightly, upbeat productions advised salesmen to subdivide their territories by school district or parish, thus making appeals to community leaders more efficient. They were to search out the head teacher, principal, or local minister and ask for advice and official support; carry larger books under their arms for comfort, thus sparing themselves in sparsely populated, far-drawn-out communities; stable their horses and walk from home to home, thus avoiding any pre-emptive breach of potential hospitality (one wonders how many salesmen lost a sale the moment the man or lady of the house saw the horse tied on the fence and subsequently pulled the blinds, fearing an afternoon wasted with a visitor who would eventually require feeding); and summon all their powers of "intelligent, earnest and glowing description" to kindle customer desire for their scriptural wares. The work was invariably described in terms both optimistic and urgent:

SEND FOR YOUR OUTFIT AND BEGIN WORK AT ONCE.
AVAIL YOURSELF OF TERRITORY ON THE WORK WHILE IT CAN BE HAD.
WHAT HAS BEEN DONE CAN BE DONE AGAIN.

WHAT HAS BEEN DONE CAN BE DONE AGAIN.

A FEW OF THE MANY REPORTS RECEIVED FROM OUR AGENTS.

Read, and don't let the Golden Opportunity pass.

Our Agent at Pittsfield, Mass., writes us, under date of June 9, as follows:

WM. FLINT & CO.—*Gentlemen:* For nine years I have been in the field as a canvassing agent for books, and during a portion of the time have had Bibles from different publishers, and always have purposed to get hold of the best. About eight months ago I was induced, through the manager of your office at Springfield, Mass., to take hold of the Home Bible, and circumstances rendered it necessary for me to go into a field I had just canvassed for an expensive Bible, and one that was regarded as first-class. I commenced with little courage, and the first hour took six orders, and in little time had taken nearly double the orders I had taken for my former Bible.

Since that time my success has always been the same, and I can truly say for myself, and in justice to my fellow canvassing agents, that I know of no work now before the people, issued from any publishing house in the Union, which is so easily introduced, so readily received, and in which there is one-half as much money to the agent as there is in your Home Bible.

From our Agent in Chicopee, Mass.

I first canvassed this place for a $20 Bible, (before I heard of the Home Bible,) and sold 80 copies. Yet in re-canvassing with the Home Bible, I have sold 130 copies.

Yours is a *grand* work, so complete a Bible library, and of such great beauty, and, too, at so low a price, delights and astonishes the people. I can exchange the Home Bible, even in the $14 binding, with nearly all those that paid me $20 for the other Bible.

From Hudson Smith, Agent.

I am meeting with good success. Each day I work I get from three to eight subscribers. Every one who has bought Bibles published by other houses, regrets it and greatly prefers yours. Some wish to exchange Bibles, for which they paid $13 and $15, for your $9 Bible. One lady had a Bible she paid $35 for, and after comparing the two together, she decided that yours was the best and most comprehensive. The most complimentary expressions for your Bibles have come from ministers of the Gospel and other leading and intelligent men, who are posted, and particularly capable of judging.

The Pictorial Home Bible is the only Bible that gives universal satisfaction, and is the book for agents to make money on.

Our Agent at Rochester, N. Y., writes:

I am doing a rushing business with your new Bible, my sales averaging about twenty-eight per week since I commenced. Bible readers purchase this Bible when they have many other Bibles on hand, for the library of information complete in a cheap form.

Our Agent at Troy, N. Y., writes, under date of May 12, as follows:

My sales of the Pictorial Home Bible for the week just past amount to $820. This beats anything I have ever before done in a seven years' experience with other books.

From John W. Dodge, 10 years a book agent, Richmond, Va.

I am, perhaps, one of the oldest book agents in the Southern States. For many years I have given much of my time to the selling of Family Bibles. I have used all my efforts to obtain the best editions—my motto being "The Best or None." I have most carefully examined all the late editions of the Bible published by other houses, and do most earnestly recommend the Pictorial Home Bible, published by Messrs. WM. FLINT & CO., Springfield, Mass., as the best edition I have ever seen. The entire arrangement is most excellent for family use. All admire it and say it is all that could be desired as a Family Bible. I unhesitatingly say it is the BEST as well as the CHEAPEST Bible known to me.

From our Agent at Montgomery, Ala.

I have sold fifteen Bibles to-day, and have averaged eight per day ever since I arrived here. I will sell three hundred Bibles in this city. I have examined and canvassed for all the recently published Bibles, and I have never seen any Bible that will at all compare with your Pictorial Home Bible. It is superior in every respect. When I say this, I speak the sentiment of all who have seen it. It is the only Bible that has a complete encyclopædia, analysis of Scripture, and an improved classified Bible Dictionary. It also contains many other excellencies not found in similar connections.

From our Agent at Union Springs, Ala.

I have sold and delivered forty-five Bibles in the last nine days—the most of them were of the finest binding. It gives UNIVERSAL SATISFACTION. I have been a book agent for years, and have carefully examined all the Bibles now in the market; and I unhesitatingly say that your Bible is by far the best, for mechanical execution and for value of explanatory and illustrative matter.

From our Agent at Wilmington, N. C.

The Pictorial Home Bible I regard a work of great merit. It is far superior to any Bible I have examined, and will impart a wider range of Bible knowledge than any similar work. It sells faster, and delivers more easily, and gives better satisfaction than any other edition of the Holy Bible ever published.

From our Agent at Opelika, Ala.

I have sold and delivered ninety-five Pictorial Home Bibles in forty days. I sold eight Bibles to one man for presents to his children. I sold to one man who already had eight Bibles.

From our Agent at Crawford, Ga.

The Bibles are received and delivered; every one is delighted with them. There has never been such a Bible sold in this country. It is the best, cheapest and most comprehensive Bible ever published. An agent, canvassing for other Bibles, admitted, in the presence of several, that your $14 Bible was superior to his $15.

From our Agent in Dutchess Co., N. Y.

I have found the Home Bible a great success. I have done better with it thus far than with anything else I ever canvassed for, in a large experience with books.

From our Agent in Fair Haven, Ct.

All I have seen and heard, and you have said, of the Home Bible, and its popularity and success, I find true. I have obtained five subscribers to-day, now at 12 o'clock M. Last shipment received, delivered, and please exceedingly.

OUR AGENT IN WORCESTER, MASS., sold one hundred and thirty-three, mostly of the $14 and $16 styles, in three weeks, his profits thereon amounting to over $700.00.

OUR AGENT AT SACO, ME., reports one hundred and six of the Home Bible sold by him alone in two weeks' canvass.

Our agent in Halifax, Nova Scotia, reports six copies sold the same day he received the outfit.

Our agent in Greenville, S. C., sold sixty-five Bibles, mostly high prices, in eight days.

Our agent in Tallahasse, Fla., sold eleven the first day, and fifty-three in one week's canvass.

Raleigh, N. C., agent sold and delivered eighty-seven in twenty-two days' time.

Eighteen were sold in one day, and sixty-five in one week's time, by our agent in Salem County, N. J., who also cleared $3,000 in one year's canvass.

Our agent in Berks County, Pa., averaged sixty Bibles a month for four months, three-fourths of them being of the German Edition.

The agent of Schuylkill County, Pa., sold Bibles enough in one year to buy a comfortable home.

Columbia, S. C., was supplied by our agent with fifty copies in five days' time.

Our agent in Columbia County, Ohio, delivered one hundred and fifty copies in three small townships.

At Nimsburg, Holmes County, Ohio, agent sold forty in six days.

A lady agent at Boston sold five copies for her first half day's work.

Our Chemung County, N. Y., agent sold forty-three Bibles within a radius of two miles.

Our agent at Syracuse, N. Y., sold one thousand Bibles in one year's time, an average of nearly one hundred a month.

WM. FLINT & CO., Publishers,

No. 420 Main St., . . Springfield, Mass.

TIME IS MONEY! PROCRASTINATION IS THE THIEF OF TIME.

46 "A Few of the Many Reports Received from Our Agents." William Flint & Co., Publishers touts the success of its salesmen, *c.* nineteenth century.

READ, AND DON'T LET THE GOLDEN OPPORTU-
NITY PASS.
TIME IS MONEY! PROCRASTINATION IS THE THIEF
OF TIME.[18]

While all sales manuals stressed the importance of having a character to match the crystalline reputation of the item on offer, they
spent more lines and energy on the techniques of confident salesmanship. There is more believe-in-yourself than believe-in-God in these
peppy handbooks. One manual, written by the J.G. Ford Company, a
Massachusetts Bible-publishing firm, began its pitch with the
following golden rule of salesmanship: "UNDERSTAND THE
NATURE OF THE BUSINESS ... You must depend on your
ability to describe the work so as first to excite an *interest* in it, and *then*
a *desire* for it." The process of kindling consumer desire began and
ended with the salesman's own words, which were rigorously scripted.

Several pages of "special instructions" provided with the kits
accompanying a nineteenth-century children's Bible advised vendors,
for example, to add the following encouraging remarks to potential
purchasers as they leafed through its pages:

> "It does not require the eye of an artist to see that these engrav-
> ings are beyond criticism."

> "It will create a taste for good literature."

> "It will cement the parental relationship and make home more
> dear when read by parents to children."

> "It will make a beautiful parlor-book."

And, most impressive:

> "It contains 9,356 square inches of engravings."[19]

It is clear from these instructions, which aimed to leave nothing to
chance in a salesman's pitch, that flattery and cajolery were devices

THE GREAT POSSIBILITIES IN THE BIBLE BUSINESS.

For many years the interest in Bible study has been increasing rapidly in this country, through the well organized Sunday School work of every Christian Denomination in every hamlet and village. A generation of Bible readers is constantly coming forward, so that you can readily see that Bibles are always in great demand, and that a profitable business can be done at all times.

WE MAKE YOU HEADQUARTERS FOR BIBLES. Usually Bibles have been sold through middlemen, and at very high prices. To satisfy the demand for every variety of Bible, makes it necessary to carry an enormous stock, running into thousands of dollars. The "International" Series of Bibles, comprises every variety of Bibles in all readable sizes of type, that makes possible the selection of a suitable Bible for all purposes. The "International" Series of Bibles is the largest line of self-pronouncing Bibles in the world. These Bibles are known the world over for their clear print, scholarly helps, and superior, flexible and durable bindings.

THE DIGNITY OF THE BIBLE BUSINESS. There is a certain satisfaction to be found in selling Bibles, that is found in very few lines of business. Every time you place a Bible in the home, you feel that you have accomplished something that is not to be shared in the dollars and cents of profit that you obtain. It also carries a dignity with it that is found in very few other lines of business, and that makes the work very pleasant, for a Bible representative is welcomed everywhere.

SURE SALES AT OUR CUT PRICES. The Bibles described in our catalog are the finest in the world and at the special cut prices at which they are listed, you are certain to do a tremendous business in Bibles alone. These prices are so low that you can defy competition even from inferior and less widely known makes of Bibles. If you will present the catalog properly, you will find that people generally will be glad to avail themselves of the opportunity of purchasing a good Bible at our remarkably low prices.

47 The Bible business, extolled to potential salesmen, *c.* late nineteenth to early twentieth centuries.

to shape a potential buyer's sense of him- or herself. The salesman painted a virtual portrait of his customer in the process of making a sale, drawing on the aspirations with which he had undertaken his *own* vocation: to be seen as moral, upright, well educated, culturally ambitious. The Ziegler catalogue concludes with encouragement to all such would-be self-made men: "Under any and all circumstances, DO YOUR BEST! DO YOUR BEST! AND IN THE END YOU WILL BE SATISFIED."[20] It was to that ideal of the respectable, ambitious family that the respectable, ambitious salesmen made their most potent pitch.

The flattery and cajolery went both ways: Bible salesmen were enticed into packing their book bags and hitting the road with lavish promises of potential wealth and customer respect. Enthusiastic sales testimonials praised the *Pictorial Home Bible* of 1873, which was sold only by subscription. "I have sold and delivered ninety-five Pictorial Home Bibles in forty days," enthused an agent from Opelika, Alabama, who also claimed to have "sold to one man who already had eight Bibles." (The *PHB* came loaded with historical maps, "authentic" illustrations of the Holy Land, and religious guidance, which might be what accounted for multiple sales to homes wherein books were generally in short supply.) A salesman from Rochester, New York, reported that he averaged twenty-eight Bible sales per week. His customers, like the people of Montgomery, Alabama (according to *their* local Bible salesman), bought the *Pictorial Home Bible* for its "complete encyclopedia, analysis of scripture, and . . . improved classified Bible Dictionary."

The Product

Bibles made sturdy corner-stones for the establishment of otherwise barely settled professions and households. By the middle of the nineteenth century, publishers had discovered a marketing opportunity embedded in a time-honored practice: using Bibles as places to record family history. In earlier printed Bibles we often find personal milestones – as well as traditional recipes for potions, potables, and pest control – handwritten into the one place, besides its flyleaves, where a Bible had always supplied a decent expanse of blank space: the left-over page and a half created between the end of the Old Testament and the beginning of the New. By the mid-nineteenth century, Bible publishers were filling up this found space with specially designed pages for record-keeping: elaborately decorated sheets inserted between Testaments emblazoned with the words *Births, Marriages,* and *Deaths* – or, more winsomely, *Our Family* – with lines beneath to keep spidery handwriting on the straight and narrow. These insets were, as one supplier bragged, "very beautifully designed, printed in gold, and affording ample space for a large number of names."[21] We can see how the family Bible could become, by these formal additions, a new kind of family artefact: uniformly custom-made, personalized rather than personal.

The advent of photography in the nineteenth century inspired the creation of "artful" Biblical Photograph Albums, "tastefully designed and neatly and securely bound in," according to salesmen's materials provided by the W.J. Holland Company of Springfield, Massachusetts some time in mid-century. "Added to the Family Record," Holland assured its customers, "it presents one of the most desirable styles of record for family use now published." The Holland Company's "Family Record," along with their other inno-vation, a "marriage certificate . . . adapted to all denominations and to every state," allowed families to turn their Bibles into more official record-keepers, something particularly important in this age of territorial expansion, where Bibles nearly always got to settlements before government did.

In any case, it would have taken any number of such interesting and useful bells and whistles to convince people to part with more of their hard-earned cash than the fifty cents it took to buy an ordinary cheap Bible. Indeed, some buyers seem to have coveted Bible add-ons more than Bible content. Charitable and pious American Tract Society colporteurs, working door to door to distribute religious materials in this period, were wont to deplore the less charitable and less pious reasons people gave for buying Bibles, reporting back to headquarters all sorts of shocking news: a Pennsylvania woman whose deepest desire was to own a Bible just like her neighbor's, and New Jersey customers who purchased Bibles only because they wanted to record their family histories.[22]

The Authorized Version sold by salesmen for the Holland Company also made new contributions to domestic scriptural edification. According to its title page, within its covers the ambitious reader could find the following:

The Holy Bible, to which are appended:
Psalms of David in Metre and Concordance
A Concise Treatise on the Evidences of the Genuineness, Authenticity,
Inspiration, Preservation, and Value of the Word of God
A Chronological Index to the Bible, A Complete List of Scripture
Proper Names, A History of the Translations Into English, Tables of the
Parables, Miracles, and Discourses of Jesus Christ
And a Variety of Useful and Valuable Tabular and Other Exploratory
and Explanatory Matter.
Together With
A New and Improved
DICTIONARY OF THE BIBLE
Compiled from the latest and best sources, with important additions.
The whole designed to facilitate the study and promote the better
understanding of the Holy Scriptures
By Rev. Alfred Nevin, D.D.
Author of "A Popular Commentary on Luke," "The Churches of the
Valley," "A Guide to the Oracles," etc. etc.
Illustrated with more than Two Hundred Maps, Plans, and
Engravings, on wood and steel

The W.M. Flint Bible Company's top seller came similarly equipped for educational improvement, inspiring the company's man in Rochester to exclaim, "Bible readers purchase this Bible when they have many other Bibles on hand, for the library of information complete in cheap form."[23]

Victorian salesmen rarely carried more than one or two entire Bibles of this sort – efficient, considering the sheer weight of some of these encyclopedic behemoths – but instead transported only those portions intended to pique the seller's interest and ensure that no book was delivered until the bill was paid in full. They carried less weighty books called "Dummies": partial models or mock-ups of their product. The dummy Bibles displayed to potential subscribers usually consisted of a sample cover, representative pages of maps or charts, and examples of additions like family record pages, photo albums, and illustrations.[24] Or salesmen lugged "portfolios": small portions of several different books complete with their covers. The whole was then bound together and folded. When opened, these sample books turned into traveling display cases, exhibiting an impressive variety of scriptural gimcracks for purchase over time.[25]

Or salesmen could simply carry catalogues into bookstores as well as individual homes. The P.W. Ziegler Company's 1918 *Catalogue of Selected Books and Bibles*, containing exhaustive and glowing depictions, with illustrations, of "THE FINEST BIBLES IN THE WORLD AT CUT PRICES," described an astounding set of variations on the familiar King James Version, now offered to the public with dozens of mix-and-match details. The catalogue, a tribute to Yankee ingenuity (the press was located in Philadelphia), is impressive evidence of the power of marketing to precisely defined market niches, their descriptions providing, in effect, so many mirrors in which a reader could find him- or herself reflected. Ziegler Bibles were named for imaginary groups of like-minded readers: the *Sunday Teachers' Bible*, the *International Christian Worker's New Testament*. They were named after pious desire: the *Words of Jesus Bible*, the *Precious Promises Bible*. They were developed and designed to be more convenient (at least according to the catalogue copy) than any other Bible on offer anywhere. One page illustrates the convenience of a soft-cover Bible by providing a drawing of a large hand holding it rolled up as if to smack an errant puppy – or child (the "limp and overlapping cover styles are so durably and so flexibly bound they can be rolled without injury to binding and sewing"); other pages tout the

48 A sample of the P.W. Ziegler Co.'s scriptural wares.

advantages of large-type ("suitable for Old Folks") or red-letter ("words printed in red catch the eye, and carry the words of Jesus to the heart of every reader") formats.[26]

Rubrication and "marked reference" seem, in fact, to have been particular selling points for Ziegler's diverse offerings. The *Precious Promises Testament* was, according to its sales blurb:

> ... marked and edited by J. Gilchrist Lawson, author of *Best Method of Bible Marking*, of the markings in the "Christian Workers Testament" and the "Precious Promise Edition of the International Bible," and of most of the markings of the "International Red-Letter Bible." Mr. Lawson has marked more Bibles and Testaments than all who have preceded him. He is the foremost authority on Bible Marking.[27]

Lawson (1874–1946) seems to have dominated a field bounded only by the range of the P.W. Ziegler Company. Despite the fact that he created *dozens* of red-letter versions of the Christian Bible, his authority rested on more than being the World's Foremost Bible Marker. Gilchrist was also a tireless author: on Christian themes (*Deeper Experiences of Famous Christians*, 1919, *The Greatest Thoughts about the Bible*, 1918, to name only two), as well as on more secular topics (*The World's Best Epigrams*, 1924; *The World's Best Conundrums & Riddles of All Ages*, also 1924; *The World's Best Humorous Anecdotes: Wit and Repartee*, 1923). He wrote books on farm animals, dog breeds, and the "102 leading sights of America." In short, Mr Lawson was an inveterate collector – of phrases, jokes, dogs, as well as the words of Jesus Christ.

Several of Lawson's marked Bibles and other books are still reprinted today (one, *The Marked Reference New Testament Chain of Reference System for Bible Study*, is advertised on Amazon.com as being co-authored "by J. Gilchrist Lawson and Holy Spirit"). One particular quote from Lawson, in *The Greatest Thoughts about Jesus Christ*, a declaration that the "historical evidences" of the existence of Jesus were stronger than any other recorded event of ancient history, is currently a feature of several Christian websites purporting to prove the existence of a historical Jesus. In these Lawson is invariably described as a "historian." The quote proves only that Lawson was a man of his age, searching for historical facts to prove the Bible's narrative veracity, collecting every interesting thing he came across along the way, and displaying these all in "encyclopedic" range and variety.

Travelers' Bibles

Salesmen generally do not forge new paths; they follow paths broken by their customers. By the early twentieth century the American migratory impulse had become a thing of automobiles and better-paved, more extensive roadways. The most significant, most characteristic, and least considered scriptural contribution to this newly mobile modern age was the "Gideon Bible." In the early twentieth century, the scriptures became an integral part of the modern era of restlessness, perhaps the only thing one could count on when on the road for business, pleasure, or a new job.

The Gideons, a non-denominational group founded for the purposes of Christian evangelism in 1899, took their name from the victorious warrior of the Book of Judges and their inspiration from an earlier, informal nineteenth-century drive to place "wholesome literature" in British hotel rooms. In 1908, they pledged to place the Bible in every hotel in America, making good their resolve by stocking the rooms of the Superior Hotel in Superior, Wisconsin. By mid-century, their charitable reach had extended to other, less comfortable, homes away from home: schools, hospitals, the armed forces, and prisons. Occasional drives to remove Gideon Bibles from schools (mostly in America) and hospitals (mostly in Britain) and the determination to place other sacred texts such as the Book of Mormon (in Utah) and Al Gore's *An Inconvenient Truth* (in northern California) have done little to reduce their ubiquity in the rooms people occupy temporarily.

Seemingly everywhere (under the local telephone book in a top drawer; in a line of a Beatles song) and nowhere (scholarly essays, in

This Holy Book, whose leaves display
the LIFE, the LIGHT, the TRUTH, the WAY

is placed in this room by

 The Gideons

The Christian Commercial Travelers' Association of America
AIDED BY
THE CHRISTIAN FORCES OF THIS CITY
With the hope also that by means of this Book many may be
brought to know the love of Christ which passeth knowledge.

A Mother, Comforted by the "Word" as expressed
on her Son's Tomb.

"My Son, aged 21. Died in his youth, but saved
by grace through faith in Jesus Christ."—Mother.
HOW ABOUT YOUR MOTHER?

The Ancient Gideon's Test and Triumph—Judges 6 and 7.
The Modern Gideon's Motto—Judges 7 : 21.
The Greatest Sermon ever preached—Matthew 5, 6 and 7.
BLESSED TRUTH—ACCEPT IT. Luke 19: 10: John 3-16.
The Supreme Sacrifice for all—Isaiah 53.
The Universal Invitation to all—Isaiah 55.

If lonesome or blue and friends untrue, read Psalms
23 and 27. Luke 15.
If trade is poor, read Psalm 37. John 15.
If discouraged or in trouble, read Psalm 126 ; John 14.
If you are all out of sorts, read Hebrews 12.
If you are losing confidence in men, read 1 Cor. 13.
If skeptical, read John 6 : 40 ; 7 : 17 ; Phil. 2 : 9-11
If you can't have your own way, read James 3.
If tired of sin, read Luke 18: 9-14; 18: 35-43; John 9.
If very prosperous, read 1 Cor. 10 : 12, 13.
The Wonderful Result—Isaiah 35—Ps. 121—Rom. 12.

We earnestly solicit free will offerings for the aid of our
Bible work.
Christian Traveling Men, Join Us, Help Us
For particulars, enquire of any man wearing the emblem, or
The Gideons
140 S. Dearborn Street   CHICAGO, ILL.

49 An early twentieth-century Gideon bookplate.

the home), Gideon Bibles are instantly recognizable by their prefatory matter. The pages outline the portrait of an occasional reader residing in an off-ramp counterculture: the hotel or motel bedroom. The transient state of a Gideon Bible reader is itself transient, of course: what has brought the traveler to this place will require the traveler to depart. But Gideon Bibles treat brief stays in unfamiliar places as prime moments for biblical intervention, and so they are prefaced with efficient guides for easily looking up specific scriptural verses. They offer the following citations under HELP IN TIME OF NEED: "Comfort in the Time of Loneliness: Psalm 23; Isaiah 41: 10; Hebrews 13: 5"; "Guidance in Time of Decision: James 1: 5, 6; Proverbs 3: 5, 6"; "Strength in Time of Temptation: James 1: 12–16; 1 Corinthians 10: 6–13." But the alluring dangers of being a stranger in a strange land seem most acute on the page entitled PRACTICAL PRECEPTS, which cites among the "Great Themes of Scripture" passages relating to "the sin of adultery," "the prodigal son," and the "consequences of forgetting God."

A shrewd understanding of those who live out of suitcases in the pursuit of sales, then, is what distinguishes the Gideons, reflecting the condition of their own lives as lay businessmen (and now, women). "The Lord has opened doors for the placement of His Word among many strategic groups of the population and in places through which large and important streams of people pass from day to day," their Bibles declare: a mission statement that brings us up with a start.[28] In it we clearly hear the echoes of medieval mendicants' and missionary footsteps, and recognize the Bible's capacity for speaking not only *to* the restless, but also *for* their equally restless purveyors.

Conclusion

While we may smile at some of the phrases, puzzle at the special attractions, and wince at under-financed attempts to make stamped cardboard Bible covers look antique, we will also have to acknowledge that, despite our condescending smiles, the world of the late eighteenth and nineteenth centuries was not all that quaint, nor all

that different from ours. The Bible's new appearances and appurte-
nances in this age reflected as well as shaped the needs of the rapidly
transforming culture of Christianity itself. As Protestantism frag-
mented into denominations, like the Methodists moving across
America, its Bibles were as fervently bought and sold as they were
read and expounded. And so, the scriptures' seemingly inexhaustible
malleability in appealing to (to quote the Gideons) "strategic groups
of the population" will be the subject of the next chapter, as we move
from the modern age to a post-modern one.

CHAPTER EIGHT

OLD WINE IN NEW WINESKINS

THE BIBLE IN THE TWENTIETH CENTURY

"Man and woman a simultaneous creation, with an equal title deed to this green earth/Gen.," wrote Elizabeth Cady Stanton inside a copy of her most famous work, *The Woman's Bible*, dedicating it to the Kearney (New Jersey) Suffrage Club. The inscription referred not only to Stanton's commitment to a woman's right to vote, but also to *Woman's Bible*'s radical re-reading of the Book of Genesis, which took as inspiration and provocation the fact that there are two versions of the Creation story. Chapter 1 of the Book of Genesis states only "male and female He created them," while Genesis 2 concludes with Adam missing a rib and declaring that Woman was "taken out of Man." For centuries, the Bible had presented its readers with two different stories of what transpired in Eden, and, unlike biblical commentators before her, Stanton was sticking only to the first one.

A collaborative work by Stanton and a committee of female scholars, *The Woman's Bible: Comments on Genesis, Exodus, Leviticus, Numbers and Deuteronomy* (published in 1895 complete with advertisements for the suffragist magazine *The National*) provided forthright, unsentimental, thoroughly unabashed feminist commentary on scripture. The committee's labors were driven, as they wrote in

Jan 15 - 1900   250 W 94
For the Members of the   N.Y.
Kearney Suffrage Club
with the Compliments of the Author
Elizabeth Cady Stanton
"Man and woman a simultaneous creation,
with an equal title deed to this green earth
Gen. chap I - 27 - 28 verse"

50 Elizabeth Cady Stanton's dedication to the Kearney Suffrage Club, 15 January 1900 found in a copy of *The Woman's Bible*.

the preface, by social acceptance of women's seemingly sanctified state of oppression:

> [T]heir clergymen told them on the one hand that they owed all the blessing and freedom they enjoyed to the Bible, on the other hand, they said it clearly marked out their circumscribed sphere of action: that [their] demands for political and civil rights were irreligious, dangerous to the stability of the home . . .[1]

The Woman's Bible is proof of what can happen when an unhappy band of domestic angels decide to quit dusting their family Bibles and start reading them with clear-eyed apprehension. Its tone was exhilarated, more gleefully engaged in the slaughter of sacred cows than was suitable for works of traditional biblical scholarship. The committee was unapologetically one-sided, providing commentary only for the passages in the Bible that referred directly to women or had special interest in or to women. The approach had its benefits: "as all such passages combined form but one-tenth of the entire

Bible," Stanton dryly noted, their undertaking was not "so laborious as, at the first thought, one would imagine."[2] Her observation expressed a feeling, growing among educated Victorian women on both sides of the Atlantic (although the American movement was more explicitly tied to religious critique, and thus by extension religion altogether, than Mrs Emmeline Pankhurst's) that the Bible, undoubtedly written by men, had been exclusively interpreted by men, who for generations had employed scripture as unassailable evidence of women's essential inferiority.

"Mrs. Stanton's Bible" was, predictably, roundly condemned by outraged clergymen and politicians who had long been willing to quote scripture to *their* own ends. They charged *The Woman's Bible* with corrupting both women and the sanctity of Holy Writ. And they had a point. In rejecting traditional biblical interpretation, *The Woman's Bible* challenged not only the authority of the messengers, but also the authority of the message, shocking many and delighting others. "The Bible is no more inspired than the dictionary," wrote a Marilla R. Richter to a Mrs Foster Morse in the flyleaf of an 1898 edition of *The Woman's Bible* – a sentiment that might have made *Mr* Foster Morse more than a bit anxious.

As for the critics who charged her with irredeemable blasphemy, Stanton blandly, if wickedly, inquired whether anyone had asked other biblical scholars "to stop their work on the ground it was ridiculous for *men* to revise the Bible."[3] Now *she* had a point. Audacious as *The Woman's Bible* seemed at the time, it had merely capped off two centuries of increasingly daring and skeptical academic scrutiny of the Bible by men: historical, linguistic, and archeological explorations that had finally led to a call for a new official version of the Bible in 1870. It was the staid English Revised Version of the Bible published in 1881, not Stanton's audacious commentary on the King James Version, that most powerfully demonstrated the loosening of the English-speaking world's ties to the Bible it had inherited from King James I.

This first significant revision of the English Bible since 1611 finally ushered in what might seem to us by now a very overdue second age of scriptural translation. The dizzying velocity of change in social institutions and communications technology, in fact, can make the twentieth century seem uncannily akin to the sixteenth in many ways: here, as then, new translations again paved the way for other, more material, forms of scriptural refashioning. But twentieth-century folk were no longer the readers envisaged by ambitious Protestant theologians and translators but *consumers*, nudged into pluralistic being by enterprising publishers and the nascent field of market research. Once the driving force behind the publishing phenomenon we now call "mass media," the Bible was eventually forced to share its audience with novels, newspapers, and magazines by the middle of the nineteenth century. It could only face new challenges in the pluralistic and diversifying religious marketplace of an even more commercial and secular twentieth century.[4]

Was nothing, then, sacred? This chapter examines relationships between the English-language Bible and the modern marketing of Bible reading, questioning how far the Bible's new styles and audiences in the twentieth century represented a sorry capitulation to secular, consumer culture. We will find, to our surprise, perhaps, that the scriptural text remained remarkably stable for a book with diverse and contested origins. The social and cultural expectations of its readers, however, did not.

A New Age of Translation

Confronted with the combined forces of university biblical scholarship and the discovery of more, and more ancient, biblical texts than had been available in the seventeenth century, the Authorized Version was starting to look well past its intellectual sell-by date by the second half of the nineteenth century. Accordingly, the Church of England convened a committee to revise the one English-language version of the Bible in extensive use on both sides of the Atlantic since the early seventeenth century. They promised "as few alterations as possible" and to keep its modes of expression in "the language of the Authorized and earlier English versions." The result of their labors was the English

Revised Version (ERV), published by Oxford University Press in 1881: the first Bible in English to be extensively and definitively revised by authority since 1611.

The ERV emerged to a din of happy anticipation that turned, within a few short weeks, into roars of British disdain. Educated clerics thought it (in the words of "Prince of Preachers" Charles Spurgeon) "strong in Greek, weak in English." Others found it (as the Bishop of Durham reported) devoid of "that ENGLISH felicity . . . which should entitle it to take the place of the Authorized Version in our national heart."[5] Britons of unequal education but equally scandalized ears suddenly all found that seventeenth-century English sounded better to them than the dry-as-dust formulations of up-to-date scholarship. They missed the style of the AV, which, after more than two centuries of ecclesiastical and domestic usage, had been bred, deeply, enduringly, and apparently permanently, into their bones. Faced with this widespread evidence of clerical and lay obduracy, the Church of England swiftly decided to make adoption of the new version optional, with the consequence that the ERV was relegated to the scholar's study (it seems only two churches in the whole of England elected to use it in their services) while the AV remained in English churches and English hearts.[6]

This new version had also been hotly anticipated in America, where it made the news – literally in the case of Chicago, where the 22 May 1881 *Daily Tribune* and *Times* both featured the entire text of the ERV New Testament, tucked behind the usual phalanx of ads touting buggies, coal, hair tonic, and upright pianos. (Newspapers of this era generally placed all their advertisements on the front page, a practice to which neither the *Tribune* nor the *Times* took exception.) One Chicago department store, Sea's, offered copies of the newspaper free to those it designated "The Pious Poor" ("3 cts. charged to those able to pay. Same nicely bound, 12 cts."), inspiring the excitable writers of the *Tribune*'s headlines to warn its readers to "COME EARLY!" to avoid the "CROWDS! CROWDS!" that would become "JAMMEDLY JAMMED!" Whether these exclamations were designed to fan excitement for the content of the English

Revised New Testament or the contents of Sea's Department Store is an excellent, if unanswerable, question.[7]

In any case, Americans were no more pleased with the new version than their counterparts across the Atlantic had been. The ERV was essentially a British product, despite the presence of a small cohort of American scholars on the revision committee.[8] The rapid spread of American-English usage, a major transformation in the English-language world since the eighteenth century, had not figured in the new translation, despite the fact that by this time America had become by far the largest domestic market for the Bible it still called the "King James." At the urgent request of the revision committee members who hailed from the United States, a substitute list of American words and phrases was hastily appended to the British version, a jury-rigged measure that then haunted the American committee for more than a decade. The committee had promised their British counterparts not to bring out an American edition of the ERV for another fourteen years, during which time, predictably, several enterprising if less scrupulous American publishers were able to employ the addendum as a cheat sheet in printing their unauthorized versions of the Bible.

Finally, in 1901, the surviving American members of the original revision committee – faithful remnant indeed, by this time – got to transfer these words and expressions, plus a significant number of other American words and phrases the British committee had not considered worth considering at all, out of the ERV's back pages and into a text they could now call the *American* Revised Version.[9] What were these characteristically Yankee locutions? Some were innocuous examples of Anglo-American differences in everyday usage: the American "wheat" for the British "corn," for example. Some seem to have traded peculiarly British forms of prudery for peculiarly American ones: "lewd" for "whorish," for example. Some gestured at nativist Protestantism, an attitude that continued to rear its ugly head with every influx of European Catholic immigrants into the US: "love" for "charity" in First Corinthians, for example, may have downplayed the doctrines of good works and intercession that many

Protestants thought defined Catholicism. And some responded to the more lurid cultural obsessions of antebellum America: "Holy Spirit" instead of "Holy Ghost," for example. (The obsession with séances and spiritualism that flourished after the American Civil War had made people familiar with the wrong sort of ghosts.[10])

But while Britain remained content with its Authorized Version, the publication of the American Revised Version ushered in a fervent half-century of translation and revision in the United States, with each new scholarly foray into Holy Writ threatening to sully the scripture's sacred nature. The Bible's sanctity seemed to rest on old sound rather than new sense, a cultural predilection demonstrated once again in 1947 with the publication in the US of the New Testament in the Revised Standard Version. Anticipating the usual resistance, the editors of the RSV wrote as much about the things they had left undone than the things they had done: "The Revised Standard Version is not a new translation in the language of today . . ." they wrote, reassuringly, in its preface. "It . . . seeks to preserve all that is best in the English Bible as it has been known and used throughout the years," they continued, intent on being regarded as conservators rather than innovators.

To some readers, the RSV revisers' promise seemed to suggest that the preservation of the Bible's sacred status was a matter of remembering its emergence in English translation, rather than its origins in Greek and Hebrew texts. In America the RSV became the most widely accepted and best known of the twentieth-century translations of the Bible (in Britain it was, like the ERV before it, simply snubbed out of all useful existence) but did not succeed in dethroning King James. In an age of rapid change in morals and mores, the sound of "thee" and "begat" voiced ancient and timeless truths to those Christians whose notion of scriptural purity became ever more stubbornly fixed on 1611.

The revision committee had eliminated much of the KJV's archaic language from the RSV, a decision that seems simply to have etched the cadences of the KJV more deeply onto the hearts of Bible-loving evangelicals and, especially and more lastingly, biblical fundamentalists. America's love affair with the KJV reminds us that the language of Shakespeare and the sonorous liturgical rhythms of the Church of England had formed an essential building block of common speech in many parts of the United States. The King James Version's elegant archaisms resonated like a cradle language in regions often lacking in high culture or higher education, out-of-the-way places where even the poorest and most unworldly Christians still hung onto stately Elizabethan imagery by the very tips of their tongues.

These days the King James Bible reigns supreme in two very different settings: mainstream British Anglican and traditionalist American Episcopalian congregations, where it pairs perfectly with the 1662 (or 1928) Book of Common Prayer; and, seemingly far to the other side of the spectrum, the fundamentalist, independent, mostly Baptist congregations that call themselves "King James Only Churches." Adherents of this movement (there are hundreds of US churches listed in telephone and website directories as "King James Only" (KJO); one international website lists six British churches), claim the King James is no *version*, liable to revision and retranslation, but a King James *Bible* – the only Bible acceptable for worship. This is not, however, merely a matter of how it sounds. One well-known proponent of KJO, Gail Riplinger, claims in her books and on her website that the KJV "teaches and comforts through its miraculous mathematically ordered sounds," but King James Only believers do not simply prefer the Authorized Version's fluent cadences or its merrie olde locutions. And they do not, like the anti-immigrant and famously corrupt governor of 1940s' Texas, "Ma" Ferguson, prefer the KJV because they think the King's English was good enough for Jesus Christ. Instead, the King James Only movement believes that the Authorized Version is the only scriptural text that can be considered inerrant for English-speaking Christians. Representing an inspired line that began with Wycliffe, ran through Tyndale, and ended at 1611, they believe it has the same direct claim to divine inspiration as scripture's ancient originals. Promulgated in heated website debates, unaccredited Bible colleges, and privately financed publications, the

NEW TESTAMENT
BAPTIST CHURCH

70478 Twentynine Palms Hwy.
Twentynine Palms, CA 92277
(760) 366-7836

Dr. William J. Pasquini
Pastor

Standing for: The KJV as God's preserved,
infallible, inerrant, inspired WORD. The deity
of Christ, His blood atonement, salvation by
faith and New Testament soulwinning.

51 Pamphlet supplied by the Twentynine Palms Baptist Church.

arguments forwarded by the King James Only movement begin with a call to remember English textual origins that possesses a certain logic (the English translation was one of the first ones accessible to English speakers, after all, predating the founding of the US – and, besides, no one has yet located the Greek and Hebrew originals). They end, however, in distinctly less rational warnings of Satanic conspiracies to water down the truth of the Gospel with new, corrupted translations of God's Truth.

Given the fervor for translating and paraphrasing that has characterized the American Bible market for the past forty years, we might figure that the proponents of King James Only are merely reacting with bad grace to the spectacle of their once familiar and nearly universal English scriptural world turned upside down. The twenty-first century future will most likely not favor the King James Version, whose discernible decline in the past three decades is less attributable to disenchantment with its quaint locutions or level of background scholarship than it is to major changes in Christian worship patterns. According to a study by the American Bible Society, to be successful scripture translations must complement the sounds and cadences of congregational worship, and even Sunday mornings are beginning to look and sound a lot different than they did in the 1940s.

These trends began with the vernacularization, in the directive promulgated by the Second Vatican Council (1962–5), of the Latin Mass, followed by a rise in alternative Protestant and, more recently, non-denominational services, all of which led to the publication of a myriad "new" translations of the Bible in the busy second half of the twentieth century: the *New International Version* (1978), the *New King James Version* (1979), the *New Jerusalem Bible* (1985), the *New Revised Standard Edition* (1989). For all their claim to improvement, however, every title tells us as much about the preservation of traditional expectations: proclaiming not newness but a mildly updated fidelity to what has always been. Take away the *New*, after all, and we are left with the *old*: the International Bible (KJV), the King James Version, the Jerusalem Bible, the Revised Standard Version.

This might sound surprising, especially if we believe the elaborate apologies for traditional scripture made by late twentieth-century Bible editors. "God never intended the Bible to be too difficult for his people," write the translators of *Revolve*, a magazine-format presentation of the New Testament (*New International Version*) aimed at teenage girls. The *ExtremeTeen Bible* (also NIV) explains the Bible's eccentricities with bravado: "It's authentic. It's extreme. No fears. No regrets."[11] Recent editorial teams assert that their translation is both intellectually sound and faithful to the closest possible approximation of scriptural origins, making the case that timeless truth can nonetheless be clothed in contemporary fashions.

The most fashion-conscious of these, the teen-magazine format Bibles *Revolve* and *Refuel*, contain the complete text of the New Testament in the *New Century* translation (NCV), a version that is explained and justified at some length at the beginning of both. (The verse on the title page of *Revolve* offers Proverbs 31:30 in NCV: "Charm can fool you, and beauty can trick you, but a woman who respects the LORD should be praised." The King James Version is: "Favour is deceitful, and beauty is vain: but a woman that feareth the Lord, she shall be praised.") For their part, the translators of the *New Century Bible* claim the Bible is currently seen as irrelevant to everyday life, a problem they blame on difficult language rather than difficult tenets. In its original form, they write, the Bible was accessible: "the authors of the Bible recorded God's word in familiar, everyday language." They now offer a "clearer" version for the sake of recognition and familiarity:

> The *New Century Version* captures the clear and simple message that the very first readers understood. This version presents the Bible as God intended it . . . A team of scholars from the World Bible Translation Center worked together with twenty-one other experienced Bible scholars from all over the world to translate the text directly from the best available Greek and Hebrew texts. You can trust that this Bible accurately presents God's Word as it came to us in the original languages. Translators kept sentences

short and simple. They avoided difficult words and worked to make the text easier to read.

The *New Century* is, then, not a translation but a paraphrase: "thought for thought" rather than "word for word." And so the translators must tout their scholarly accuracy and the purity of their base texts even more vehemently, while at the same time providing exactly the same sorts of reassurance we have seen offered by revisers of translations. Where the Bible is concerned, to claim to be radically new (as opposed to simply "radical," as is common in new Bibles designed for teens and older children) is still, it seems, to commit a kind of heresy, even at the end of the twentieth century. We have heard these concerns before: from John Wycliffe, William Tyndale, the translators working for King James I of England, and the translators of the ERV, the ARV and the RSV.

Old Wine in New Bottles

While Protestants spent the twentieth century dividing into even more churches, their Bibles multiplying into even more translations and paraphrases, Roman Catholicism underwent a far more radical transformation. Although Catholics had access to the vernacular Bible throughout the modern era, they had not been encouraged to read the Bible privately and their church services were still organized around the performance of the Mass rather than the preaching of the Word. The second Vatican Council changed all that, not by shifting the focus of worship but instead by directing that the Mass now be delivered in the languages of everyday life. The liturgy in English now contained the Bible in English, and Catholic educators and priests were soon calling for a large-scale program in biblical education.

One material result of this call was the printing of one of the first mass-produced modern study Bibles, and surely the most intriguing given the history of Catholicism's historic restrictions on direct lay reading of the Bible: *The Catholic Study Bible* of 1970.[12] "From the beginning of its existence," its editor, Donald Senior wrote, frankly acknowledging the fractious relationship Catholicism often had with lay scriptural interpretation and access, "the Bible has been the object of intense study, prayerful reading, and even heated debate." That study, reading, and debate had been conducted almost entirely in priestly circles, but now

> that trend has been radically reversed. The Second Vatican Council gave a strong impetus to a biblical renewal in every dimension of Catholicism . . .

The *Catholic Study Bible* thus represents a major shift in official attitudes to lay Bible reading: orientation to access through study is meant to replicate the intensely scholarly examinations of scripture once undertaken only by priests and seminary students. "The Bible is not meant to be a coffee-table book," Senior states briskly, and the *Catholic Study Bible*'s appearance – textbook-sized, paperbacked, and bristling with in-depth scholarly apparatus – surely supports the assertion.

On the other hand, this Bible is also a manual of Catholic tradition, which continues to regard Bible study as a corporate, rather than individual, act. "The Bible is the Church's book, not a private library," Senior reminds readers:

> Whatever approach one takes to reading and praying the Bible, it is important from a Catholic perspective that it not be done in isolation. Only in the context of the Church's faith and tradition as a whole can the full meaning of the Bible be discovered . . . Some Christians who isolate themselves from common sense and from the sound wisdom of the Church community can interpret the Scripture in a bizarre and even destructive manner.

The verso of the title page is inscribed with *nihil obstat*, signifying that the Church has approved the publication of this Bible and endorses its use by Roman Catholics. This study Bible – carefully prepared and intellectually challenging – was not, then, designed to inspire individual interpretation, which might lead a reader into the thickets of unorthodox doctrine. Once again we are reminded, as we were in the history of the reformation Bible, that increased access to scripture does not necessarily mean an increase of liberty in its interpretation.

Unless, of course, we factor in another historic truism: once the Bible gets into people's hands, there's no telling what they'll think once they have read it – and, indeed, where the Bible will go next. Evangelical publishing houses in America have lately produced an impressively large and ever-proliferating number of translations, paraphrases, and packaged versions of the Bible, each tailored to meet the specific cultural expectations of conservative Bible readers living in a secular world: a world that can seem, to some evangelicals, oppressively hostile, and, to others, worth learning from. Evangelical marketing makes good use of both these attitudes at the same time, producing a kind of counterculture of familiarity. Its scripture publishers ply their wares with a cleverly defiant panache that has entirely eluded other, more liberal, Bible markets. Currently, then, the hotter sort of today's Protestants can buy Bibles with eye-catching bindings that look like cheerful, ingratiating teen magazines, and Bibles in plain covers meant to prevent curious onlookers from discerning the Bible reader in their midst. Both are advertised as choices necessary to the public practice of evangelical piety.

In a world obsessed with " new and improved," certain changes to the Bible are inevitable. Increasingly sophisticated marketing strategies have made it possible for publishers to design Bibles with a wide variety of editorial additions and precisely aimed and calibrated study aids and commentaries. The market now also boasts a dizzying array of Bibles in which scriptural content can be tailored, with a set of interchangeable insert "modules," to the needs of particular age and ethnic groups: the *Women of color Study Bible (King James Version)* or the *Promise Keeper's Bible for Men*, as well as Bibles designed for "special interest groups": recovering addicts

52 Teaching module insert for the Book of Acts, *Women of Color Study Bible.*

(*The Twelve-Step Bible*), pre-pubescent romantics (*The Princess Bible for Girls*), hormonally addled teenagers (*The True Love Waits Bible*), computer-gaming middle-schoolers (*KidsBible.com*). There is even a set of products – including specially designed covers and excerpted Bibles for children and teens – named for *What Would Jesus Do?*, which not only trades on the acronym once so predominant on rubber wristbands, but also seems, at least to *this* writer, a bit redundant.

This catch-them-where-they-live approach defines the market strategies of the Bibles designed for older children and teenagers by innovative Bible publishers, which (almost without exception) tend to socially and theologically conservative views. These views they package as countercultural, in a world characterized as hostile to evangelical beliefs and offensive to its sensibilities. Pre-adolescence and adolescence can be stormily disobedient times; the new teen

Bibles package conformity to parental and church mores as a form of edgy, radical behavior. "God inspired a book that . . . gave us a picture of the out-on-a-limb life that is the life of faith," state the editors of *Revolve*, the magazine Bible first published in 2003. "The whole Bible is really about God connecting with us through Jesus Christ. He was the truest revolutionary of all time. He lived through a life just like ours, with its frustrations and hard times . . . THIS BIBLE IS A SURVIVAL GUIDE."

The new teen-oriented Bibles are not exactly anti-cultural, however. To define and attract this audience calls for a careful incorporation of current secular phenomena: hip-hop; extreme sports; video game geekery; text-messaging; lip gloss (these trends, of course, have changed more than once in the time it took for me to finish this chapter – and will continue to, dozens of times, before it comes out in print) while stressing that the truly Christian teen is never ultimately in thrall to secular fads, but only to Jesus. This leads, unsurprisingly, to some intriguingly mixed messages (for which reason alone they probably make a lot of sense to adolescents, who spend their junior high and high school years being treated as independent consumers umbilically connected to parental purse-strings). The removable sticker on the metallic cover of one such teen Bible solemnly announces: "The world is a rapidly changing place, but some things will always remain the same. Truth is truth. Time doesn't change it. The Bible may be old, but so are the ideas of Plato, Aristotle, and Socrates. Real wisdom is timeless. That's what you'll find in here."[13] It has been designed to resemble a pop-top soda can.

Likewise, *Revolve* is a flimsy, disposable teen magazine in look and feel (and intention), but each issue contains the full text of the New Testament. The product of extensive market analysis, *Revolve* (whose advent in 2003 was breathlessly covered in most sectors of the print media, including especially bemused commentary from the *New York Times* and the *New Yorker*) comes complete with scripturally informed tips for teenage girls seeking guidance on such issues as dating, piercings, strict parents, and obnoxious little brothers. The editors describe the extra-scriptural format:

53 The 2003 cover of *Revolve* magazine.

Each book [of the Gospels: Matthew, Mark, Luke, and John] has an *Introduction* written specifically to help answer these kinds of questions. There are other special features to help you get as deep inside the Bible as you can. *Blabs* are questions and answers with experts on a variety of topics important to you every day. *Promises* point out the commitments that God makes to us. *Learn It and Live It* gives real-life application of tons of Bible verses. *Bible Bios* tell the stories of real-life girls who lived during the Bible times. *Beauty Secrets* shows ways you can beautify your inner-self. There are notes on *Relationships* and *Issues* that you deal with daily. *Guys Speak Out!* gives you the opinion of real-life teen guys on questions you wonder about. There's just a ton of info for you to learn from. It's all here – truth, inspiration, bottom-line *actual* reality. Are you up for the challenge?

"Actual reality" in *Revolve* demands responses that in an earlier age might have been covered in the monastic counsels of perfection: chastity and obedience make frequent appearances, with denial, if not exactly poverty, also entering into the marginal discussions. These imaginative conversations (there is no way of knowing exactly where, or from whom, the editors got their interlocutors) are not, as a skeptical observer might expect, relentlessly simplistic and oppressive, but nuanced: the only approach, if you think about it, that would satisfy teens faced with a book less fallible and more authoritative than a strict parent. On the issue of body art, to cite one example, the girl who writes "is it OK to get a tattoo?" is told that, if she considers only the words of scripture on the subject, she will find none to help her: "tattooing" is not specifically banned in the Bible. Disobedience, on the other hand, *is*; parents are to be obeyed in all things not specifically prescribed or proscribed in the Bible if not in "things against God." The inquiring girl is advised to ask her parents and to accept their decision, in a spot-on, if teen-oriented, demonstration of scriptural comparison and exegesis.

Published in its first edition one year later, and aimed at adolescent boys, the magazine-format New Testament *Refuel* features sidebars that teach everything from how to change the oil in your car to how to wrestle an alligator (this last written, if not meant, in all seriousness). Like *Revolve*, *Refuel* also features tips for everyday life, only these are called, pointedly (as if adolescent boys need to be hit between the eyes with the two-by-four of direct command at all times), *Dos and Don'ts* rather than *Revolve*'s gentler *Learn It and Live It*. The strictures are rough and ready, concentrating on basic hygiene rather than Maybelline and employing snarky humor to lighten the bossy tone: "*Do* use Deodorant/ *Don't* Surf in Shark-Infested Waters."

While obviously modeled on *Revolve* in terms of both approach and format, *Refuel* is self-consciously guyish, with advice columns like: "Ten Non-Girly Ways to Make A Friend Feel Better." Its warnings center on steroids, STDs, driving and drinking, with one blurb on date rape. *Refuel* shows an equivalent amount of concern with pre-marital chastity as *Revolve*, but speaks more of the risks of disease than of pregnancy. It touts the excitement and worth of foreign mission with an enthusiastic, tub-thumping regularity one only finds in *Revolve* on matters of modest, if stylish, dress (*Revolve* girls are not encouraged to take up mission work with the same intensity). This defensive, Christians-are-*not*-wimps-or-nerds persona takes a breather in the Christian music reviews, which are briskly informative.

The teens gracing the magazine covers of *Revolve* and *Refuel* are very attractive, with bright and open smiles: an image that underscores the magazine Bibles' assertion that the young evangelicals created by sidebars, asides, and commentary on the inside are confident in their public selves. Their embrace of the social mores of evangelical Christianity is packaged as daring and revolutionary. The non-Christian world they stand out against (which, the magazine's commentaries suggest, constitutes a powerful and oppressive cultural majority in America) can be summed up in a few cultural stereotypes: non-chastity, homosexuality, drug use, and relativisms, both social and religious.

This last is, to be sure, carefully parsed. While conceding that the Bible contains some proscriptions that are universal and others that

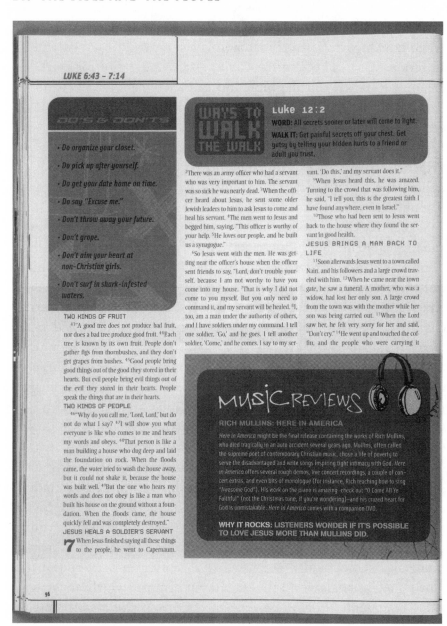

54 A page from *Refuel's* Book of Luke.

only made sense in the context of the culture that produced it, homosexuality and unbelief are unequivocally condemned – and so become inextricably bound up with each other. Teen readers are counseled without qualification that they are not to associate with gays, even as platonic friends. They are also instructed not to associate with non-Christians except to pray for them and "share their faith" with them as well as they can. Other religions are described as invalid (this last particularly uncompromising as presented in *Refuel*, with its concentration on foreign mission work). Going farther, both magazines insist that the Bible says that Christian churches that do not teach specifically that people "must be saved" are not true churches, thus making stark distinctions even between different denominations and iterations of Christianity.

Overall *Revolve* and *Refuel* are stylish versions of the Gospel. They sport a jazzy look, spout an affable and irreverent tone, and possess a clever, throwaway appeal placed alongside their "timeless message." The magazine format makes it possible to update and reset the commentary and blurbs, thus nimbly gauging the current teen-cultural scene and playing to it, while keeping the words that run down the center of both pages sacrosanct. Here we see evidenced, then, the fact that, no matter how much novelty it employs to deliver its message, religious radicalism is nearly always, at its heart, religiously and socially conservative. These Bibles resemble nothing more than the Geneva Bible of 1560, which was also a translation nearly overshadowed by *its* marginal notes, prefaces, charts, and adjunct material – all designed to draw the portrait of a true Christian in the second half of the sixteenth century, a time of social and religious peril for the newly emergent evangelicals called "Protestants." A teen magazine Bible, uncommonly innovative from the viewpoint of modern book publishing, uses its innovations to promote a traditional reading of the Word. It seems a fitting if retrograde end: while the twentieth century opened with scripture supporting a radical suffragist political program, it ended with the upholding of traditional mores.

Conclusion

While the Bibles considered in this chapter sported new physical formats, came tailored for several enthusiastically developed niche markets, were articulated in new versions – not only new translations, but also revisions and paraphrases – and spanned one hundred fast-moving years, there are actually few significant differences between them. Wildly disparate in style and tone, none has in any significant sense transformed the general meaning of the scriptures, nor have any recast the basic narrative of the Christian Bible. Their small number of superficial disparities merely points out the remarkable stability of the Christian Bible as a text – a collection of words that, more often than not, supported social tradition rather than social change.

This was not a matter of scriptural inviolability. It was a matter of a modern culture's expectations of a book – the only text in western culture that projects an aura of both diversity and stability – and the powerfully conservative bent of a modern commercial culture intent upon profit. We will now turn, briefly, to the media revolutions of the past decade to see if this timeless conservatism can still hold true for the Bibles of the future.

CONCLUSION

And so *this* book, chronicling the long, symbiotic history of a book and its readers both real and imagined, will close with two very different episodes, related if disparate examples of where Bible culture is tending in this new century.

The first begins with remarks I overheard while shamelessly eavesdropping on visitors at the Huntington Bible exhibition in late 2004. It stars two Bibles and two people:

> Two woman are peering intently into a glass case containing the last exhibition item of the show – a gorgeous 2003 facsimile of *The Lindisfarne Gospels*, a medieval manuscript Bible owned by the British Library.
>
> *First Woman* (decidedly): "I like this one" [pointing to the reproduction] "better than those" [pointing to a set of original teen bibles in magazine format]
>
> *Second Woman* (nodding vigorously): "it's a *real* Bible, isn't it?"

Well, maybe. It is, in fact, a copy of one of the treasures of the British Library, one of the literary and artistic wonders of the medieval world, and one of the masterworks of the western scriptural tradition. It is

also exquisitely, heartstoppingly, beautiful. The Gospel's radiant illuminations, precise script, and intricate pictorial devices are so singular
as to allow scholars to trace this manuscript's origin to a particular
time, place, and artist-scribe: the early eighth century; a Benedictine
monastery situated off the northeast coast of England; a bishop
named Eadfrith of Lindisfarne.[1] It is thus both easily categorized and
highly idiosyncratic, and its words and images, full of discernible
character and energy, provide us with a rare perspective on the past.
To view this book in its horizontal gallery case at the British Library
is to grasp at that thread of desire that connects our twenty-first-
century selves to the early Middle Ages – no matter the breadth of
our historical knowledge, the depth of our biblical understanding, or
the purity and pitch of our religious feeling.[2]

This can also be true for those whose vocations require them to
analyse the Lindisfarne Gospels with an intellectually reassuring
measure of critical distance. Even the Curator of Manuscripts at the
British Library occasionally departs from the standard argot of
scholarship in her commentary on the manuscript:

> How, and why, did one person invest so much sustained effort into
> producing such an encyclopaedic masterpiece? . . . What must it
> have been like to claw back enough time and energy to undertake
> this body-racking, muscle-aching, eye-straining task? . . . this book
> is the physical expression of a devout, deep spirituality . . . in which
> one individual creature endeavors its utmost to seek union with
> his/her maker through a labor of love, a quest which answers a
> deep-rooted human need.[3]

Warm words from an academic! Dr Brown's initial analysis of the
Gospels calls up to our mind's eyes the image of heroic religious duty.
Her harsh-edged descriptions – "claw[ing] back," "racking," "aching"
and "straining" – strive to express the significance of a life spent in spiritual devotion, intellectual aspiration, and physical effort. Such an existence might seem to us lost to the murky recesses of an almost
unrecoverable historical moment, but still Brown has managed to

capture something of the exacting and exhilarating reality of a medieval scribe's work. And to be sure, the modern-day curator actually has something in common with the eighth-century monastic – with, in fact, every person who has ever held and studied the *Lindisfarne Gospels*. Touching its pages, poring over its words and pictures, today's specialist links his or her eyes and hands to thirteen centuries of attentive and reverent handling.

Like the Huntington Library's less showy Gundulf Bible,[4] the Lindisfarne gospel book has a biography: a verifiable, traceable record, although, as is so often the case with religious biographies (whether of books or of saints), the story can be mythic at times.[5] After Lindisfarne, like all British monasteries in the sixteenth century, was closed, its monks dispersed, and its properties made over to Henry VIII's government, the Gospels traveled south, where we eventually find them living a less fabulous life in the late sixteenth-century booklist of one Robert Bowyer, Clerk of the Parliaments for King James I of England. The eminent English bibliophile Sir Robert Cotton obtained the manuscript from Bowers some time before 1613, the date the *Gospels* first appear in Sir Robert's library catalogue. It was here the book took on a second name, one of the famously site-specific pressmarks of the renowned Cotton manuscript collection: Nero D. iv. The imperial designation describes the book's exact location on Robert Cotton's library shelves: fourth shelf down, fourth book from the left, directly below a sculpted bust of the ancient emperor.[6]

In 1702, when Cotton's library was dispersed by his heirs, Cotton MS. Nero.D. iv became the property of a nation newly engaged in the business of displaying its pre-modern heritage. The Lindisfarne Gospels became one of the first items selected for the foundation collection of England's newly established national museum. Since their move to a national collection, the Gospels have left the security of the British Museum (now Library) only five brief times since 1757.[7] They have also taken on one more role: as public artefact, exhibited to attract and instruct yet another very different audience.

The manuscript also bears witness to the precocious nature of Britain's vernacular culture. Like so many other hard-working books of scripture belonging to the medieval Church, the Lindisfarne Gospels show the handwritten evidence of generations of clerical ownership and use. In their case, however, the evidence goes well beyond the usual corrections or additions, making the Gospels as famous for their marginalia as they are for their illuminations. Two hundred years after their creation, between every line of the original Latin of the Gospels, a monk named Aldred painstakingly added word-for-word translations of Matthew, Mark, Luke, and John in Anglo-Saxon. This makes the Lindisfarne Gospels the oldest known English translation and the first known text written in the English language.[8]

That this text is a translation of scripture brings us full circle. Like the Gundulf Bible with which we began, the Lindisfarne Gospels is no mass-produced, printed book, but a hand-copied and -illustrated one: the product of a single scribe-illuminator, the witness to countless expressions of devotion, the inspirer of desires sacred and secular, rare beyond monetary calculation. Its jeweled binding and decorated pages have provided an imposing shrine for sacred text, making this manuscript, with its astonishing visual beauty and massive, glittering materiality, an object of physical veneration. Over thirteen hundred years of a charmed existence, its neatly inked text has testified to the majesty of the Christian Word. And, literally in between the lines, another neatly inked text testifies to the very human urge to render those magnificent words in accessible, homely, vernacular translation.

In recent centuries, however, the accessibility of the Lindisfarne Gospels has been recalculated and re-mediated. Research institutions like the British or Huntington Libraries do their work constrained by two paradoxical and equally essential mandates: to preserve rare books, and to make them available to scholars – and, since the Library also exhibits the finest of its holdings, to the public. While a select few specialists may still handle the book outright, access to the Gospels is rare, conducted under strict guidelines formulated to protect it not only from the kind of marginal elaborations that would once have been common scholarly practice, but also now from the inevitable damage even the most reverent handling will cause even the hardiest book.

The *eyes* of the public are less deleterious. The Gospels, owned by Great Britain and maintained by taxpayers and Lottery revenue, are on view most days of the year, seven days a week. Encased and on display, this once portable, one-of-a-kind, book is confined: not only to a horizontal case in the Treasure Room of the British Library in the Borough of Camden in London, but also – and most inextricably – to its singular identity as a unique, irreplaceable national treasure.

Or is it?

Consider the following ad copy from a direct mail campaign of 2003:

Masterpieces of book production of the past as bibliophile treasures of today

Explore and own a treasure from The British Library

Even among the wealth of treasures in The British Library, the *Lindisfarne Gospels* (Cotton MS Nero D. iv) have always maintained a special status as a relic. The *Lindisfarne Gospels* are kept and preserved under rigorous environmental and security conditions. For the first time ever this precious Gospel book is now recreated in the original format of $13\frac{1}{2} \times 9\frac{3}{4}$ in. in colour and in its entirety.

In addition to the 16-page canon table sequence, five sumptuous carpet pages, six Incipit pages and four portraits of the Evangelists adorn a total of 259 leaves. Several lavishly decorated ornamented initials and over 200 colour-filled initial letters subdivide a total of 518 pages, including the text written in Insular half-uncials in two columns, between whose lines Aldred diligently inscribed his Old-English translation. This, the oldest translation from Latin into English, makes the *Lindisfarne Gospels* a precious linguistic monument.[9]

What exactly is on offer here? The hasty reader might be forgiven for feeling concerned that the British Library has fallen upon hard times and been forced to sell off its most valued holdings. The sharp-eyed

55 Lindesfarne Gospels (facsimile) advertisement (2003).

reader, however, will note an advertising pitch of enormous appeal. The adage we encountered in the world of the nineteenth-century Bible salesman operates as well in this recent brochure. What is for sale here is not primarily a book – not an eighth-century book, certainly, but not even a twenty-first-century book. What is for sale is the idea of holding something incalculably precious, a dream of possession made possible by twenty-first century technology.

And, of course, deep pockets. Tucked into the impeccably accurate description of the original is the word "recreated," a term heralding the next, generative phase in the life of this singular text: its reproduction and distribution. Can a "treasure" actually be "recreated," produced and sold in multiple copies, without losing its allure, its humane power?[10] The brochure argues it can, trading on the valiant aspects of the Gospels' first creation and the uncanny accuracy of its technical re-creation to underscore the value of investing in just such a book. And priced at $10,368.56 per copy, this facsimile of the Gospels surely qualifies as a serious investment.[11]

The original Gospels were first an ecclesiastical, then a private, and now a treasured public attraction, and so it is fitting that the gospel book offered here in facsimile is identified as a "relic," a material object that has taken on transcendent nature. The Gospels have been deposited in a secular reliquary called "a display case" and set in a nationally sacred space called "The British Library." They have been exhibited to public view under carefully crafted conditions that both ensure their continued preservation and highlight their rarity and power. In a secular age and a secular setting, the Gospels continue to serve the very human desire for encounter with objects that imbue immediate human experience with meaning and awe.

Which brings me from the sublime to, perhaps, the ridiculous: a YouTube video, freely available on the web, recently sent to me by a former student. (If you want to be entertained in this life, tell your friends and acquaintances you are writing a book on the Bible.) It is a parody of an infamous video of the 1990s that featured a rapper, Sir Mixalot, performing a memorable and catchy paean to the abundantly curvy female. The YouTube update speaks to a desire for something equally physically impressive, according to *this* rapper, Sir Readsalot: his girlfriend's great, big, enormous . . . Bible. Readsalot wants his scriptures, and the people who read them, to live *large*. And he is just as adamant about what he doesn't like: "weenie" Bibles on compact disc, pocket-sized scriptures, paraphrases, girls who carry flimsy paperback Bibles. He wants "ribbon bookmarks," "big red letters," and, yes, the King James Version (letters he wears emblazoned on his chest in gold). In short, he wants a nineteenth-century Bible.

Once I stopped laughing hysterically, caught my breath, and thought about this, I realized just how little things have changed in Christian Bible culture. Protestants were eventually convinced not to put their faith in dead wood and even deader bones after many years of careful preaching and teaching, but since then, as we have seen, their embrace of the culture of the Bible never let go of the object. So I have anchored this history of the Bible in the many evidences of this material attachment between people and a book – hundreds of copies and versions produced over one thousand years of a mutually sustaining relationship, passing through a phalanx of human hands. To acknowledge this in no way casts doubt upon the spiritual claims made by Christianity; in fact, it highlights and confirms them. Christianity is a profoundly historical religion; its otherworldly concerns have always and necessarily been connected through the words of its sacred text to verifiable events and real people operating in human time. Its narrative is, therefore, necessarily plotted on various forms of physical evidence, evidence that has time and again inspired the response of faith.

I'm not entirely sure that it's possible to conclude a book on the Bible, any more than it is possible to conclude a reading of the Bible. A reader can turn all the pages, and close the covers, but this is one book that has always resisted closure in every sense. In any case, this book has been selective in its topics from the start. I began with a discrete collection of physical objects: Christian Bibles, nearly all of them in English, and all of them produced by Anglo-Americans. To write the cultural history of such a book required a primary sense of it as a human artefact, a thing of pages and covers, even while I would concede and even celebrate the fact that somehow this ever-changing material object has taken on sacredness in western culture.

What makes a book sacred? For Christians, it has never been, as it is for Islamic followers of the Koran, the idea that the sacred text must remain in its original language. There are no originals of the books of the Christian Bible, a text that, arguably, owes its sacred status to two cheeky acts of translation: the determination, in the first century, to add a second set of texts to the Hebrew Bible (thus transforming, for Christians, the intrinsic impact of its historic texts); and then, in the fourth century, the determination to translate a composite text written in Greek and Greek translations of the Hebrew, into one coherent and narrative Latin text.

For this reason, perhaps, Christians do not celebrate a holiday named for Bible reading, as Jews do at Simchat Torah, a yearly holiday that marks the end of the reading-over of the entire Torah and the start of the next. Christian churches read the Bible by fits and starts: no lectionary covers every one of its chapters and all of its verses. To read it from beginning to end, then, is more likely to be an individual effort, with all the singularity of interpretation that such an enterprise suggests. Thus uniformity of interpretation is neither a determinant nor a consequence of the Christian Bible's claim to sacredness.

The Bible and the People has traced two seemingly antithetical claims. The first concerns the increasing accessibility of the Bible, even in centuries that church historians and Protestant theologians have told us were characterized by the scripture's Latinate impenetrability in a largely illiterate and vernacular western culture. This, as we have seen, was simply not true. The Bible was familiar to medieval people in a variety of rich ways, preaching, theater, and personalized, vernacular devotional texts among them. The Reformation, with its projects of biblical translation and explanation, further enlarged the circle of the biblically literate. And the modern era of the Bible can be mapped onto a plethora of commercial interventions, all aimed at increasing access to the ideas of the Bible. In fact, we saw all these projects, in every age, instantiated in physical format. The Bible became easier to obtain, carry, own, and read over every century of its existence: smaller, more clearly marked, more uniform in content, more winsome in design, more tailored to the diverse markets of a diverse Christian culture. Along the way we also watched the Bible make a move across the Atlantic, where religious disestablishment, the rapid spread of evangelical Protestantism, and a commercial market for Bibles second to none have eventually made America the major exporter of modern and post-modern cultures of scriptural print.

And yet, this book has also argued for something else, and quite passionately: the intrinsic strangeness of this text, its intractable foreignness; its stubborn narrative resistance. How can this be? How can the central text of western religious culture, the central text of western culture, period, if truth be told, be both so accessible and so inaccessible? Which of its strange names and deeds, its ancient uncertainties, its narrative divergences and contradictions, can have possibly formed the basis for Christian doctrine and morality,

Christian surety, Christian theologies of God's unswerving and unfolding plan for human salvation?

It was my observation, in the fourteen years I taught History of Christianity at a liberal Protestant seminary, that my most engaged and intellectually curious students were invariably more interested in emergent work by academic scholars on non-canonical texts like The "Gospel of Thomas" or the "Gospel of Judas," an extension of their conviction that "real" Christianity should not have to be restricted to the narrow confines of the early Church's "orthodoxy." My students loved heretics more than they did church administrators, an approach that never failed to warm my heart and make me pull my hair out when grading papers. In fact, over fifteen hard-working years for all of us, I failed miserably at the task of getting them to recognize, at least, the attractions of officialdom, of institutionalization, or of living by the rules. This love of the unorthodox came from their liberal theologies: their passionate conviction of the Church's diversity and of its openness to all sorts of people. And so they were drawn to Gospels like Judas and Thomas, which enshrined broader approaches (if sometimes narrower ideas) to early church membership and doctrines than the Bible did.

Same with the novel that took the reading world by storm a few short years ago, Dan Brown's *The Da Vinci Code*. (When I curated the Bible exhibition, I had to read the novel myself, and for a simple reason: it was always the subject of the first question I was asked when leading a curator tour, giving a media interview, or speaking publicly on the history of the Christian Bible.) With its not so subtle streak of anti-Catholic-institutionalism and its cracking good but entirely cavalier way with historical facts and documented works of art, the novel speaks to the longing of at least some of its readers (perhaps most of its readers) for a Church that had always looked like many western Churches today: with women included in the ranks of leadership and priests and ministers that marry and have families. But it also simply speaks to the mysterious nature of Christian scriptures, the perennial work of the Bible's readers to make sense of the maddening and thrilling document of their faith.

This book has attempted that same daunting task. Beginning in the Middle Ages, we examined manuscript Bibles produced as working texts for cathedral and monastic personnel, illuminated Psalters produced for wealthy landowning patrons, and manuscript copies of vernacular plays produced by illiterate laypeople who, when judged on their own terms, were engagingly astute on issues of theology and the scriptures. We marked the impact of the early modern printing press and its not so silent partner, the vernacular translation, moving from illicit and sophisticated Wycliffite manuscript Bibles to state-sponsored Protestant scriptures. We watched the uncertain and politically agonizing progress of the English Bible from the execution of the great translator William Tyndale in the reign of Henry VIII to the achievement of the team of translators working for James I less than one hundred years later.

We charted the seventeenth-century voyage of King James's Bible to a new world, mapping its increasingly sure hold on American speakers of English across the pages of the *Bay Psalm Book* and the Aitken and Carey Bibles – but noted as well its tentative and troubling grip on the Native Americans for whom the Reverend Eliot translated the scriptures. We accompanied Bible salesmen as they stepped onto the nineteenth-century doorsteps of prairie homes with their colorful and overpriced wares, available by subscription. And we saw the Bible extend its long and various reach into the current Bible marketplace, which now provides a seemingly endless variety of Bibles designed for every type of household and every sort of person – from African American women in after-church study groups, to computer-savvy six-year-olds, to guitar-fixated adolescent boys who would sooner surrender their right to the keys to the family car than be caught reading something that looked *anything* like a Bible in public.

Perhaps the Huntington Library's sixty-six-volume *Kitto Bible*, created from the excised pages of a vast array of European Bibles and crammed thick with over thirty thousand European and British watercolors and prints, stands as the most impressive reminder of something the examination of every other Bible in this book has also, if less spectacularly, demonstrated: that over the past millennium, the book known as the Bible has been endlessly trimmed and expanded, refashioned by its readers to meet the needs of religion, politics, and popular demand. It has permanently moved beyond the institutional worlds of Church and University to play a powerful and sustaining role in everyday life, whether public or private. Yet at the heart of all these formats, no matter how startling, no matter how singular, is a remarkably stable text – the same work so painstakingly copied by hand onto vellum one thousand years ago.

Which is why I will close, selfishly, with a personal anecdote. My maternal grandmother, who did not go to college, was the first bona-fide scholar I ever observed in action. Every Saturday evening after supper (I was an undisputed mistress of the art of wheedling my parents into letting me go to my grandparents' for overnights) my grandfather and I would plot out another exciting evening of TV watching (westerns) and Barbie-doll fashion shows (I had cornered the market on those little plastic shoes). My grandmother was made of sterner stuff. She would get down her Bible, which was covered in a soft, tooled, brown leather, much worn: King James Version, with the words of Jesus picked out in red, one of those ribbon bookmarks, and gold index tabs. A dictionary, pronunciation guide, and a set of brightly colored maps of the Holy Land could be found in the appendices. Grandma would then locate her copy of *Strong's Exhaustive Concordance of the Bible*, the most recent issue of *The Upper Room* (a pamphlet, published monthly, with prayers and Bible verses listed for daily meditation), and a packet of curricular materials provided by the Southern Baptists for assistance in yearly adult education. Consulting, marking, and collating all this information, taking notes furiously, my grandma would prepare her weekly Sunday School lesson for the Adult Women's Class of the First Baptist Church of De Soto, Missouri. She taught that class for over twenty years, and while I quickly learned the verses she loved best, I am guessing she never said the same thing about them twice.

I named this book *The Bible and the People* with her in mind.

NOTES

Chapter One: The Eye of the Beholder: The English Bible, *c.* 1066–1200

1. Scraping was the method by which mistakes on vellum could be, imperfectly, erased.
2. Augustine was particularly taken with this ability of Ambrose's, remarking that he "never read any way but silently." Alberto Manguel, *A History of Reading* (London: HarperCollins, 2003), 41–3. Ambrose was ahead of his time, according to Paul Saenger, who posits that silent reading as a widespread practice emerged in what he calls the "spaces between words" devised by the monastic scribes of Ireland and England in the seventh and eighth centuries: *Space Between Words: The Origins of Silent Reading* (Palo Alto: Stanford University Press, 1997), 83.
3. This dual purpose was rare but not unheard of in British Christianity after 1066. It reflected the policies of the powerful Norman churchmen who served as Archbishops of Canterbury in the era between the Conquest, which effectively ended the power of the Anglo-Saxon Church, and the Reformation, which effectively ended the power of the monasteries. While all bishops have a direct jurisdiction over the secular Church, their authority over monastic houses was diluted through the authority of often powerful and nearly autonomous abbots. Now no such impediment to Gundulf's power existed.
4. *Cambridge History of the Bible* (Cambridge: Cambridge University Press, 1963), II: 142.
5. Huntington Library (hereafter HEH) MS 62, vol. I, fol. 1 rr.
6. "PRIMA PARS BIBLIE PER BONE MEMORIE GUNDULFUM ROFFEN[SEM] EP[ISCOPU]M. LIBER DE CLAUSTRO ROFFENS QUEM QUI INDE ALIENAV[ER]IT ALIENATU[M] CELAV[ER]IT VEL HUNC TITULU[M] IN FRAUDEM DELEV[ER]IT EXCOMMUNI-CATUS EST * FERENTIB[US] SENTE[N]CIAM [DICTO] S[AN]CTO

EP[ISCOPO] PRIORE [ET] SING[U]LIS P[RE]SBITERIS CAPITULI ROFFENSIS."
I am indebted to Consuelo Dutschke and Mary Robertson for aid in translating this anathema as accurately (and menacingly) as Gundulf's heirs would have wished.

7. Lumley's library has been studied by Sears Jayne and Francis R. Johnson: *The Lumley Library: the Catalog of 1604* (London: Trustees of the British Museum, 1956).

8. HEH MS 62, vol. I, fol. 1 rr.

Chapter Two: On the Road and in the Street: The English Bible, *c.* 1200–1500

1. This is certainly what is usually argued by scholars of Protestantism, from Martin Luther to, more recently, David Daniell: *The Bible in English: its History and Influence* (New Haven: Yale University Press, 2003).

2. *Treatise of the Manner and Mede of the Mass*, cited by Virginia Reinburg in "Liturgy and the Laity in Late Medieval and Reformation France," *Sixteenth Century Journal* 23, no. 3 (1992), 530.

3. *Oxford Dictionary of the Christian Church:* "heresy." The exception that proves this rule would have to be Albigensianism, or Catharism, a system of thought so distinct from Christianity that it almost ought to be considered as a non-Christian religion in competition with Christianity rather than an incorrect interpretation of it.

4. The monks' Bibles were instead given to them (or the money to purchase was given them) *ad usum* – for their use but not their property. Christopher De Hamel, *The Book: a History of the Bible* (London: Phaidon, 2001), 135.

5. What follows has been written in more detail and with admirable technical proficiency by several scholars of the medieval manuscript: Richard and Mary Rose, and Christopher De Hamel chief among them. I am especially indebted in this brief section to the plethora of information contained in De Hamel, 140–65; and in Chapters 6 and 8 of R. Rouse and M. Rose, *Authentic Witnesses: Approaches to Medieval Texts and Manuscripts* (Notre Dame, Indiana: University of Notre Dame Press, 1991), 191–220; 259–340. The Rouses and De Hamel can't agree on the market for these French Bibles, alas. The Rouses argue for university students and De Hamel, more persuasively, for the new mendicant friars.

6. De Hamel, 120–1.

7. So-called not because they weren't religious in nature, but to distinguish them from monastic houses, which were organized around a "Rule" and thus called "regular" (the word "rule" is from the Latin *regula*).

8. De Hamel, 131.

9. Not all of these folk would have been able to read Latin, even haltingly. There were plenty of pictures in most Psalters, however, and by the fifteenth century we see more of them appearing in the vernacular. Merchant-class Psalters were much less sumptuously made than the version on display here. Murray McGillvray, *Four Medieval Manuscript Leaves and a Caxton Leaf*, University of Calgary Libraries Special Collections Occasional Paper Number 9 at www.ucalgary.edu/libraries.

10. This is the opening Psalm of the "festial canticles," which appear in the Ellesmere Psalter at fol. 175 verso, directly after the Psalter proper.

11. Huntington Library (hereafter HEH) MS EL 9 H 17 ("Ellesmere Psalter"), fol. 175 verso; *Huntington Library Catalogue of Medieval and Renaissance Manuscripts*, 30–3.
12. Ibid., fol. 46 recto.
13. Michael Camille, *Image on the Edge: the Margins of Medieval Art* (Cambridge, Mass.: Harvard University Press, 1992), 9.
14. Andrew Taylor, "Into his Secret Chamber: Reading and Privacy in Late Medieval England," in James Raven, Helen Small, and Naomi Tadmore, eds, *The Practice and Representation of Reading in England* (Cambridge: Cambridge University Press), 43.
15. R.M. Lumiansky and D. Mills, eds, *The Chester Mystery Cycle: a reduced facsimile of Huntington Library HM2* (Leeds: University of Leeds School of English, 1980), xiv.
16. Both were calculated from the date of Easter, which accounts for their movable position in the seasonal calendar.
17. The 1555 reference is in the archives of the Edinburgh "Hammermen," a guild that, true to its name, incorporated all workers with hammers, especially forge-men: *Oxford English Dictionary* (hereafter *OED*).
18. Chaucer uses the term in this manner in the Pardoner's Tale (1390): *OED*.
19. The notion of reading "past" something is the conception of *New Yorker* essayist Adam Gopnik, whose essay on the Book of Esther and his first attempt at *Purim spiel* is an engaging account of wrestling with an exotic biblical text: "A Purim Story," in *Through the Children's Gate* (New York: Knopf, 2006), 60.
20. Laurence Clopper, ed., *Chester* (Records of Early English Drama) (Toronto: Toronto University Press, 1979), 4.
21. *REED: Chester* cites a Mayor's list of 1555: "The old and Antient Whitson playes in this city of Chester were first made Englished . . . in . . . Anno 1268 . . .": 3.
22. The stage directions read: ". . . and on the boards all the beasts and fowls hereafter rehearsed must be painted so that their words agree with the pictures."
23. This longer stage direction is not in the Huntington Library MS but a later, 1607 manuscript copy. HM 2 has, instead, "Then shall Noah shut the window of the ark and for a little space within the boards he shall be silent and afterwards opening the window and looking around about saying . . ." The 1607 directions suggest that this may have been the cue for the company to sing the metrical version of Psalm 69 as found in the Psalter set to meter by Thomas Sternhold and John Hopkins. David Mills, *The Chester Mystery Cycle* (East Lansing, Mich.: Colleagues Press, 1992), 59.
24. In Chester they continued well into the reign of Elizabeth, eventually angering the Privy Council, the Archbishops of Canterbury and York, and the Bishop of Chester. Various plans to "Protestantize" them eventually came to naught: *Chester Mystery Cycle*, xvi.

Chapter Three: The Politics of Translation:
The Bible in English, *c.* 1500–1700

1. *The Gospels of the Fower Evangelistes, translated in the olde Saxons tyme out of Latin into the vulgare toung of the Saxons* (London, 1571), sig. *P* ii r.
2. Anglo-Saxon Bibles were the creation of the Irish and Scottish monks of the fourth and fifth centuries who had converted the island's Teutonic conquerors by

preaching to them from scriptures translated into their pagan tongue. David Daniell, *The Bible in English* (New Haven: Yale University Press, 2003), 44–55.

3. *Fower Evangelistes*, sig. A ii. r. Foxe also included a large dose of the Anglo-Saxon New Testament in several editions of his enormously popular *Actes and Monuments of these latter and perilous tymes*, a mordant and vividly bloodthirsty "there but for the grace of God go we" account of Protestant courage under Catholic persecution. One common link between these two texts was the printer John Day, who owned the Anglo-Saxon types. While undoubtedly a number of other considerations – his own religious opinions, for example – must account for Day having the right to print so many lucrative Protestant texts, it is also important to realize that, first and foremost, he also had the specialized equipment to produce them: J.M. Garnett, "The Study of the Anglo-Saxon Language and Literature," in *The Addresses and Journal of Proceedings of the National Educational Association Session of the Year 1876* (Salem, Ohio: printed by Allan K. Tatem, 1876), 147.

4. The Dudley copy of *Fower Evangelistes* is housed in Special Collections at Honnold Library of the Claremont Colleges, Claremont, California. Other books printed by Parker with Leicester's coat of arms suggest that the printer made presentation copies for Leicester. I am indebted to Bill Sherman for this detail.

5. Huntington Library (hereafter HEH), RB 92534.

6. This is not to claim that there were no Bibles in other vernacular languages prior to the sixteenth century; unofficial Bibles were produced in many European languages, reflecting local and regional variations in enforcement and censorship. Elizabeth L. Eisenstein, *The Printing Press as an Agent of Change* (Cambridge: Cambridge University Press, 1979; rpt. 1980), 346.

7. Disputed elections in the fourteenth century (1309–77) had led to the Church's having more than one Pope and two established papal residences (the second in Avignon), which left claims for the singular authority vested in one man severely damaged.

8. A point made by Margaret Aston: *Lollards and Reformers: Images and Literacy in Late Medieval Religion* (London: Hambledon Press, 1983), 71–2.

9. John Fines, "Heresy Trials in the Diocese of Coventry and Lichfield, 1511–12," *Journal of Ecclesiastical History* 14 (1963), 165, quoted in Aston, 71.

10. But see also Daniell, 79.

11. Daniell offers the most masterful précis of this process: ibid., 76–85.

12. HEH MS 134, fol. 38 r. I have modernized the spelling.

13. In an article about twenty-first-century translations like the *New International Version*: Daniel Rodosh, "Marketing the Good Book," *New Yorker*, 18 December 2006: 54–8.

14. Paul L. Hughes and James F. Larkin, *Tudor Royal Proclamations* (New Haven: Yale University Press, 1964) I: 193–7. Emphases are mine.

15. His additional preface to the reader in the 1534 edition continues this work by describing in detail his travails with George Joye, who had "secretly" corrected ("by what occasion," Tyndale complains, "his conscience knoweth") Tyndale's translation and sent it to the printer without informing Tyndale of that fact.

16. New Testament, * i v.

17. *Biblia: The Byble, that is the Holy Scrypture . . . faythfully translated in Englysh. MDXXXII* (Sowthwarke: for James Nycolson: [1535]), title page.

18. *The Bible and Holy Scriptures conteyned in the Olde and Newe Testament* (hereafter Geneva Bible); (Geneva: Printed by Rouland Hall, 1560), Dd iii v.

19. Geneva Bible, h ii v.
20. The first to number verses in a manuscript Bible was Stephen Langton, a professor at the University of Paris (and later Archbishop of Canterbury), in 1205. Robert Stephanus, a Paris printer, numbered his Latin Vulgate Bible of 1555. Stephanus worked in Paris until his patron, Francis I, died. Stephanus had enemies in the Church and so fled to Geneva, where the Geneva Bible was produced. H. von Soden, *Die Schriften des Neuen Testamentes* 2 vols (Göttingen: Vanderhoeck Ruprecht, 1911–13), I: 484.
21. In some states, at least, according to Kevin Finn, the manager of "Book People" in Austin, Texas, who explains the phenomenon by saying "maybe people think the Bible should be for free . . . an average King James Bible with zipper is about thirty-five bucks": *Barre-Montpelier Times Argus*, Vermont Sunday Magazine, 1 August 2006.
22. Adam Nicholson, *God's Secretaries: The Making of the King James Bible* (New York: HarperCollins, 2003), 121.
23. Ibid., 209–10.
24. *The New Testament of our Lord and Savior Jesus Christ translated out of the Latin Vulgat by John Wiclif . . . Prebendary of Aust in the Collegiate Church of Westbury, and Rector of Lutterworth, about 1378* (London, 1731), a v.

Chapter Four: Missions and Markets: The Bible in America, *c.* 1600–1800

1. Instruction website, United States Immigration and Naturalization Service: http://usgovinfo.about.com.
2. See Michael Winship for the important point that Puritans were not particularly bound to the Geneva Bible after the advent of the AV. The Word of God was the Word of God, and (as this chapter argues) the Church of England employed the AV, and Puritanism was not, in the main, a separatist movement. Michael Winship, *Making Heretics: Militant Protestantism and Free Grace in Massachusetts, 1636–1641* (Princeton: Princeton University Press, 2002), 231–3.
3. *Dotrina christiana en lengua española y Mexicana: hecha por los religiosos dela orden de Sancto Domingo.* Mexico [City]: en casa de Juan Pablos, 17 January 1548. Huntington Library (hereafter HEH) RB 106426.
4. *La Biblia, que es, Los Sacros Libros Del Vieio y Nuevo Testamento* [Basel: printed by Thomas Guarinus], 1569. HEH RB 40932
5. Theodor de Bry, *Das vierdte Buch von der neuwen Welt.* Frankfurt am Main: printed by Matthias Becker's widow for Johann Theodor de Bry, 1613. HEH RB 122161.
6. *Portrait of John Eliot.* Unknown artist. [Purportedly painted 1659 or 1660.] HEH HG 27.219.
7. *The Holy Bible . . . Translated into the Indian language, and ordered to be printed by the commissioners of the United Colonies in New-England, at the charge, and with the consent of the Corporation in England for the Propagation of the Gospel amongst the Indians in New-England* (Cambridge, Mass.: printed by Samuel Green and Marmaduke Johnson, 1663).
8. Jill Lepore, *The Name of War: King Philip's War and the Origins of American Identity* (New York: Knopf, 1998), 31.

9. This account is drawn from David Paul Nord, *Faith in Reading: Religious Publishing and the Birth of Mass Media in America* (Oxford and New York: Oxford University Press, 2004), 10–23.

10. *The Massachusett Psalter . . . with the Gospel according to John, in Columns of Indian and English* (Boston: printed by B. Green, and J. Printer, 1709).

11. Governor Winthrop's Journal mentions two texts printed prior to the *Bay Psalm Book*, a tract and an almanac; both have been lost to posterity, and, strictly speaking, neither is a book in any case: Bradford Swan, "Some Thoughts on the Bay Psalm Book of 1640," *Yale University Library Gazette* 22, no. 3 (January 1948), 51.

12. Francis Quarles, *Emblemes* (1635), which is a useful reminder that even Protestants recognized the symbolic power of images to instruct the inquiring mind. One radical Protestant writer influenced by Quarles was John Bunyan, whose *Pilgrim's Progress* of 1678 famously made use of emblematic imagery in the scenes set in "the House of the Interpreter." John Bunyan, *The Pilgrim's Progress*, ed. Roger Sharrock (London: Penguin, 1965, rev. and rpt. 1987), 389, n. 51.

13. Reprinted in David Cressy and Lori Anne Ferrell, *Religion and Society in Early Modern England* (London: Routledge, 1996), 192. Psalms also featured in the seventeenth-century music books designed for secular and domestic recitals.

14. Thomas Sternhold, *Certayne Psalmes chosen out of the Psalter of David, and drawen into English metre*. London: printed by Edward Whitchurche, [1549?]. HEH RB 48300; *The Whole Booke of Psalmes: collected into English meeter, by Thomas Sternhold, John Hopkins, and others, conferred with the Hebrew, with apt notes to sing them withall . . .* London: printed for the Companie of Stationers, 1627. HEH RB 96519.

15. *The Whole Booke of Psalmes faithfully translated into English metre* (Cambridge, Mass.: printed by Stephen Day, 1640).

16. Cotton Mather, *Magnalia Christi* (1702); also quoted in Wilberforce Eames's introduction to *The Bay Psalm Book: Being a Facsimile Reprint of the First Edition, printed by Stephen Daye, At Cambridge, in New England, in 1640* (The New England Society in the City of New York, 1912), vi.

17. *Bay Psalm Book* facsimile: sig. *2 recto.

18. *Bay Psalm Book* facsimile: sig. **3 verso.

19. Quoted in Swan, 59. The verse is in the hand of Increase Mather, and is held at the Historical Society of Pennsylvania. There is a later, more elegant – and thus less original – version quoted by Cotton Mather in his *Magnalia Christi*: Swan, 58.

20. John Alden, "The Bible as Printed Word," in E.S. Frerichs, ed., *The Bible and Bibles in America* (Atlanta, Georgia: Scholars Press, 1988), 13.

21. *Biblia, das ist: die Heilige Schrift Altes und Neues Testaments* [Luther's translation]. Germantown [PA]: gedruckt bey Christoph Saur, 1743. HEH RB 48160.

22. New York: printed for T. Allen, [1792]. HEH RB 112418.

23. Reprinted in David Daniell, *The Bible in English: its History and Influences* (New York: Yale University Press, 2003), 585.

24. A point made by Daniell, ibid., 584–6.

25. *The Holy Bible* [King James Version]. Philadelphia: printed and sold by R. Aitken, 1782. HEH RB 35443.

26. John Paul Cadden, *The Historiography of the American Catholic Church, 1785–1943. Studies in Sacred Theology no. 82* (Washington, DC: Catholic University of America Press; rpt. New York: Arno, 1978), 3–4.

27. *The Holy Bible* [Douai version]. Philadelphia: printed and sold by Carey, Stewart, and Co., 1790. HEH RB 112350.

Chapter Five: On Not Understanding the Bible

1. Hugh Latimer, *The sermon made by the Reverend Father in Christ, Mr Hugh Latimer, Bishop of Worcester, made to the convocation of the clergy before the Parliament began, the 9th day of June, the 28th year of the reign of our late King Henry the Eighth. Translated out of the Latin into English, to the intent that things well said to a few may be understood of many, and do good to all them that desire to know the truth.* Reprinted in George Elwes Corrie, ed., *Sermons by Hugh Latimer* (Parker Society, Cambridge, 1844), 33–40. It has been reprinted more recently in David Cressy and Lori Anne Ferrell, *Religion and Society in Early Modern England* (London: Routledge, 1996), 15–19, and can also be found on the web on countless denominational sites, including one that purports to reprint only "Anglican Ethereal Sermons."

2. Genesis 14.1; Exodus 6.24; Revelation 1.11. All from the King James Version printed by Collins Clear Type Press, London and New York, 1939. This version has "helps," one of which is the syllabic division and phonetic accenting of all words like the ones above.

3. This is beginning to change in feminist treatments of the story of Tamar, although these rarely get pulpit outings. The fig tree anecdote is considered "probably symbolic but not clear" by the editors of the *Oxford Annotated Bible*.

4. This is a reference to, and paraphrase of, the famous seventeenth-century declaration by William Chillingworth that the "Bible . . . was the religion of Protestants." See Patrick Collinson, *The Religion of Protestants* (Oxford: Clarendon Press, 1982), viii.

5. Quoted in Willam H. Sherman, " 'This Book Thus Put In Every Vulgar Hand': Impressions of Readers in Early Modern Bibles," in Kimberly Von Kampen and Paul Saenger, eds, *The Bible as Book: The First Printed Editions* (London: British Library and Oak Knoll Press, 1999), 125. This essay inspired not only many of my treatments of the marked-up Bibles shown in the Huntington's 2004 exhibition, but has gone on to play a powerful role in the shaping of this, and the next, chapter of the present book. And Sherman's monograph on this topic, *Used Books* (Philadelphia: University of Pennsylvania Press; 2008) has made the topic of personal annotation and handling of books his own.

6. In the Huntington Library's copy of *The New Testament of Our Lord Iesus Christ, translated out of Greeke by Theod. Beza . . . Englished by L. Tomson.* (London: printed by Christopher Barker, 1582; first edn, 1577). For such "used" Bibles, see William Sherman, in *The Bible as Book*: 128–9.

7. *The New Testament of Our Lord Iesus Christ, translated out of Greeke by Theod. Beza.* I have regularized the spelling.

8. Robert John Thornton, *The Lord's Prayer, Newly Translated from the Original Greek . . .* (London: Sherwood & Co.; Cox; and Dr. Thornton, 1827).

9. *The Holy Bible* [King James Version] (New York: J.C. Riker, 1845).

10. See Heidi Brayman Hackel, *Reading Material in Early Modern England* (Cambridge: Cambridge University Press, 2005).

11. St Paul, Epistles, with Anselmian gloss *Pro altercatione*. Manuscript written in Italy, middle of the twelfth century. Huntington Library (hereafter HEH) MS 56.

12. Paul Saenger, *Space between Words: The Origins of Silent Reading* (Palo Alto: Stanford University Press, 1997), 90–7.

13. Humanist scholars corrected the attribution, which for centuries had been to the great Church father and Catholic saint, Ambrose. Erasmus dubbed the anonymous author "Ambrose the Lesser," which name served to distinguish this commentary from that point on.

14. Ambrosiaster, *Commentary on the Epistles of Paul*. Manuscript written in England, *c.* 1130–40. HEH MS 52434.
15. *The Holy Bible* [King James Version] (London: printed by J.W. Pasham, 1776).
16. *An Harmonie Upon the Three Evangelists, Matthew, Mark, and Luke, with the commentary of M. John Calvine: Faithfullie translated out of Latine into English, by E.[usebius] P.[aget]. Whereunto is also added a commentary upon the Evangelist S. John, by the same authour* (Londini impensis Geor. Bishop. 1584), sig. (˙,˙) r. Emphasis is mine.
17. Ibid. (˙,˙) 2 r.
18. Francis Roberts, *Clavis Bibliorum. The Key of the Bible . . .* (London: printed by T[homas]. R[atcliffe]. and E[dward]. M[ottershed]. for George Calvert, 1648).
19. *The Creation of the World. Being the first chapter of Genesis* (London : printed by John Hammond, 1646); William Samuel, *An Abridgement of Goddes Statutes in Myter . . .* London: printed by Robert Crowley [i.e. Richard Grafton] for Robert Soughton [i.e. Stoughton], 1551. HEH RB 89066
20. E. Beecher, *The Christian School, or Scripture's Anatomy . . .* London: printed by T.D. for the author, and are to be sold by Hen. Broom, 1676. HEH RB 13407
21. Alexander Ross, *An Exposition on the Fourteene First Chapters of Genesis, by Way of Question and Answere . . .* (London: printed by B[ernard]. A[lsop]. and T[homas]. F[awcet]. for Anth: Vpphill, 1626). Ross, a poet of such proud and prolific mediocrity that he was satirized in Samuel Butler's *Hudibras*, wrote on a large number of topics secular and sacred.
22. *Nolens Volens: or, You shall make Latin whether you will or no . . . Together with the youths visible Bible . . .* third edn. (London : printed by J.R. for T. Basset, and J. Brome, 1682).
23. Robert Williamson, *Sha'ar ha Rivshon 'o Petach Hechivson 'el L'Shon Hakodesh: The First Gate, or the Outward Door to the Holy Tongue, Opened in English* (London, 1654).
24. Hugh Broughton, *A Concent of Scripture*. [London: printed for Gabriel Simson and William White? 1590?].
25. Joseph Mede, *The Key of the Revelation, searched and demonstrated out of the naturall and proper charecters [sic] of the visions . . .* London: printed by R.B. for Phil. Stephens, 1643. HEH RB 146818
26. John Bunyan, *The Pilgrim's Progress* (rpt. and rev. edn 1987, London: Penguin Books, 1965), 46.

Chapter Six: Extra-Illustrating the Bible

1. A "codex" is a manuscript or book, rather than a text written on a scroll or tablet.
2. *New York Times*, 1 August 2004, The Magazine, 16.
3. Joan Evans and John Howard Whitehouse, eds, *The Diaries of John Ruskin, 1848–1873* (Oxford: Clarendon Press, 1958), 487–8. This hard work was of long duration, and required more than simply excision. The day before, Ruskin reported putting "two pages of missal in frames."
4. Christopher De Hamel, *Cutting Up Manuscripts for Pleasure and Profit: The 1995 Sol M. Nalkin Lecture in Bibliography* (Charlottesville: Book Arts Press, 1996).
5. The Huntington Gutenberg is missing the final leaf in each of its two volumes. I am grateful to its Curator of Early Printed Books, Stephen Tabor, for the point about Wells's "Noble Fragment."

6. Barbara Shailor, "Otto Ege: His Manuscript Fragment Collection and the Opportunities Presented by Electronic Technology," *Journal of the Rutgers University Libraries* vol. LX, 1–22. Shailor mentions Ege's collection of "black letter" printed pages as well as his several collections of manuscript treasures.

7. So-called by its outraged Puritan critics, disgusted at what they saw as blatantly Catholic behavior passing itself off as ultra-Protestant piety: see, for example, *The Arminian Nunnery: Or a Brief Description and relation of the late erected monasticall place, called the Arminian Nunnery at Little Gidding in Huntingdon-shire. Humbly recommended to the wise consideration of this Present Parliament* (London, 1646).

8. De Hamel, *The Book*, 250–1.

9. J.E. Ackland, *Little Gidding and its Inmates in the Time of King Charles I. With an Account of the Harmonies Designed and Constructed by Nicholas Ferrar* (London: SPCK, 1903), 39. Emphasis is mine.

10. Any repeated words or passages (of which there are plenty, especially among the synoptic Gospels) were distinguished by typeface: the whole of the work was in roman type, with repetitions in black letter. In this way it was possible for readers to follow the topic (by subheading) or the evangelist (by marginal letter). Ackland, *Little Gidding*.

11. De Hamel, *The Book*, 250. On the de-illustration of the Bible, see also Lori Anne Ferrell, "Transfiguring Theology: William Perkins and Calvinist Aesthetics," in C. Highley and J.N. King, eds, *John Foxe and his World* (Aldershot: Ashgate, 2002), 177–9.

12. Found in Matthew 18:6; Mark 9:42; Luke 17:2.

13. Reproduced but not explicated in De Hamel, *The Book*, 250.

14. Ibid., 251.

15. It is not clear how many the community made altogether; there are eight Little Gidding Harmonies extant. I have examined the copies owned by the British Library and Harvard University.

16. Forrest Church, "The Gospel According to Thomas Jefferson," in *The Jefferson Bible* (Boston: Beacon Press, 1989), 4–16.

17. Ibid., 18.

18. Lori Anne Ferrell, "Grasping the Truth: Calvinist Pedagogy in Early Modern England," in C. Helmer and K. De Troyer, eds, *Truth: Interdisciplinary Dialogues in a Pluralist Age* (Leuven, Belgium: Peeters, 2003), 139–45.

19. While he never indulged in this particular pastime, Mr Huntington was nonetheless captivated by the art of extra-illustration. He purchased most of the approximately 1,000 extra-illustrated books and sets – including Granger's *History* – currently owned by the Huntington Library.

20. Marcel Roethlisberger, *European Drawings from the Kitto Bible: An Exhibition at the Henry E. Huntington Library and Art Gallery, San Marino, California. November 1969 through February 1970* (Huntington Library Publications, 1969), 1r.

21. Lucy Peltz, "Engraved Portrait Heads and the Rise of Extra-Illustration," *The Walpole Society*, vol. LXVI (2004): 23–5.

22. David Knott of Reading University is currently working on constructing the biography of this elusive man. I am grateful to him for sharing his preliminary findings with me.

23. Roethlisberger, 3.

24. Robert N. Essick, *The Works of William Blake in the Huntington Collections* (The Huntington Library, 1985), 121–2.

25. Or, as Peltz puts it, "more than a sum of its many parts": 16.
26. Essick, *Works of William Blake*, 90.
27. Job 1:17, Kitto XXII: fol. 4046 r–v.
28. Job 2:7; Kitto XXII: fol. 4057 r.
29. Job 3:25; Kitto XXII: fol. 4108 v.
30. Job 13:15; Kitto XXII: fol. 4130 r.
31. Job 19: 25–7; Kitto XXII: fol. 4136 v.
32. Job 38:2; Kitto XXII: fol. 4167 v.
33. Job 41:1; Kitto XXII: fol. 4186 r.
34. In presenting these excerpts as an extracted conception of the whole, I am borrowing a page, and a method, and rather shamelessly, from Louis A. Ruprecht, Jr.'s *Tragic Posture and Tragic Vision* (New York: Continuum, 1999), whose work on narrative has informed my treatment of these issues.
35. Robert Essick calls this work "one of Blake's most important visual commentaries on the Bible," Essick, *Works of William Blake*, 122.
36. Although not every entry in the series is keyed in this way to the text. The exception is the final verse, which faces an engraved print by Cole entitled "Behemoth seu Hippopotamus, Iobi. XI. V. 15 & C.": Kitto XXII: fol. 4185 v; the page from the *Kitto Bible* is inlaid into fol. 4186 r.
37. Kitto LVIII, fol. 10556 v. 10557 r.
38. Kitto XLIII.
39. Authorized Version.
40. Adam Gopnik, "A Purim Story," in *Through the Children's Gate* (New York: Knopf, 2006), 56–72.

Chapter Seven: Traveling Companion: The Bible in the Nineteenth Century

1. As quoted in Kevin Starr, *Americans and the Californian Dream, 1850–1915* (New York and London: Oxford University Press, 1973), 79.
2. Ibid., 78.
3. *The Comprehensive Bible* [King James Version]. (Philadelphia: J.B. Lippincott, 1860).
4. George Eliot, *Adam Bede* (rpt.edn: Oxford: Clarendon Press, 2001), 462–3.
5. Anthony Trollope, *The Warden* (1855; rpt: Penguin, 2004), 65, 67.
6. *The Christian's Complete Family Bible* [King James Version], new edn (Liverpool: printed by Nuttall, Fisher, & Dixon, 1808).
7. Trollope, 67. Robertson Davies, *The Salterton Trilogy* (London: Penguin Books, 1980).
8. Colleen McDannell, *The Christian Home in Victorian America, 1840–1900* (Bloomington: Indiana University Press, 1986), 83–4. See also chapter three of her *Material Christianity* (New Haven: Yale University Press, 1996), 67–102, *passim*.
9. *The Illuminated Bible* [King James Version] (New York: Harper & Brothers, 1843–6).
10. The 1843 frontispiece is reproduced in Scott Casper, Jeffrey Groves *et al.*, eds, *A History of the Book in America, vol. 3: The Industrial Book 1840–1880* (Chapel Hill: University of North Carolina Press, 2002), 202.
11. An argument made recently by Paul Gutjahr in *An American Bible* (Stanford, Calif.: Stanford University Press, 1999), 49–56.

12. Gustave Doré, *The Bible Gallery . . . with . . . Descriptive Letter-press by Talbot W. Chambers, D.D..* (London: Cassell, Petter, Galpin & Co., 1880). Salesmen's dummy for J.L. Sooy, *Bible Talks with Children: Or, the Scriptures Simplified for the Little Folks* (Philadelphia: P.W. Ziegler & Co., 1889).

13. *The Child's Bible* [King James Version] . . . (London: Cassell, Petter & Galpin, [*c.* 1870?]).

14. Ruth Bottigheimer, *The Bible for Children: From the Age of Gutenberg to the Present* (New Haven: Yale University Press, 1996), 86–8.

15. Starr, 77–83.

16. According to Paul Gutjahr, by 1855 these three societies accounted for 16 percent of all books printed in the United States: "Diversification in American Religious Publishing," *A History of the Book in America, vol. 3*, 194.

17. David Paul Nord, *Faith in Reading: Religious Publishing and the Birth of Mass Media in America* (Oxford and New York: Oxford University Press, 2004), 9.

18. *A Few of the Many Reports Received from our Agents* [Philadelphia, Cincinnati, Springfield: William Flint & Co., 1873?].

19. Leaflet inserted in salesman's dummy for *Bible Talks with Children* (*c.* nineteenth century).

20. *The Agent's Manual.*

21. Salesman's dummy, W.J. Holland & Co. Springfield, Massachusetts.

22. As reported in Nord, 138–9.

23. *A Few of the Many Reports Received from our Agents.*

24. Salesman's dummy for *The Holy Bible* [King James Version] . . . *Together with a new and improved dictionary of the Bible . . . by Rev. Alfred Nevin. . .* (Springfield: W.J. Holland & Co. [1870s]).

25. Canvasser's sample book, possibly from National Publishing Company, Philadelphia, *c.* 1905.

26. P.W. Ziegler Co., *Illustrated Catalogue of Selected Books and Bibles.* (Philadelphia, *c.* 1918), 3, 7, 9.

27. Ibid., 3.

28. "Who are the Gideons?" insert in hotel New KJV Bible (Nashville, Tennessee: Gideons International: 1983), n.p.

Chapter Eight: Old Wine in New Wineskins: The Bible in the Twentieth Century

1. Elizabeth Cady Stanton, *The Woman's Bible* [with the Bible in the King James Version], Part I (third edn) and Part II (first edn). (New York: European Publishing Co., 1898), 8.

2. Ibid., 5.

3. Ibid., 10.

4. This thesis has recently been persuasively advanced by David Paul Nord: *Faith in Reading: Religious Publishing and the Birth of Mass Media in America* (Oxford and New York: Oxford University Press, 2004), 6–7 and *passim.*

5. Quoted in J.S. Kerr, *Ancient Texts Alive Today: The Story of the English Bible* (New York: American Bible Society, 1999), 147.

6. Ibid., 148–9.

7. The front page of the *Tribune* is reproduced on p. 148 of Kerr.

8. *The New Testament* . . . [English Revised Version]. (Oxford: at the University Press, 1881).
9. *The Holy Bible* . . . [Revised Standard Version]. (New York: Thomas Nelson & Sons, 1901).
10. Kerr, 149.
11. *Revolve* and *ExtremeTeen* are both *New Century Bibles*, the version currently popular with evangelical Bible houses.
12. *Catholic Study Bible*, ed. Donald Senior *et al.*: with the Bible in the New American Bible translation (1970, NT revised 1986, Psalms revised 1990). (New York: Oxford University Press, 1990).
13. Holy Bible (New Living Translation): Metal edn (Wheaton, Illinois: Tyndale House, *c.* 1996).

Conclusion

1. It is now thought that Eadfrith's scriptorium partner (there were nine scribes working at Lindisfarne in the eighth century) was Bede, who spent his time on the island penning his ecclesiastical history: "Gospel Truth: Research Throws New Light on Lindisfarne Manuscript," *The Guardian*, 14 May 2003. Many thanks to Shandra McGlasson for this reference.
2. David Daniell describes in awed detail the exact path from the entrance of the British Library at St Pancras to its John Ritblat Gallery (which in David Daniell's words sounds like Aladdin's cave), where the case displaying this manuscript stands: *The Bible in English: its History and Influence* (New Haven: Yale University Press, 2004), 19.
3. Michelle P. Brown, *The Lindisfarne Gospels: Society, Spirituality, and the Scribe. Cotton MS Nero D iv* (Lucerne and London: Faksimile Verlag Luzern and The British Library, 2003), 4. Hereafter *TLG*.
4. See Chapter One.
5. I am indebted to Brown's exhaustive account for the details of the fate of the original Gospels: *TLG*, 84–149.
6. Brown, *TLG*, 4–5.
7. Ibid., 139–43.
8. This is the claim of the British Library and its Curator of Manuscripts Michelle Brown. Daniell gives a different opinion, counting a glossed translation of the ninth-century Vespasian Psalter (a book of psalms designed for liturgical use) into a Mercian dialect as an earlier biblical translation.
9. From the advertising catalogue of 2003 tucked into the Huntington copy of the facsimile.
10. This question was first asked of photography, famously, by Walter Benjamin, in "The Work of Art in the Age of Mechanical Reproduction," in *Illuminations* (Frankfurt, 1955; English trans., 1968), 217–51.
11. Huntington Library invoice and catalogue slip. The copy owned by the Huntington Library is catalogued as a rare book, thus placing it under restricted access.

INDEX